Soldier with No Past

Soldier with No Past

*The Struggle of an
Amnesiac World War I
Veteran to Reclaim His Life*

EVANGELINA M. PALMER AND
JAMES J. JIMENEZ

McFarland & Company, Inc., Publishers
Jefferson, North Carolina

ISBN (print) 978-1-4766-9647-8
ISBN (ebook) 978-1-4766-5504-8

LIBRARY OF CONGRESS DATA ARE AVAILABLE

Library of Congress Control Number 2024057101

© 2025 Evangelina M. Palmer and James J. Jimenez. All rights reserved

No part of this book may be reproduced or transmitted in any form or by any means, electronic or mechanical, including photocopying or recording, or by any information storage and retrieval system, without permission in writing from the publisher.

Front cover images: a worn, tattered, and weathered photograph of Hector F. Perez as a young man; At close grips with the Hun, we bomb the corkshaffer's, etc., during World War I (Library of Congress).

Printed in the United States of America

*McFarland & Company, Inc., Publishers
Box 611, Jefferson, North Carolina 28640
www.mcfarlandpub.com*

Evangelina M. Palmer: To my cousin,
James J. "Jimmy" Jimenez,
whose collaboration helped make
this factual story possible.

James J. Jimenez: To all the "lost" military
personnel who have suffered from PTSD.

Acknowledgments

Evangelina M. Palmer

To my brother, Dr. Gabriel F. Palmer-Fernandez, for his manuscript review and enthusiastic support.

To William "Bill" Atkinson, Sr. (1929–2023), for sharing his recollections of our deceased family members with complete honesty.

To Bill's daughter, my second cousin, Dinorah Anne "Dinni" Allred, (1954–2024), who assisted in conveying her father's treasured memories to us.

Table of Contents

Acknowledgments (Evangelina M. Palmer)	vi
Preface (Evangelina M. Palmer)	1
Introduction (James J. Jimenez)	7
One. The People	11
Two. The Events	18
Three. La Familia	25
Four. History of Wars	35
Five. In the Service of His Country (Charles E. "Charlie" Perez)	43
Six. In the Service of His Country (Hector Perez)	60
Seven. Public Sentiment	97
Eight. Bill S. 851—A Partial Victory	131
Nine. The Final Three Decades	144
Ten. Understanding Wartime Trauma	164
Epilogue (James J. Jimenez)	178
Appendix	185
Chapter Notes	203
Bibliography	225
Index	241

"Winners never quit, and quitters never win."
—Vince Lombardi

Preface

Evangelina M. Palmer

It all began with a series of unrelated events that eventually gave rise to how the idea of this story, and the need I felt to document it, came together. In 2017, following the sad and expected death of my mother, Clara Maria "Bibi" Fernandez y Perez, a truly remarkable woman, my sisters and I began the unenviable task of sorting through her personal effects in order to follow her wishes as to who would retain ownership of her few items of jewelry, clothing, letters, files, and other personal items. There was one folder in particular that caught my eye due to what appeared to be scribbling on its cover. As I looked more closely, I saw that it was a handwritten note addressed to my mother from one of her Key West, Florida, cousins, Margarita (long since deceased), dated September 24, 1992. I became intrigued, as I remembered Margarita fondly from two visits my mother and I paid her in the 1980s. The folder contained information about our maternal granduncle, Hector, of whom my mother had spoken when she mentioned snippets of a wild story about him throughout our childhoods. Neither of my sisters had an interest in retaining the folder, and my brother lived out of state and was not present, so I decided to keep it.

Sometime after the numbness of my mother's passing subsided a bit, I decided it was time to review the contents of the folder. I was stunned as I read it. It struck me as a story of a man whose life changed dramatically when he voluntarily enlisted in the U.S. Army in 1917 and was later burdened with a series of unimaginable challenges; yet he, unbelievably, seemed to have overcome them. This was a miracle in my view, and I think you will agree after reading this book.

I pondered Hector's story for many weeks. His memory engulfed my very existence. He was with me wherever I went, whatever I did, even in my dreams. I was consumed, and, yes, I even spoke his name. I was in awe and admiration of the man who overcame such adversity and insurmountable obstacles. As my understanding of what he had been through grew, my love for him deepened.

I then turned my thoughts to the details of how Hector and his wife Grace overcame these challenges, and I felt compelled to uncover all the facts of their improbable journey. I often thought to myself that I was not certain whether I could have accomplished what they did, nor whether anyone else I knew could either. The time he spent in the trenches of the battlefields during World War I consumed and changed his entire life. Later, when faced with the reality of his dire situation, he could have chosen a different, darker path and ended it all, as many before and after him had done. Fortunately, he did not, and I believe his faith in his God was what deterred him from choosing that tragic ending.

For me, this story needed to live on—not just for posterity but also so that others may benefit from the knowledge detailed in the pages of this book. For those who suffer from seemingly insurmountable challenges that life has placed in their paths, this story might help them not to give up. These acts of bravery, valor, persistence, determination, virtue, grit and fairness were intermingled with injustice, hopelessness and despair.

It soon became plain to me that Hector's amazing wife Grace was vital to their success. I believe his accomplishments would not have been possible without her involvement, guidance and love. What they successfully endured, to right all the wrongs that befell them, was nothing short of miraculous.

I knew I had to uncover further details about the facts than what I had up to that point in my life. So, my first step was fact finding—filling in my family trees.

My paternal lineage was easier to research than my maternal lineage, as the former line had resided on the same island for hundreds of years. They hailed from Mallorca, the largest of the Balearic Islands and a part of Spain. I had certified copies of civil registry pages detailing the births and deaths of my father's ancestors that were obtained during visits to the island in the 1990s through the late 2000s. My father's family history was easily found there, dating as far back as the 1530s, after his ancestors arrived from Italy. In 1905, my paternal grandfather, Gabriel Palmer Bestard, a young marine carpenter, left Mallorca for Cuba. He would eventually build a small empire in the island nation, working every day of his life until his death in 1959. He never forgot his roots. After becoming a wealthy man, beginning in the 1920s he traveled frequently with his young family back to his hometown of Estellencs to improve the infrastructure by paving roads, building an electric plant, and renovating parts of the town's Catholic church and other public and private improvements; he was honored by the town as their prodigal son, and his wife Eulalia, their adopted prodigal daughter, due to their good works.

My father was thankful that his father died before he could see Fidel Castro confiscate all the family's assets in Cuba, including his palatial family home in the Miramar section of Havana, named "Villa Eulalia" after his wife (today, it is a boutique hotel operated by the Cuban Government and on the U.S. State Department's List of Cuba Prohibited Accommodations), and, most important, the largest shipyard in Cuba, situated in Havana Harbor. Since its inception in 1918, this shipyard serviced not only the international and Cuban maritime sectors but also the Cuban government's naval vessels. Every government of Cuba since 1918 was our customer, including Castro's own Revolutionary Army (we had no choice in the matter). The shipyard continues in operation to this day, having been confiscated by the Cuban government in 1960; it is now managed by the Cuban Ministry of Transportation. But that is a story for another time.

Researching my maternal lineage was not as straightforward. That line originally hailed from Spain before migrating to the Canary Islands; later, branches migrated to Cuba and the United States. The Canary Island line was explored by a maternal uncle, the Honorable Judge Carlos B. Fernandez (RIP), in the 1970s and early 1980s on his many vacations, which he used as "genealogical fact-finding missions." He discovered much. The Cuban trail is where the details are not as clear, since records are not accessible due to governmental restrictions that the communist country imposes on citizens and non-citizens alike. Located in the West Indies, Cuba is the largest single island in the Caribbean archipelago and is governed by an authoritarian regime in which political opposition is punished by imprisonment. Fortunately, I had many conversations with my mother and an older cousin of hers in the 1980s, at which time I took contemporaneous notes, and they both shared vivid recollections of their lives in pre-Castro Cuba, as well as their family's ancestors who had arrived in Cuba from the Canary Islands, with a branch of the family immigrating to Florida in the mid- to late 1800s. Much of what I learned from my mother and cousin was corroborated by records I found on Ancestry.com.

A pivotal event was when a distant cousin, James J. "Jimmy" Jimenez, and I connected online because of our independent DNA testing. We had both uploaded our test results to various sites and eventually found that we were a match. Jimmy's maternal great-grandmother, Rosario Castellanos y Velasco, was the younger sister of my maternal great-great-grandfather, Jacinto Velasco y Valdez. Jimmy and I communicated via email, and our ancestral histories matched up exactly, as we had suspected they would. I mentioned our common relative Hector Perez and his story, along with my endeavor to build and document his life's story. Jimmy was unaware of this story, since he was not as (genealogically) close to Hector as I was. I shared with Jimmy how I wanted to chart Hector's life, from his birth in Florida to his travels to New York City and from his days as a soldier fighting in France during World War I through the remainder of his life in Massachusetts.

Jimmy was stunned after hearing the story, just as I had been. He was moved by the tenacity displayed by Hector. I learned that years earlier, Jimmy had written a book for his family about his immediate family's genealogy, which included a chapter on our Velasco ancestors. I was very impressed with his chapter on our relatives. I was also impressed by his writing style.

Based on the information I provided to Jimmy at the time, he wrote a five-page story titled "A Wrong Righted, Finally," which was posted to a private family website. The purpose was to share the story with our relatives for their own edification. The write-up summarized Hector's enlistment in the U.S. Army just before our country's entry into World War I, at which time he fought with the Allies on Europe's Western Front against the Central Powers. Many of the battles are legendary and among the bloodiest the world has seen. Jimmy's short story covered Hector's return to America and his meeting with the physically disabled young woman who would later become his wife. In addition to describing their marriage, it explained Hector's years-long struggle resulting from his war-induced illness. It also detailed their extensive, noble efforts to restore Hector to some normalcy.

At that point we both felt compelled to compile a story about Hector's journey because we knew it was powerful and worth sharing.

We were excited to work together on researching and documenting our findings. While I had some background in research and basic forensic accounting, I had no experience in writing a story. Yet I felt I had the necessary knowledge handed down to me and requisite skills to add to the story and give it the emotional charge it deserved. After all, I am a Latina; emotion and the gift of gab is in my DNA. I shared all the information I had in my folders with Jimmy, and we agreed to research every scrap of evidence and document it. We took a genealogical approach to our project, developed leads, and determined the steps each of us would take, sometimes overlapping. We created charts, tables and timelines to use in cross-checking our data, and we began writing the narrative. Our intent was to collect everything we could about Hector and test its veracity.

We discovered our talents were complementary. I provided the basic details, we determined the course of action, and Jimmy's broad strokes began to paint the picture. I then compared and refined that picture with our detailed data, old and new, along the way verifying, validating and corroborating our findings.

Luckily, I had interviewed relatives who had first-hand knowledge of Hector and his immediate family decades earlier, which we used after corroborating facts. We then pored over ancestral databases; newspaper archives; military archives; U.S. censuses; U.S. city directories; immigration passenger lists (military and civilian); army transport lists; state marriage records; state divorce records; birth and death certificates and records; public and private state aid organizations in Massachusetts, Washington, D.C., New York, and Florida; Social Security records; U.S. congressional records from 1931 to 1935; national professional musician organizations; and my family photographs and letters that were contained in the original folder, as well as from a first-hand source, Hector's nephew (and my mother's first cousin), William "Bill" Atkinson, Sr., a nonagenarian who sadly passed away five days before Christmas 2023.

Additionally, we gathered information about the diagnoses given to Hector between 1917 and 1932. We referenced material about the subject from both contemporaneous times through to more recent times to enhance the reader's understanding of these diagnoses. What was known and believed in 1917 and 1932 is not the same as what is understood today.

It is our intent that readers understand exactly what happened to Hector and Grace, beginning with the injustice, followed by the convoluted twists and turns and layers of complexities they had to contend with, all while both of them suffered from their own handicaps. We felt this biographical account of our relative's life had to be factual to the greatest extent possible. While parts of this story may seem unbelievable, the details we uncovered prove it to be undeniably true.

Collaboration with Jimmy helped make this story possible. While neither of us are writers at heart, we created a pathway toward sharing this story from the facts and from the details we uncovered. Our journey together seems to have been destined, like how Hector and Grace's was, though our journey was nowhere near as important or life altering as theirs. Once all the facts are revealed, it will become clear that this is a tale to be remembered and used as a beacon of light when things get dark and unbearable. Such information is what family legacies are made of.

At this point, I'd like to take a moment to share three caveats with you. First, due to the poor storage conditions and age of our photographs, documents, and letters, the reproduction of their images will be substandard at best. Hundred-year-old paper suffers deterioration quickly if not handled properly. Our publisher cannot be blamed for the poor quality, as they normally would not even print most of these items, and we are grateful that they are doing so. Second, news articles and genealogical records published online often exist behind paywalls and require a subscription to access digitally. We have included as much as possible in our notes to assist in accessing the materials. Lastly, we felt the need to change the names of a few individuals to protect their living descendants' privacy concerns. My direct ancestors' names have not been changed. The few names this decision affected were very distant via marriage over a century ago and were not related to me by blood.

So now I hope you, the reader, will turn the pages and see for yourself how these two young people, Hector and Grace, each with their own handicap, overcame dark, hopeless years fighting against a bureaucracy that seemed immovable and unchangeable, and against an illness that was invisible and yet palpable in every breath they took, until reaching their goal. At the end of this true story, I believe you will always remember our amazing Grace and irrepressible Hector.

Fredericksburg, Virginia
December 28, 2023

Introduction

James J. Jimenez

This is a historical account of an individual and his family, based on personal memories captured in verbal stories, handwritten notes, and letters passed down within the Velasco and Perez families over multiple generations. This story is corroborated by these family notes and letters, as well as by governmental and genealogical records. These include medical and military records, accounts from military personnel, letters from veterans' associations, the American Red Cross, the Associated Charities, the American Disabled Veterans (now called the Disabled American Veterans), and state, civic, and social agencies. There are also numerous newspaper accounts and records of congressional action taken on this individual's behalf.

The story is being told by the grandniece of Hector Perez, who was a World War I veteran, because of its importance to her and members of her extended family. Her name is Evangelina "Lina" Palmer. She and her family were forced to flee their native Cuba during the rise of the Fidel Castro regime, when she was almost three years old, at which time they immigrated to the United States.

In 2017, after her mother's passing, Lina discovered a folder among her mother's personal effects containing newspaper clippings and correspondence about her granduncle. She remembered hearing snippets of a family story about the unusual and harsh circumstances that her maternal granduncle had endured and the unimaginable injustice he suffered at the hands of the U.S. Army in the 1920s. Lina realized that over time, the number of people with knowledge of these events continued to decrease, as they took place about a century ago. She felt the need to record and document her granduncle's life and his struggles, the official charges brought against him as a mentally challenged soldier by the U.S. Army, and the eventual justice he received. She reconstructed his life based on what she knew and then set out to learn more and corroborate it so she could

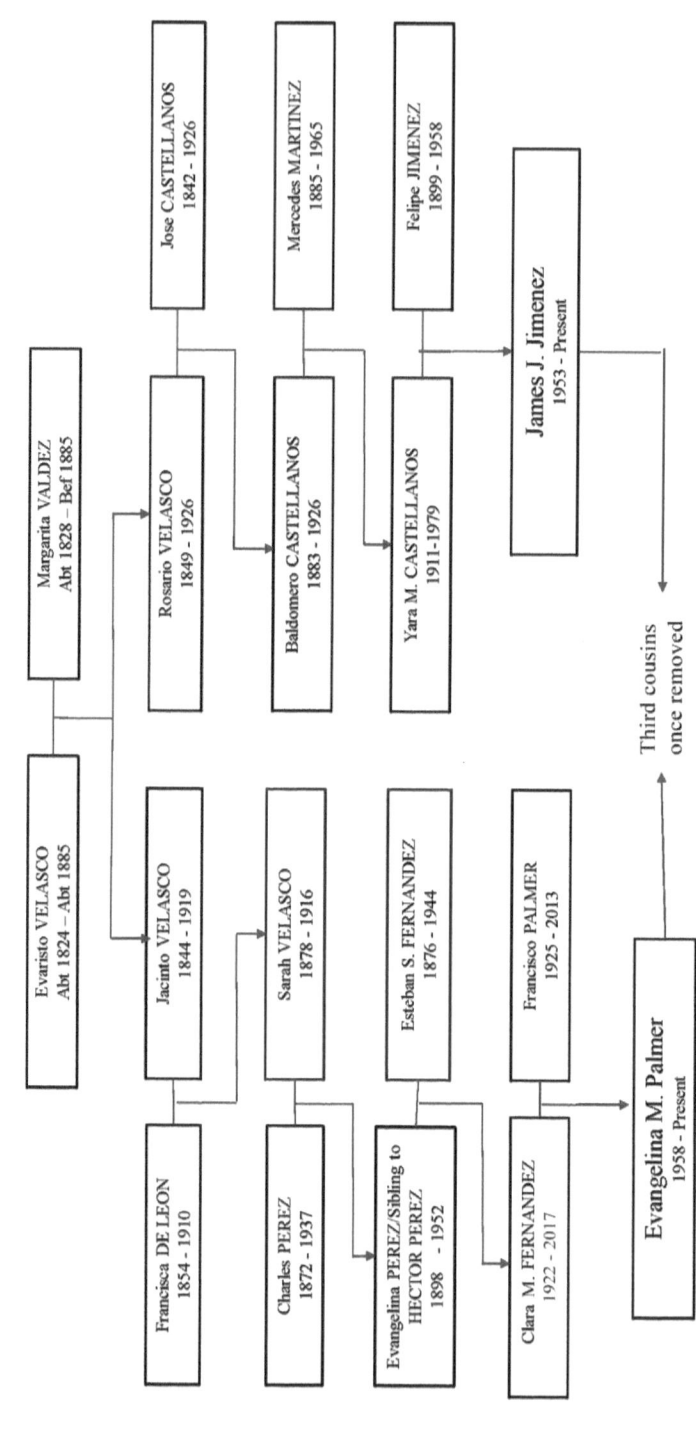

Figure 1: Family tree showing the relationship of Lina Palmer, Jimmy Jimenez, and Hector Perez.

preserve this part of her family history. Lina soon realized how powerful and emotional this story was and how veterans' experiences need to be shared and made public so the U.S. Army and its bureaucracy can learn from past antiquated procedures and implement better practices for their treatment of the people who serve today as well as those who will serve in the future. She felt this story would resonate with people at all levels of society and help some get through their own difficult challenges. Lina shared this story with a family member who had not previously known about it and who was deeply touched, and together they set out to document the facts. She did this in collaboration with your narrator, James J. Jimenez, a third cousin once removed (see figure 1). During this research, we also learned that our common ancestors in Cuba were people who fought for their country's liberation from oppressive and unjust rule. This story includes important historical notes about the struggle for freedom of two nations and several wars with global impact.

Ultimately, this story is about an irrepressible, patriotic young man, a second-generation American whose life was irreversibly impacted by World War I. It is about a man who volunteered to fight for his country, a man whose family had fought for their native country's liberation a few decades earlier. It is about a man who lost all memory of his past life, including the bloody battles he was in and who he was. Whether you believe there were preexisting psychological issues involved or not, by the end of this story, you will see how the effects of combat and the ensuing military injustice altered the lives of many. Covering six decades, this historical account traces the journey of a man who vanished and was "lost" to his family for 15 years.

ONE

The People

The Setup

Things were slow to happen in the early 1920s. It was a time of confusion, oblivion, and uncertainty. Life presented unusual complications that needed to be worked through. Times were tough and replete with ambiguity. There were many unanswered questions and no easy answers. The unforeseen impacts of evolving events were broad and deep. The problems encountered were profound and tragic, putting lives on a collision course with an unimagined destiny. As events unfolded, no one could have guessed what was to happen next. A brief, chance encounter of but a few minutes gave rise to a host of problems that would seem insurmountable. Lives were abruptly upended in dramatic fashion. New complications were continually emerging as all traces of normalcy in their lives disappeared. It was disorienting. Efforts to remedy matters were not immediate, and progress came much too slowly. Things were shrouded and unclear, like murky waters.

Resolving complex issues of such profound importance would require a multilayered approach. Action would need to be taken on several fronts by the proper parties. There would be great reliance on the goodness of human nature to try to bring things back to normal. The triumph of good over evil would be foundational to setting lives back on track. Compassion and understanding would be needed, as would patience. The remedy to this conundrum would require a confluence of movers and shakers, along with someone to bring it all together. The proverbial straw that stirs the drink is a fitting axiom.

A newly married couple, each with their own disability, with no experience in complex matters, would now have to spearhead efforts to overcome the failures and inequities they became victims of. They would need to be the catalyst and overarching champions to make things right, and they would have to push all the right buttons to fix this problem. Coordinated efforts were key. They needed to identify the issues and take appropriate action. There was much work to be done to restore their lives to what they were before these injustices took place. To make matters worse, the two people leading the efforts were neophytes with no clear idea of how to set their lives back on track. Needless to say, the odds were against them.

To compound the situation, telephones were still under development and not yet widely used by the public. Written correspondence was sent by postal mail. Though life was slow compared to today's pace, the U.S. mail was speedier and more efficient in the management of sorting and delivering mail than it is today. A matter of only a few days would pass between an inquiry and an answer.[1] However, the postal service of the early twentieth century was by no means as immediate as today's electronic mail or overnight delivery methods are, especially for urgent issues that were of such profound consequence.[2]

The much-needed actions to effect change could only come about by getting advocates to work on the case together. The question became a matter of how much responsibility people and groups were willing to take on to undo a wrong, to make things right, and fully restore lives back to as normal as possible. In the end, the actions of those at the center of the drama demonstrated how they continuously struggled for years trying to rectify the injustices that were inflicted on them. They were nothing if not irrepressible. They soon learned that an essential and critical interdependence between individuals and organizations working together would be needed to resolve and remedy unjust governmental actions. Sometimes an act of Congress is the only answer. In this case, it would be. But would it go far enough?

The Principals (1920–1928)

It is best to unravel this story beginning in May 1928 in Worcester, Massachusetts. A married couple in their early thirties were walking down Main Street. The woman was the former Grace Marie Dale. Genealogical records revealed the family name was changed from Daley to Dale during her father William B. Dale's generation, sometime between when he left his native Edinburgh, Scotland, in 1882 and his arrival in the United States later that year. Records from Scotland indicate William's surname was Daley at the time of his birth.[3] The ending "y" was dropped after he arrived in the United States. It is a well-known fact that many immigrants changed the spelling of their surnames on arriving in the United States to better fit in. Sometimes their names were inadvertently changed by others involved in the immigration process for various clerical reasons.

Grace's mother was the former Elizabeth A. Dolan, a native of Ireland who immigrated to the United States in 1883.[4] Both of Grace's parents arrived in their new country when they were around the age of eighteen. Elizabeth met and later married William in Worcester, Massachusetts, in 1886.[5] Worcester became the Dales' newly adopted home. Their six children were born there, and they remained in Worcester their entire lives. William and Elizabeth would eventually be buried there, as would most of their immediate progeny.[6]

Grace was born on June 1, 1895.[7] She was best described as reserved, introverted, and well educated. She was physically handicapped, having worn an artificial right leg from the age of six for unknown reasons. Attempts to learn more about the cause of this disability from known Dale family descendants have proven unsuccessful. She was the second youngest of William and Elizabeth Dale's six children. Grace earned a high school diploma and had a university education in business that included certification in elementary accounting principles.[8] Interestingly, in the United States in 1920, people aged twenty-five and over averaged a median of 8.2 years of schooling, and only 60 percent of females had a high school diploma.[9] When it came to formal education, Grace was ahead of the curve in comparison to her contemporaries.

Grace married Alfredo Velasquez Sanchez, who was referred to as "Alfred" by her family. He was also identified as such in a few newspaper articles as well as in other documents we found. Subsequent interviews with members of Grace's family would later corroborate this fact. Grace and Alfred married in July 1921, after meeting in Worcester, Massachusetts, a year earlier. It is not known how they met or the exact day in July they were married, only that it was in 1921. On meeting him, Grace was charmed by Alfred and was described by others as being "carried away" by him. He had an agreeable and pleasing personality. Her handicap was not an issue for her husband. We learned that he cared for her deeply. In letters we found, Grace would say her husband was always "polite and caring."

Soon after meeting her husband, Grace discovered that he was an accomplished pianist. She learned he was quite fond of entertaining others with his talent and enjoyed playing the piano very much. If he became moody, which he did from time to time, he would go off by himself and play the piano. He found comfort and solace in this practice. He was well liked by others and was popular with those he met. Alfred possessed many attributes Grace admired.

They courted for about a year. A short announcement was found in the *Worcester Evening Gazette*, a local newspaper, on July 7, 1921, under the heading of marriage intentions.[10] The information was garnered from city hall records stating that Alfred and Grace were to be wed, but no date was given. In this announcement, he was referred to as Alfred, though his surname was misspelled as "Lauchez." His age was correct at 25 years old. He was reported to be a machinist, and his home address was given as 63 Coral Street in Worcester. Grace's age was also correct in the article, which listed her as 26 years old. She lived on Franklin Street, her family home at the time. Their residences were about a mile apart. According to the 1920 U.S. Census, Grace was a 23-year-old telephone operator who lived with her parents on Franklin Street. Grace's age was reported incorrectly in the census, as she would have been 25 years old at that time, having been born in 1895.[11] The other information on the census is correct.

Alfred moved in with Grace and her parents at their Franklin Street home following the marriage in 1921. We found their marriage recorded in the database titled "Index to Marriages in Massachusetts 1921–1925," on the sixth line from the top for Alfredo.[12] Halfway down the page we found the record for Grace.[13]

In an unrelated newspaper article printed in the *Worcester Evening Gazette* on August 29, 1927, Alfred Sanchez was reported to have had his automobile stolen over the weekend. The article went on to say that his vehicle was located and returned to him.[14] This event occurred about six years after their marriage. They remained at the Franklin Street address during this entire period.[15]

The Heart of the Matter (1921–1928)

Grace had the education and skill to compete in the job market, but her husband did not. Alfred was always able to find work but did not last long at any of his jobs for varying reasons, all related to poor job performance. He was respectful of others, personable and talented, but it would not take his employers long to discover that Alfred had issues getting his work done. This was the case with every employer he had, and his employment would always be terminated due to this one issue.

So, what was it that caused Alfred to have such a spotty work record? At the core of Alfred's problem was his absentmindedness. He would willingly do exactly what he was instructed to do, and things would start out well, but he would soon forget some aspects of what he was told to do. He could not fully complete all his assigned tasks, as he failed to recall fully all the instructions he was given. For instance, he got a job at a local eatery and was assigned to close the restaurant at night, but he would forget to lock the door. To keep Alfred on the payroll, his employer changed his job assignment, having him open the restaurant instead, but then Alfred would forget to make the coffee first thing in the morning. It became evident that Alfred was willing to work; he just would not or could not remember all the assignments he was given. This pattern of behavior was demonstrated at many of the jobs he held, all for only short periods of time. The reason for his dismissal was always the same: failure to complete all his assigned tasks. According to his employers, there were no other factors that led them to terminate his employment. He was always found to have a pleasing personality, and he got along well with others. Alfred was well liked by his peers and superiors. These factual details were outlined in correspondence dated June 9, 1930, between state social agencies and are discussed in detail later.

One might think that Grace would grow weary of her husband's inability to retain steady employment after some time, but she supported Alfred every step of the way. Grace was unconditionally devoted to her husband and wanted nothing more than to make their marriage a success. She was not a contrarian and was more guided by the spirit of unity in her marriage than anything else. Overall, she remained supportive of her husband throughout his struggles. She collaborated with Alfred in approaching the challenges they faced. They loved one another and did their best to work together. They supported each other. She remained at his side as an equal partner during this entire ordeal; in fact, we soon discovered that she was the driving force behind the many efforts to help Alfred address and resolve his issues. She was his staunchest ally.

We do not know for certain whether there was a particular reason for Grace's unwavering loyalty to her husband in the face of his ongoing struggles. Being physically handicapped, she may have seen her husband's lapses in memory as a handicap, too, and therefore had a deeper understanding than most. Maybe her upbringing caused her to be more empathetic than most folks might be in similar circumstances. Her acceptance of and tolerance for what Alfred was going through were unusual. It may have been that he was her only suitor, and she considered herself fortunate that he had asked her to marry him, considering her handicap. During our research, we learned a Dale family relative had experienced mental challenges at an early age, which may have taught Grace to be more empathetic than most. A 1910 Worcester State Asylum census revealed this fact.[16] A 1918 death record at line number 208 reveals the diagnosis and cause of death.[17] A Find a Grave memorial shows the final resting place was with the family.[18] We surmise that Grace did all she did out of love for her husband. It was her own self-perseverance that drove her. Whatever the reason, together they formed an alliance and were going to get through whatever life had in store for them. To her credit, and in the face of the reality of her situation, Grace had the intelligence, education, and wherewithal necessary to make smart choices. These talents and abilities enabled her to hold down a job while being promoted regularly.

It turned out that Grace knew very little about her husband. Over the year they courted, she was unable to elicit much definitive information from him about his past. She knew nothing of her husband's former life, having only met him in 1920 as a young adult man. She could not learn anything about his family since Alfred could not remember. She made inquiries into his past, asking him where he was from and about his family roots. Alfred was never able to provide any information about his birth, childhood, or family, other than his belief that he was born in Tampa, Florida. He did not remember names and could not recall much else about his past. Grace was perplexed by his vagueness. His former life was shrouded within a whole host of mysteries when she married him due to his inability to recall basic aspects of his past. He was simply unable to remember even the most fundamental events of and people in his former life. Yet we know he remembered how to play the piano.

Due to his inability to hold any job for long, the couple decided to relocate in the hopes that a geographical change would improve Alfred's ability to hold onto a job. Alfred and Grace moved to Newark, New Jersey, hoping this would be the cure. He had little difficulty finding work after relocating, but, once again, he never lasted more than two to three months at any job.

One evening around two years after moving to Newark, Alfred was brought home by the police. They informed Grace that they had found him in a confused and dazed state when they questioned him. He told them he did not know who he was or where he was from. We have not learned how the police ascertained Alfred's identity or residential address, so we assume he had some form of identification on his person or was known to them. It was at this point that Grace decided she and her husband would return to Worcester, and so they did. Grace realized she could not depend on Alfred for financial support. She returned to her previous job as a switchboard operator at Memorial Hospital in Worcester with a salary of $12.00 a week. Her salary alone was insufficient for the two of them to get by on, so Alfred got a job at a fur shop and found work as a restaurant helper. However, he was soon dismissed from both jobs. The reality of what was happening to them had set firmly in by now.

At times Alfred had bouts of unusual and inexplicable behavior. As mentioned earlier, he would go off on his own at times, not returning home as expected. Then, on his return, he could offer no reasonable explanation for where he had been, nor could he provide any explanation for his actions. For a short period of time, they lived with Grace's parents. Grace found herself in a position of having to "look after" her husband and indicated on more than one occasion that she would "always try to take care of him." In terms of tolerating her husband's issues, she was always supportive of him. At the same time, she was a realist. Grace was aware of the challenges that marriage to Alfred presented to her. Figuratively speaking, she did not live life seeing things through rose-colored glasses.

Alfred could not have been easy to live with, but he knew Grace would help him. He loved her deeply for this support. Grace wrote in her letters to a family member that he was a gentleman and a kind husband to her. They were well suited for one another. Although they were merely trying to make ends meet, theirs was indeed a union of mutual commitment. This was their love story.

Two

The Events

A Chance Meeting Spells Disaster (May 1928)

Back to that fateful day in May 1928 in Worcester, Massachusetts, when Grace and Alfred were walking on Main Street. At this time, the couple had been together since 1920. They were approached by an unknown stranger who knew Alfred. The only problem was that the stranger greeted him with a different name. On seeing Alfred, the stranger referred to him as "Perry." Alfred and Grace wondered why the stranger called him by that name. The stranger informed Alfred that "Perry" was the surname he had used when they served together overseas. The two had met while fighting for the U.S. Army in France during World War I. Grace listened to the stranger intently. Alfred had no recollection of fighting in France during the war, nor could he recall his military service. Equally puzzling was that Alfred did not recognize his former "war buddy" in the least.

World War I was simply known as the world war or the Great War at that time since it was the first global conflict.[1] The war lasted from July 28, 1914, through November 11, 1918, and was one of the deadliest global conflicts in history. It was fought between two coalitions: the Allies (primarily France, the United Kingdom, Russia, Italy, Japan, and later the United States) versus the Central Powers (led by Germany, Austria-Hungary, and the Ottoman Empire). Fighting occurred throughout Europe, the Middle East, Africa, the Pacific, and parts of Asia. An estimated nine million soldiers were killed in combat, plus another 23 million wounded, while five million civilians died due to military action, hunger, and disease. Millions were killed as a result of genocide, while the 1918 "Spanish flu" pandemic was exacerbated by the movement of so many combatants during the war.

While World War I broke out across Europe in 1914, the United States remained neutral until April 6, 1917, when war was declared. Congress voted to approve U.S. entry into the war for several reasons. The first was the sinking of the *Lusitania* by a German submarine, coupled with continued German submarine warfare; second was the infamous Zimmermann telegram, which revealed Germany's offer to help Mexico regain territory lost to the United States in the Mexican-American War—namely, Texas, New Mexico, and Arizona. Until that time, most Americans did not feel the country had an interest in the war. Following these events, American sentiment was now different.[2]

Prior to U.S. involvement in the war, the army had 133,000 soldiers, not enough for fighting a war. Therefore, the United States reinstated the military draft for the first time since the Civil War; Congress passed the Selective Service Act on May 18, 1917, through which 2.8 million men were inducted into the army, along with another two million volunteers.[3] By the war's end, the United States had sent two million troops to the Western Front. All these facts were reported in the daily news stories and were very sobering for the public.

During the encounter with the "war buddy" in Worcester, Grace informed the stranger that her husband's name was Alfred Velasquez Sanchez, not "Perry." While she had known her husband for only a year before they were married, Grace told the stranger that her husband used this name when they were married and had done so ever since. Naturally, Grace had no reason not to believe Alfred. Her husband said he believed that was indeed his name when the two first met in 1920. While speaking, Alfred also said he vaguely remembered the name "Perry" but did not know why. Alfred then asked the war buddy whether he knew when he, Alfred, got out of the army. The stranger responded that he did not know.

Shortly after that chance meeting on Main Street, the couple hired a Worcester attorney by the name of William C. Bowen, who recommended Alfred contact the War Department to inquire about what they had learned. Alfred and Grace wondered whether the military could help shed light on his identity: Was he really Alfredo Velasquez Sanchez or Perry? They thought the military could reveal his true name, tell him where he was from or advise him about who his family was so that he could contact them. His family, if he had any, could easily think he had been killed in action and not identified. Alfred and Grace followed the attorney's advice and wrote to the War Department. The couple was eager to learn more about Alfred's past, his family, and many other things he was not able to remember, and they felt this opportunity might be a dream come true. What was obvious to all was the reality that Alfred was "lost."

The Army Gets Their Man (May 1928)

Their letter elicited a response from the War Department. Alfred was instructed to report immediately to Fort Adams, Rhode Island. Without having a copy of that letter, we must make an educated guess regarding the army's intent here. Alfred may have been seeking answers, but the military had other priorities. The army was intent on exacting justice. On his arrival at Fort Adams on May 29, 1928, Alfred was promptly arrested and charged with desertion. He was brought before a general court-martial, found guilty and sentenced. He was then placed in confinement until the verdict could be approved before the reviewing authority. The sentence that was handed down was a dishonorable discharge, with forfeiture of all pay and allowances due or that would become due, and to be confined at hard labor for one year. His case was slated to go before the reviewing authority on September 20, 1928. He would be confined for four months awaiting final review and adjudication by the commanding officer and tribunal.

Alfred was never advised of his military status until his arrival at Fort Adams. Furthermore, according to the War Department, the person claiming to be Alfredo Velasquez Sanchez was known to them as "Hector H. Perry." While it is unclear how the army made that assessment, Alfred had in fact enlisted as Hector H. Perry, as we will soon see (see appendix).[4] Yet his name was not Hector H. Perry, either. It would take another three-plus years and herculean efforts on the couple's part to find out that Alfred's real name was Hector Perez, which makes the story that much more incredible.

As a deserter, Hector H. Perry stood trial before a general court-martial, which is the military's highest-level trial court.[5] It tries service members for the most serious offenses.

Although the Uniform Code of Military Justice did not yet exist in May 1928, desertion carried a maximum punishment of a dishonorable discharge, forfeiture of all pay, and confinement of five years.[6] If desertion occurred during a time of war, the death penalty could be invoked at the discretion of the commander and general court-martial members.[7] If the accused was found guilty, the sentence would be adjudicated based on when the act of desertion occurred.

World War I officially ended at the eleventh hour on the eleventh day of the eleventh month in 1918, which became known as Armistice Day. Simply put, November 11, 1918, was the date the war ended. As we learned from the historical record, Hector deserted well after that point. His official date of desertion was June 26, 1920, which was the date he was due to return from his approved furlough, which began nine days earlier, on June 17, 1920. As the war was over, the imposition of a death sentence would not have been an option at his general court-martial.[8] The young couple was grateful for that.

Hector went to Fort Adams as instructed, expecting answers. Instead,

Two. The Events

the army took physical control over him since he was the person they identified as Hector H. Perry, and, as far as they were concerned, he was a deserter. He was now theirs to deal with as they saw fit.

To this day, it remains a mystery as to why Hector Perez enlisted in the army in 1917 under the assumed or adopted name of Hector H. Perry. As detailed later in this book, his mother died in Tampa, Florida, on January 21, 1916, prior to his enlistment, so her disapproval of his enlistment could not have been a factor as to why he would assume a different name at that time.[9] We also learned he enlisted in New York City in March 1917.[10] What transpired in Hector's life during the year and two months between his mother's death and his enlistment in the military is unknown. In addition, we learned that he left his hometown of Tampa, Florida, after his mother's death; his whereabouts during the subsequent year are also unknown. There is no one living today with personal or first-hand knowledge of what transpired during that period. One must wonder what prompted him to adopt the name Hector H. Perry at the time of his enlistment and why he chose to enlist in New York City.

Theories can be postulated, but nothing can be proven. Nothing has been discovered that would give a clue as to why Hector used the name he did at the time of his enlistment. Nor were we able to find evidence of the reason for his going to New York in our research. We postulated that he may have gone to visit family in New York after his mother passed away. His father had been born in New York (we will discuss this subject in chapter 3), so a visit would have been understandable.[11] We wondered, aside from his parents, was there anyone from whom would he want to hide his enlistment to the point that he changed his name and enlisted in a distant city. He was twenty years old at the time of his enlistment and an adult; therefore he could make such decisions on his own, without needing parental or anyone else's approval. So it is doubtful that he was hiding his enlistment from anyone.

Or could it be possible that Hector was already exhibiting signs of mental issues at the time of (or prior to) his enlistment due to his mother's death or some other trauma? Or did he change his name purposely to "fit in" by adopting a more anglicized surname? There were no family stories passed down over the years about Hector having any psychological or emotional issues prior to his enlistment. As we previously indicated, Hector declared that he had no recollection of having served in the army and did not know why he used the name Perry when he enlisted. There must be a plausible reason why he ended up in New York and enlisted there. Unfortunately, the answer to that question remains enigmatic.

As far as family genealogy buffs and those with close family ties know, no one was even aware that Hector had a middle name or used a middle initial. "H" was the middle initial shown on the army records; what did it stand for? Later, we will reveal how this detail connects to other data.

During his period of confinement, while Hector awaited a decision on whether the sentence would be approved, modified, or remitted by the reviewing authority, he faced the reality that his previous dream of the army helping him learn his identity had turned into a nightmare. Due to his desire to unravel the mystery of his past, he was now confined and separated from Grace, all due to a crime he could not remember committing.

Between June 26 and July 27, 1928, during his confinement, army psychiatrists assessed Hector. The diagnosis was a "constitutional psychopathic state, inadequate personality." This diagnosis seems to have influenced and sufficiently moved all the tribunal members who sat for his general court-martial, as evidenced by the following letter they wrote to their commanding general, which has been transcribed verbatim.

Clemency Letter (August 1928)

Fort Adams, Rhode Island,
August 3, 1928.

Subject; Clemency:

To: The Commanding General, First Corps Area, Army base, Boston, Mass.

The members of the General Court martial, which sat in the case of private Hector H Perry, who signed their names below, are of the opinion that clemency should be granted as follows, namely, remission of dishonorable discharge and six months of the confinement.

Signed,

O. S. Wood, Major 13th Infantry
A.D. Johnson, Capt. 13th Infantry
S.C. Thompson, Capt. 13th Infantry
G.L. Prindle, Capt. 13th infantry
N.D. Young, 1st Lt. 10th C.A.
J.E. Dooley, 1st Lt. 13th infantry
N.E. Smith, Jr., 2nd Lt., 13th infantry
Defense counsel

All the officers who sat for and heard the general court-martial case (as well as the defense counsel) recommended clemency, which included remission of the dishonorable discharge and six months of confinement.[12]

Not even a week later, the army brass felt Hector should undergo further psychiatric assessments. During August 9–12, 1928, Hector endured another battery of tests. The diagnosis this time around: psychoneurosis, hysteria, acute (constitutional psychopathic state, inadequate personality). Could the reason for these new tests be that Hector exhibited concerning signs of further mental deterioration during his period of confinement? He had undergone a solid thirty days of psychiatric observation and evaluation, and this second round of tests produced the same diagnosis as the first, though more severe.

The Final Verdict (September 1928)

Hector remained confined for four months. Then, on September 20, 1928, while remanded by the army and in custody at Fort Adams, the reviewing body partially approved the sentence. Hector was dishonorably discharged with forfeiture of all pay and allowances due now or that would become due. The only modification was that confinement was remitted. This was a tiny bit of good news along with the terrible news. The approving body considered the four months he served in confinement and counted it as time served toward his prison sentence, but the remainder of the recommendations in the clemency letter were not adopted.

The members of the general court-martial saw the various diagnoses as something that concerned them in reviewing Hector's case and thus felt he should be granted clemency. We learned from newspaper reporting that it was the commanding officer, General Preston Brown, First Army Corps, who had the last word.[13] His veto was all that counted. In general court-martial trials, the commanding officer has the final say. All the military officers hearing the matter believed the dishonorable discharge and the sentence should be set aside, except for General Brown. Rank is the overriding factor in determining final judgment, regardless of the recommendations of the officers hearing the case. The trial officers heard the evidence and deliberated logically and fairly, whereas the ranking officer read the documents and all on his own decided he knew better. Two axioms come to mind: rank has its privileges, and might makes right.

We would later learn that the army, in their recordkeeping and reporting, was not forthcoming when they stated in a letter dated July 3, 1931, almost three years later, responding to a congressional inquiry, that Hector "surrendered."[14] They referred to him as "returning to military control."[15] (This letter is transcribed verbatim and displayed in chapter 7.) This version of events made it sound like he was captured. Technically, Hector did not "surrender," as he had no idea that he deserted in the first place, and his deserter status was not communicated to him until he arrived at Fort Adams and was immediately taken into custody. He was not captured *per se*, and he was not avoiding apprehension. For eight years he was living his life as any normal citizen would and was not attempting to keep his identity a secret. He did not know who he was. This fact should have been plainly evident on hearing the particulars about how he arrived at his current state. To make matters worse for the army, the letter in question revealed a previous mental illness diagnosis made while Hector was still overseas. The general court-martial members should have been made aware of what was known at that time from Hector's military medical record showing this diagnosis from April 1919 prior to sailing home in July 1919.[16] Hector and Grace should have been informed of it as well during the trial.

We will follow, document, and compile the records to demonstrate how Hector and Grace reacted to this "death sentence" and formulated a plan to right this wrong, which pitted them against the bureaucracy of the 1920s U.S. Army.

Three

La Familia

The "Lost" Hector Perez and His Family

The essence of this story does not really shift at this time. It has always been about our principal, a man who served his country in some of the bloodiest battles our nation had fought up until then.[1] He suffered an emotional or mental breakdown while serving that led to amnesia. He did not even know whether he had family or where they lived. He was alone and lost. He miraculously found a partner who accepted him. She had all the traits they would both need to succeed as a couple and later helped him solve the mysteries of his forgotten past. Most important, she helped him fight to get the charges against him reversed. This partner, as we like to call her, was Hector's "amazing Grace." She and her family had accepted Alfred, now Hector H. Perry, with open arms since their marriage in 1921. We learned these were the people he felt closest to and considered his family. Hector and his adopted family would not learn of his true "identity" until three years later in 1931.

This story is not about Alfredo/Alfred Velasquez Sanchez or Hector H. Perry; it is about Hector Perez, his wife Grace, and the most unusual, unjust, and unimaginable challenges they had to overcome to right the wrong committed against him. These three identities were the same person, and that person entered the world as Hector Perez. The other two names are fabricated: one from the mind of an amnesia victim and the second for unknown reasons.

From this point on, insofar as this story goes, the identity of Alfredo/Alfred Velasquez Sanchez no longer exists, except for historical reference. Hector H. Perry (the name by which the army knew him) was on trial. Even though the life of Hector and Grace as a couple had been a challenge from the very beginning, it was about to take a dramatic turn for the worse. Their lives would never be the same. The difficulties they had endured over their first eight years together would pale in comparison to the difficulties they would experience over the next three.

The personal knowledge of living family members as well as the numerous documents in the genealogical record prove unequivocally that Hector's maternal predecessors were the descendants of Evaristo and Margarita Velasco. Along with many fellow Cubans, the Velasco family immigrated to the United States in 1869, at the onset of the Ten Years' War (1868–1878) in their native Cuba.[2] They brought with them their five children, the oldest being Hector's grandfather Jacinto V. Velasco (coauthor Evangelina Palmer's great-great-grandfather), along with their only daughter Rosario (coauthor Jim Jimenez's great-grandmother) and three younger sons. Four of the children were adults when the family immigrated. The family chose Key West, Florida, to escape the Spanish oppression in their native country and begin their lives anew. Hector's mother, Sarah Velasco, was one of Jacinto Velasco's sixteen children; she was born in Key West in 1878.[3]

Family records, census reports and genealogical records confirm that Hector's paternal predecessors were the descendants of Jose Isabel Perez and Claudia R. Mora. The Perez family, like the Velasco family, also immigrated to Key West from Cuba in 1869.[4] They arrived with a one-year-old daughter, Dolores (nicknamed "Lola"), and, according to the 1870 U.S. Census, had been married since 1860.[5] Uncorroborated but well-known family history attested that Jose Perez was politically active in the struggle for Cuban independence. He was assigned to fundraise in New York City. Immediately after his arrival to the United States, along with his wife and infant daughter, they traveled up the Eastern Seaboard to New York. Charles Perez (Hector's father) was born in New York City in 1872, as evidenced by the 1880 U.S. Census, his U.S. passport application (dated June 15, 1930), several other census reports, and family records.[6] Jose, Claudia, and their two young children traveled to and lived in Lancaster County, South Carolina, for a brief time, where another son was born in 1873, who they named Ramon.[7] By 1875, the couple was back in New York City, at which time they welcomed a third son named Agusto.[8] The 1880 U.S. Census verifies the birthplaces for Dolores, Charles, Ramon, and Agusto, corroborating at least part of the family lore.

In the 1900 U.S. Census, Claudia Perez (Hector's paternal grandmother) was asked "how many live births to date" she had experienced; she answered "seven." To the next question ("how many living?"), she answered "two."[9] We know the two living children were Lola and Charles. The two brothers Ramon and Agusto died between the censuses of 1880 and 1900. We found no evidence of the other three births or deaths in the United States, so we must assume those other three children were born and died in Cuba. It was clear that the Perez family traveled between New York City and South Carolina for a few years before heading back to Key

West. By 1880, they were living in Key West, where they remained for the rest of their lives. Jose passed away in 1901, and Claudia died in 1910.[10]

Both sets of Hector's grandparents were born in Cuba, and both parents (Charles Perez and Sarah Velasco) were born in the United States. Hector's mother, Sarah, was a classically trained and highly accomplished pianist, and her husband Charles was a cigar maker. The two were married in Tampa, Florida, on February 15, 1896, and had four children, two boys and two girls.[11] They named the children Hector; Evangelina; Charles E. (Ernest), who was referred to as Carlos in one early document, though later in life he went by the nickname "Charlie"; and Dinorah M.

Hector Perez was born in Tampa, Florida, on December 16, 1896, ten months after his parents married.[12] He was the oldest of the Perez children. Hector's three younger siblings were all born in Key West. His sister Evangelina was born eighteen months after him in 1898, his brother Charlie was born in 1899 and his sister Dinorah was born in 1903.

On a few occasions Hector would inform his wife, Grace, that he had no recollection of Tampa. Setting aside his absentmindedness, we know Hector's family moved from Tampa to Key West when he was a toddler. All four Perez children were raised in Key West.

Following the Family

According to the 1900 U.S. Census, both the Velasco and the Perez families lived in Key West. The census record for the Velasco family reflected fourteen people living together at 306 Elizabeth Street, with the head of the household being Jacinto, along with his wife Francisca de Leon y Silvera.[13] Jacinto's occupation was listed as carpenter. Living with Jacinto and Francisca were their daughter Sarah, her husband Charles, and their three children, Hector, Evangelina, and Charles (Dinorah, the fourth child, had not yet been born). Jacinto's other children living with him at that time were aged nine through eighteen. We learned that in 1901 Jacinto developed a safety appliance system to prevent railroad cars from going off their tracks. He applied for and was granted a U.S. patent for his invention (figure 2).[14] Displayed below is a photograph of Jacinto V. Velasco (figure 3). His wife Francisca died in February 1910, and Jacinto died nine years later, in May 1919.

The 1910 U.S. Census revealed that Charles, Sarah (figures 4 and 5), and their four children lived at 910 Winden Lane in Key West.[15] At that time, Charles was employed as a cigar maker, and Sarah was a music teacher. Four years later, in 1914, the city directory listed the family living at 1926 Seidenberg Avenue in Key West.[16] Like his father, Hector, was

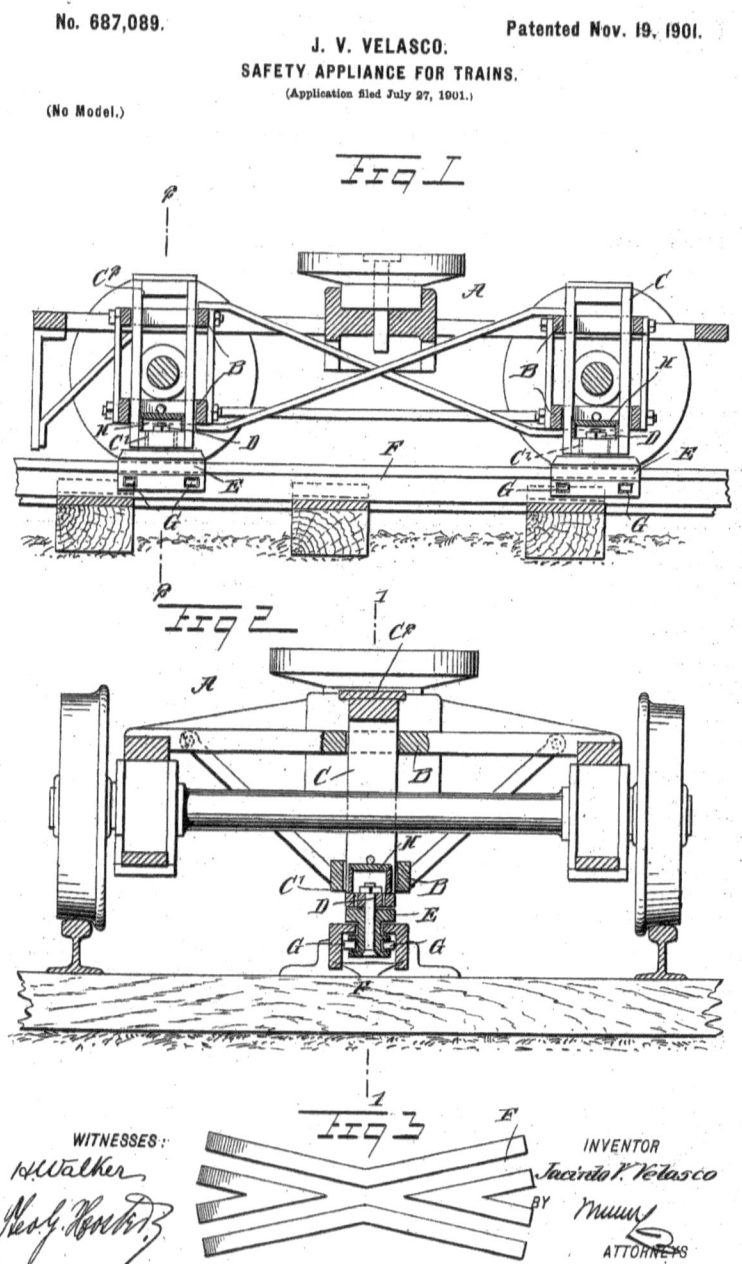

Figure 2: Image of the 1901 U.S. patent granted to Jacinto V. Velasco for a safety appliance for trains.

employed as a cigar maker at that time and lived at the same address on Seidenberg Avenue; his sister Evangelina can be found several lines above Hector's name, listed as a student.[17] He was eighteen years old. We know from family lore that the Perez household was filled with music, as Sarah could be found at the piano every day while instructing her children as well as students. Both Hector and Evangelina were classically trained, and Sarah had them on a rigorous schedule. We learned the family owned a cat that would sit on the piano whenever someone played. By all accounts, their home pulsed with musical activity and was described as warm and inviting. Sometime between 1914 and 1915, the family moved to Tampa, Florida.

Figure 3: Jacinto Velasco y Valdez, born July 11, 1844, in the city of Havana, Cuba. He immigrated to Key West, Florida, with his family in 1869 to escape Spanish oppression. He was a carpenter by trade and a well-known tinkerer who invented a railcar safety device for which he was granted a patent in 1901. He spent his entire life in Key West from the time of his arrival to his death in 1919.

Hector's mother, Sarah Perez née Velasco, died at her home at 408 East Michigan Avenue in Tampa.[18] She succumbed to tuberculosis at the age of thirty-seven on January 21, 1916. Life expectancy at that time was fifty-four years for women.[19] During the nineteenth and early twentieth centuries, tuberculosis (TB) was one of the leading causes of death in the United States and one of the most feared diseases in the entire world. Formerly called "consumption," tuberculosis is characterized externally by fatigue, night sweats, and a general "wasting away" of the victim.[20] Sarah's obituary was published in the *Tampa Tribune* on January 22, 1916. It was a scant two-line item. Funeral services were held that morning at 9:00. Sarah was interred at Woodlawn Cemetery in Tampa.

Hector was nineteen years old at the time of his mother's death. His brother Charlie was sixteen. Sarah's two daughters, Evangelina and Dinorah, were eighteen and twelve, respectively. After their mother's death, the girls went to live with their Velasco aunts, who also resided in

Tampa. They had a large extended family there consisting of many aunts, uncles, and cousins, especially female cousins of similar ages to them.

As mentioned earlier, Hector's father, Charles Perez, was born in New York City. We found no evidence of any known relatives living in New York City after Sarah's death in 1916. Charles later remarried in 1925, nine years after Sarah's death. He lived in Key West, Florida, with his second wife. We learned she accidentally poisoned herself on August 18, 1932,

Photo by Telegram Staff Photographer
Hector Perez of 9 King street and his father, Charles Perez of Key West, Fla.

Figure 4: Charles Perez was born December 18, 1872, in New York City. His father, Jose I. Perez, was an organizer and fundraiser in the struggle for Cuban independence. Charles was reserved and mild mannered; he worked as a cigar-maker his entire life. He married Sarah Velasco, and they had four children. After the death of his second wife, Mercedes, he moved to Cuba to live with his oldest daughter Evangelina and her family. He died and was buried in Cuba in the late 1930s.

and died ten days later. Two newspaper stories reporting details of the accident and its aftermath were published in the *Key West Citizen*.[21] The first story appeared on August 18, 1932, and reported that Mrs. Charles Perez had accidentally ingested a strong solution of bichloride of mercury, after which she became seriously ill. Mercury bichloride is absorbed into the bloodstream and organs, where it damages the kidneys and intestinal tract, causes internal bleeding, and, at a high enough dose, is deadly. The incident occurred during the night when Mrs. Perez thought she was taking medicine she had used in the past but grabbed the bottle of poison instead. The following morning, she was reported to be suffering in terrible agony. A physician was called to the house and stated that in his opinion she had ingested poison. An examination and the subsequent use of a stomach pump proved the doctor's diagnosis was spot on. Charles Perez told the *Citizen* that afternoon that his wife was much better, and they hoped for her recovery.

On August 29, 1932, the second story was printed in the *Key West Citizen*, which reported that Mrs. Perez had died at her residence at 414 Louisa Street the prior evening after taking a dose of poison by mistake. Funeral services were held that afternoon from the residence of her sister at 1117 Duval Street.

Figure 5: Sarah Velasco y Leon was born in February 1878, in Key West, Florida. She studied piano from an early age. She married Charles Perez in 1896, and they had four children. She taught piano her entire life. She tutored two of her four children to play the piano. Her home was said to always be filled with music, and she was described as a contented woman. She died in 1916 from tuberculosis at the age of 37.

Sometime after this tragedy, Charles moved to Cuba and lived with his daughter Evangelina and her family. He died in Havana, we believe, during the latter part of 1937.

The Velasco family was musically inclined, with several members being accomplished musicians in their chosen instruments. Sarah's brother, Antonio, played the cornet (a brass instrument like the trumpet) and was depicted in a photograph of the "Russell's Cornet Band of Key West" taken in 1904 and available for viewing in the Florida Keys Public Library Archives.[22] The quality of the photograph, unfortunately, is not suitable for printing. One of Sarah's younger sisters, Eliza, was a classically trained pianist as well.

As an accomplished pianist, we know Sarah gave piano instruction to two of her four children. Hector and his sister Evangelina studied piano under their mother's tutelage up until her death. Family members recounted that they both played beautifully. It was in Tampa that Evangelina (figure 6) met her future husband, Esteban Silvestre Fernandez Quintanal Barroso, when she began working as a cashier at a pharmacy that he managed in Tampa, known as

Figure 6: Evangelina Perez y Velasco was the second child of Charles and Sarah, born on June 28, 1898, in Key West, Florida. She was known as a brilliant piano player and described as a "happy soul" (translated from the Spanish "una alma feliz"). She married an older professional man, Esteban S. Fernandez. Their only daughter, Clara "Bibi" Fernandez y Perez (Hector's only niece), recounted that "her mother was a forward-thinking woman for her time and enjoyed using and mastering the modern public transportation (buses) available in Havana, much to her husband's chagrin." She had three children. Her family moved to Cuba in the mid-1920s. She was known to cook special meals for the family's German shepherd nicknamed "Navy" (short for British Navy) three times a week. She was the piano player at her local Methodist church in Cuba and died in 1952. She is buried in a family plot.

the "Latin American Pharmacy." They married two years later in July 1918, when she was about twenty years old and he was forty-two. That year they moved to Macon, Georgia, where Esteban managed the "Terminal Pharmacy." Their first child, Esteban, was born in Georgia, and by 1920 they returned to Florida. They resided in Tampa, where Esteban returned to managing the Latin American Pharmacy.[23] We found evidence showing that later that year, in August, they left Tampa, visited family in Cuba, and then arrived in Key West. Their stay was "indefinite," as records show.[24] They resided there for five years while Esteban managed yet another pharmacy, this one located on Duval Street. During this time, they

Figure 7: Dinorah M. Perez y Velasco was the youngest of the four Perez children and was born on June 24, 1903, in Key West, Florida. She was known as an entrepreneurial, energetic young woman, married a budding hotelier, and had two children. In addition to serving as a community volunteer, she worked in the hotels her husband managed and lived in Winter Park, Florida, where she was laid to rest in 1980.

had two more children: Carlos, who was born in 1920, and Clara "Bibi" (coauthor Evangelina's mother), born in 1922.[25] By the mid–1920s, the family relocated to Cuba. Esteban was returning to where he was born and where his family was located; after having managed several pharmacies for many years in the United States, he was ready to open his own. He opened a state-of-the-art pharmacy in Havana based on the American and French models of the day.[26] Evangelina eventually became the head organ and piano player in her local Methodist church, of which she was a lifelong member. Esteban died in 1944, and Evangelina died in 1952 in Havana, Cuba.

Sarah and Charles' youngest daughter Dinorah (figure 7) attended high school in Tampa. She would later return to and live with relatives in Key West, where she was born and raised for most of her life. She married William C. Atkinson in Dade County in 1929, lived in Miami in 1930, and by 1935 moved to the Orlando area, where she remained for the rest of her life. She became very active in her community and was a founding member of the Orlando–Winter Park Pilot Club. Pilot International was a national organization, whose members volunteered in aspects of health or welfare work as community service projects. Dinorah's husband was in the hospitality industry and operated several hotels. She had two sons who lived most of their lives in the area. Dinorah passed away in Orlando, Florida, in 1980.

Hector's only brother, Charles Ernest "Charlie" Perez, enlisted in the U.S. Army in January 1917, two months before Hector enlisted. Records indicate Charlie resided in New York City when he enlisted. Charlie served valiantly, as we will detail later in chapter 5. He married in New York in 1936 and had no children. By 1942, the couple had moved to Florida and divorced that year. Charlie died in Florida in 1950.

The four Perez children had differing physical appearances. According to Hector's World War II draft registration card (and family reports), his complexion was ruddy, and he had brown hair and blue eyes.[27] As a young woman, Evangelina had dirty blonde hair and green eyes. Charlie had a very dark olive complexion with brown eyes; in one census report that was taken in 1920, he was erroneously designated "mulatto."[28] Dinorah was very fair skinned with blue eyes.

FOUR

History of Wars

Cuban Conflict and Immigration to the United States

In 1492, prior to the arrival of the Genoese explorer, Christopher Columbus, the island of Cuba was inhabited by various Amerindian cultures.[1] After Columbus' arrival on a Spanish expedition, Spain conquered Cuba and appointed Spanish governors to rule in Havana. The Cuban administrators were subject to the viceroy of New Spain and the local authorities in Hispaniola. The history of Cuba is characterized by dependence on outside powers: Spain, the United States, and the Soviet Union.

Hispaniola is in the West Indies, Greater Antilles, and is situated in the Caribbean Sea. It is the second-largest island in this region. It is politically divided into the Republic of Haiti in the west and the Dominican Republic in the east.[2] When Columbus landed on the island, he named it "La Isla Española." During Spanish colonial times, the island's position on the northern flank of the Caribbean Sea provided an excellent location for control of Spanish expansion to Cuba, Mexico, Panama, and South America.[3]

In 1762–1763, Havana was briefly occupied by Britain before being returned to Spain in exchange for Florida.[4] A series of rebellions between 1868 and 1898, primarily led by General Máximo Gómez, failed to end Spanish rule.[5] However, it was the Spanish-American War (1898) that resulted in Spain's withdrawal from the island; following three and a half years of subsequent U.S. military rule, Cuba gained formal independence in 1902.[6]

Anyone of Cuban descent or versed in Cuban history and migration patterns knows that many Cubans left their native land after one of the three major struggles for independence. These wars all took place in the latter half of the nineteenth century, starting in 1868 and continuing intermittently for the next thirty years at varying levels of intensity. The first wave of significant immigration of Cubans began in 1868 following the first outbreak of the Cuban struggle against Spanish dominance. Many of Hector's ancestors were among these freedom fighters.

On October 10, 1868, what was known as "El Grito de Yara" ("The Cry of Yara") in Cuba signaled the beginning of what proved to be many years of conflict whose aim was to achieve social and political reform.[7] Yara is a small town and municipality in the Granma Province of Cuba, located halfway between the cities of Bayamo and Manzanillo, in the Gulf of Guacanayabo. Yara means "place" in the Taíno language.[8] The Taíno originated in South America and the Greater Antilles and, as such, were historic Indigenous people of the Caribbean. They spoke Arawak, and at the time of Christopher Columbus they were the most numerous Indigenous people of the Caribbean and may have numbered one or two million at the time of the Spanish conquest in the late fifteenth century. The Taíno Cacique (chief) Hatuey was burned at the stake in Yara on February 2, 1512, after he organized a guerrilla war against the Spaniards. Hatuey is known as "Cuba's First National Hero."[9]

Prior to the first rebellion in 1868, Cuba and Puerto Rico remained two of Spain's colonies in the New World and were governed from Madrid, as was a third colony, the Philippines. The first phase of this conflict plunged the island into a long and bloody civil war that produced an emigrant flow of Cubans to Key West, Florida. It began with the unsuccessful "Guerra de los Diez Años" ("Ten Years War"), which took place between 1868 and 1878. The rebellion was sparked by dissatisfaction with the corrupt and inefficient administration from Spain, the absence of native Cuban political representation, repression, and high taxes. In the struggle, at least 200,000 lives were lost. Many Cubans began their exodus to Key West in October 1868. The Velasco and Perez families were among those arriving in 1869. Of note, we found references to Jacinto V. (Valdez) Velasco in the book *The History of Havana*, by Dick Cluster and Rafael Hernandez.[10] Chapter 6 is of special interest to us, as this is where we found him mentioned for his political activities in Havana in January 1869. In a crowded theater, he voiced support for Carlos Manuel de Cespedes, the Oriente plantation owner turned general who led the rebellion against Spain. According to this source, Jacinto was later fined two hundred pesos and warned not to repeat the subversive action. The timeline of his departure from Cuba and arrival in the United States is corroborated by census records.[11]

The second uprising became known as "La Guerra Chiquita" ("The Little War") and began in August 1879.[12] It was quelled by superior Spanish forces in the autumn of 1880. Lacking organization and significant outside support, the rebels agreed to an armistice in the "February 1878 Pact of Zanjón," the terms of which promised amnesty and political reform.[13]

Spain pledged that native Cubans would have representation in their parliament. The pact also abolished slavery in 1886. Other promised reforms, however, never materialized. This failure led to continued unrest on the island.

The third rebellion was fought from 1895 to 1898 and became known as "La Guerra de Independencia Cubana" ("The Cuban War of Independence").[14] This would be the last of the three wars Cuba fought against Spain. Tensions came to a head in 1894 when Spain canceled a trade pact between Cuba and the United States. The imposition of more taxes and trade restrictions pushed the economically distressed Cubans too far, and in 1895 they launched their war of independence, a resumption of the earlier two struggles. The final three and a half months of the conflict escalated to become the Spanish-American War, with U.S. forces being deployed in Cuba, Puerto Rico, and the Philippines against Spain.[15]

While the official position of the United States was to avoid getting actively involved in the Cuban crisis, many forces were discreetly at work in Key West, Tampa, Jacksonville, and New York City (among other cities), providing financial, military, and logistical assistance to the Cubans. When the USS *Maine* sank in Havana's harbor in February 1898 after a mysterious explosion, the United States now had its pretext for going to war, and the Spanish-American War officially began. By the time official U.S. intervention began in April 1898, the war proved to be brief and one-sided. It was over by August 12, when the United States and Spain signed a preliminary peace treaty, the "Treaty of Paris," on December 10, 1898.[16] Spain's dominance was over, and it withdrew from Cuba. But it turned out that this event was the beginning of internal power struggles among Cubans that would last decades. In later years, up through 1959, growth, innovation, infrastructure modernization, improved access to education, and a raised standard of living led Cuba to be called the "Pearl of the Antilles."[17]

Many predecessors in Hector's direct family as well as other branches of our family provided aid to and fought for Cuba's liberation. These individuals include coauthor Jim's great-granduncle Charles Diaz, who was born in New York City and joined the U.S. Navy in 1883 at the age of fifteen and later, at the request of the U.S. War Department, ran filibusters in and around Cuba with other ship pilots, like the future nineteenth governor of Florida, Napoleon Bonaparte Broward. Diaz and Broward, along with daredevil types such as "Dynamite" Johnny O'Brien, outmaneuvered Spanish gunboats and U.S. Revenue cutters to keep the Cuban rebels supplied with weapons and recruits in the 1890s. Charles Diaz left the U.S. Navy and was commissioned (figure 8) a captain in the Cuban Liberation Army (a copy of his certificate of service from the Cuban government is held in the family archives). He served from September 1896 through August 1898, prior to the official U.S. engagement in the Spanish-American War. He owned and operated a hotel near Jacksonville, Florida, and then served as a commissioned officer in the U.S. Army as part of the American Expeditionary Forces in France during World War I, in which he was the head stevedore. After the war, Charles later returned to Cuba as a civilian for several years; he was employed by a multinational business enterprise and served as harbormaster in Havana. He later returned to Tampa and became harbormaster there for several years before he retired.

Cuban loyalty and sentiment run deep. There are several publications titled *Mis Recuerdos* (*My Memories*), which capture the remembrances of their home country by several Cubans. One of two timepieces from this era is by Juan Perez Rolo and another is by Salvador Bermudez de Castro y O'Lawler, Second Duke of Ripalda, Marquis of Lema.[18]

Over the decades, some of our family members made the supreme sacrifice and lost their lives in the ongoing struggle. Some fought guerrilla-style alongside the rebels in the hills of Cuba. Some who were unable or unwilling to fight donated money to help the cause. Most were discreet about their involvement for fear of governmental retaliation if their activities became known. They were fearful of reprisal and aimed to be inconspicuous about their opposition to the Spanish government. Their concern for their own safety was well founded.

During the early part of the migrant exodus, Cubans established themselves in Florida, mostly in Key West and later in other areas, such as Tampa and Jacksonville.[19] They formed significant political, economic, and social connections within Florida. In Monroe and Hillsborough Counties, Cubans began to exert decisive influence in political affairs.[20] They became the economic backbone of the community. Studies in Cuban history that have examined Cubans in Key West and Tampa have highlighted their activities in relation to the history of their native homeland. However, the cross-cultural aspects of the Cuban presence received little attention.

The establishment of a large Cuban community devoted to winning independence for its homeland exerted a powerful impact on all aspects of life in Key West and Tampa. The potential for economic success and independence increased the flow of immigrants into Florida. Familiarity with the cigar industry was an added attraction, as the emerging cigar industry founded by Vicente Martinez Ybor, a Spanish tobacco capitalist from Havana, now had a presence in Key West and Tampa.[21] The cigar industry was booming, and factories attracted Cuban workers, adding to the immigrant population. By February 1869—the same year in which the Velasco and Perez families arrived—a Cuban colony was thriving in Key West.

Revolutionary clubs were organized with the goal of raising funds as

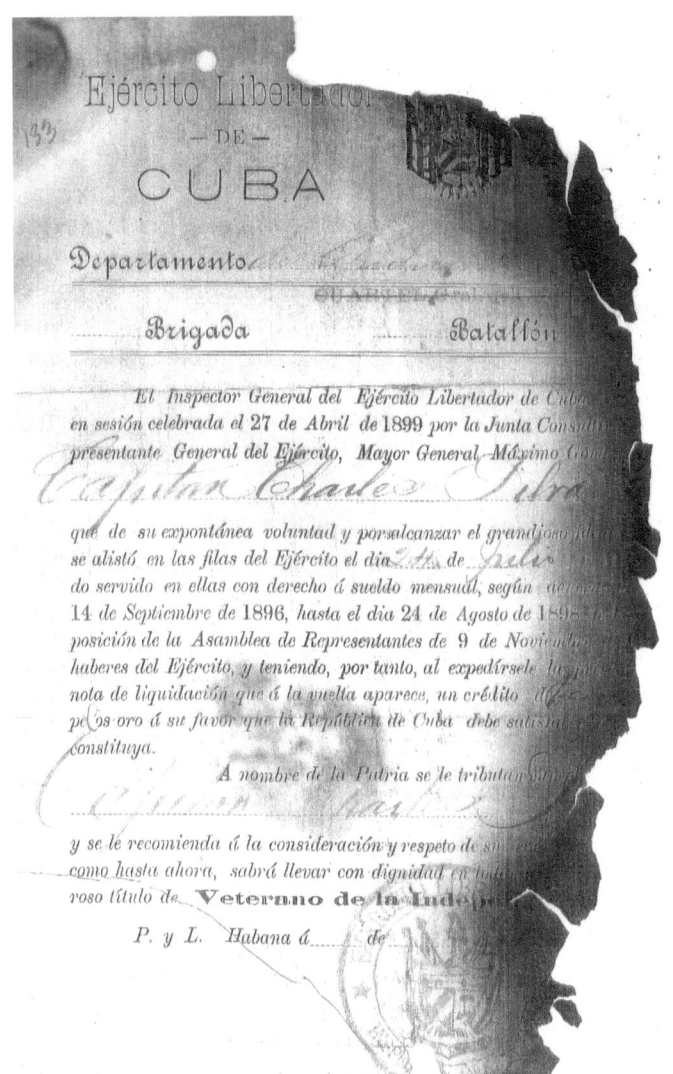

Figure 8: A reproduction of the restored certificate awarded to coauthor Jim Jimenez's great-granduncle Charles Diaz for his service with the Cuba Liberation Army (Ejército Libertador de Cuba) in the Cuban War of Independence (La Guerra de Independencia Cubana). He served as a captain with the Cuban forces from September 14, 1896, through August 21, 1898, a week after the war was won. This document was restored after it was damaged during the 1973 fire at the National Archives that destroyed much of Diaz's military records. Charles Diaz had enlisted in the U.S. Navy in 1883 in New York City at the age of 15. Prior to his service in the Cuban army, he ran filibusters in and around the island and provided manpower and ammunition to the rebels, working subversively under the direction of Vice Admiral William T. Sampson of the U.S. Department of War.

well as arming men who were sent to join the Cuban loyalist forces being formed in New York. As previously mentioned, Hector's paternal grandfather, Jose I. Perez, was said to have been an organizer tasked with raising funds in New York City for the Cuban cause. Key West became a major hub for support of the Cuban revolutionary effort. According to reports from Cuban residents at that time, in Key West, nothing was discussed more than the revolution. A population of 5,675 in Key West in 1870 more than tripled to over 18,000 twenty years later.[22] The Cuban proportion also increased, from approximately 25 percent to more than 50 percent. These factors could not help but affect the political landscape in the community. Almost every Cuban home could be considered a conspiratorial center in which virtually all that was discussed around the kitchen table was how to achieve liberty for their homeland.

Immigration radically altered the demography of Monroe County in the years after the U.S. Civil War. State laws regarding residency for eligibility to cast a ballot in elections, along with poll taxes, literacy tests, and a declaration of intent to become a citizen, affected almost every county in Florida. Once these requirements were satisfied, the Cuban emigres could vote, and a new electoral element began to evolve and exert influence.

Unexpected Outcomes of World War I

World War I began in Europe on July 28, 1914.[23] The United States entered the war on the side of the Allies in April 1917. In June 1917, the first U.S. troops began to arrive in France, forming the American Expeditionary Forces (AEF).[24] However, the American units did not enter the trenches in divisional strength until October 1917.[25] Hector H. Perry enlisted in the U.S. Army in March 1917, one month before the United States entered the war, and his younger brother Charlie enlisted in the army in January 1917.[26] On May 18, 1917, Congress passed the Selective Service Act, which authorized the federal government to temporarily expand the military through conscription.[27] The draft eventually required all men between the ages of 21 to 45 to register for military service. These two young brothers enlisted of their own volition, before the act was passed.

The war was devastating, leading to around 20 million deaths worldwide.[28] It ended on November 11, 1918, nine months after the first cases of what was referred to as the "Spanish flu" were reported in the United States. Against the backdrop of the war, the 1918 influenza pandemic surged at a time when people were already experiencing scarcity in everyday supplies and coping with having loved ones serving and dying overseas. Deaths from the 1918 pandemic were far more staggering than the loss of life due to the recent SARS-CoV-2 (COVID-19) pandemic. At least 50 million people died worldwide from the misnamed "Spanish flu," even though the number of domestic deaths was lower, estimated at 675,000.[29] But the legacy of World War I overshadowed the pandemic, making the unprecedented loss of life from the flu seem like an afterthought.

It was reported that in 1914, during the early stages of the war, soldiers deployed with the British Expeditionary Force began to report medical symptoms after combat that included tinnitus, amnesia, headaches, dizziness, tremors, and hypersensitivity to noise.[30] While these symptoms resembled those that would be expected after a physical injury to the brain, many of those reporting sickness did not experience or show signs of head trauma or other physical wounds. After the war, many returning soldiers suffered from what was then called "shell shock."

Shell shock was the medical term given to a type of post-traumatic stress disorder (PTSD) before the expression PTSD was coined. It was a term that was used to reflect an assumed link between the symptoms and the effects of explosions from artillery shells. It was thought to be a reaction to the intensity of the bombardment and the fighting that produced a sense of helplessness, which manifested in symptoms such as panic and fright, taking flight or avoidance, or an inability to reason, along with walking or talking in one's sleep. The intensity of such occurrences under wartime conditions, such as combat, was believed to cause intense stress-induced mental or emotional trauma.[31]

Those afflicted were considered disabled. It was difficult to dismiss the horrors experienced in such a war. It was reported that one prominent army physician went to great lengths to encourage shell-shock patients to reconstruct their experiences in conversations. He would use films and other sensory simulations to help the stricken patients confront their traumatic memories. These were called "talking cures," which emphasized the cognitive and behavioral symptoms of trauma. Those who used these treatments began to have a much better success rate than their predecessors had in treating and helping the afflicted. The "talking cures" method seems to have originated between 1880 and 1882 with the Viennese physician Josef Breuer (1842–1925).[32]

One can see the devastating level of worldwide deaths caused by the war and the 1918 flu pandemic, which was being spread by the vast number of travelers and the confinement of soldiers in close quarters (trenches); shell-shock symptoms arising from the conditions of war were further unexpected outcomes in this war. The many lessons learned in the treatment of diseases, including shell shock and its symptoms, and their acceptance by the medical community were critical to the advancement of medicine for the overall public health sector.

Unexpectedly, the war also rewrote the world map. Breaking with the isolationist foreign policy of the past, President Woodrow Wilson framed American involvement as a means of supporting the free people of Europe, mainly Britain and France. America's assistance was pivotal in securing Allied victory, as the democracies of Western Europe prevailed due to robust American support. Had the authoritarian Central Powers won the First World War, a push toward autocracy worldwide would have replaced liberal democratic aspirations. America's participation as a great power preserved the democratic norms and helped shape its future international role.[33]

Other unexpected outcomes of the war that we found were expressed clearly by Nicholas J. Cull, historian in the USC Annenberg School for Communication and Journalism: "World War I is an amazingly important and underappreciated moment in history.... The war ended when people were able to articulate a vision of the future, an optimism about how things were going to be better with nations working together."[34] The European Union, NATO and the United Nations would never have taken shape in an authoritarian-dominated Europe.

Another thing that was forever changed by the war was medicine. Prior to World War I, both trauma care and military public health care were primitive by today's standards. In the American experience, the Civil War (1861–1865) and the Spanish-American War (1898) helped develop military medicine, which in turn spilled over into the general medical sector. Casualty care was much improved from any previous war. Specialized military units—ambulances—were in place transporting wounded soldiers from the battlefield to nearby aid stations; triage emerged and advanced from the need to treat the wounded in the trenches to establishing field hospitals. Communicable diseases and venereal disease prevention and treatments became much improved, as did radiology.[35]

Psychiatry made huge strides during this period, mainly from the observations of Dr. Thomas W. Salmon, a pioneer in treating shell shock and combat stress disorders. After the war, the hard lessons the army learned were soon forgotten but luckily were rediscovered during World War II.[36]

On a personal level, the unexpected outcomes that Hector experienced from this war for which he volunteered in 1917 can be seen in the same vein, in that it first had deleterious effects which then led to many hard lessons learned.

FIVE

In the Service of His Country (Charles E. "Charlie" Perez)

The Military Career of Charles E. "Charlie" Perez (1917–1922)

Hector's younger brother, Charles Ernest "Charlie" Perez (figure 9), was born in Key West, Florida, on September 30, 1899, when his mother was twenty-one years old, and his father was almost twenty-seven.[1] As previously mentioned, according to the 1900 U.S. Census, he and his family lived with his maternal grandparents (Jacinto and Francisca Velasco) and their extended family of fourteen at 306 Elizabeth Street in Key West.[2] Ten years later, at the age of eleven, according to the 1910 U.S. Census, he lived with his parents and immediate family at 910 Winden Lane in Key West; they were no longer living with his maternal grandparents.[3] His grandmother, Francisca, had passed away in February, two months after the 1910 census was taken, and his grandfather, Jacinto, was living with only two sons by this date, a twenty-five-year-old who was a cigar maker and a twenty-one-year-old who was a carpenter and builder, just like his father.[4]

U.S. Veterans' Association Master Index Records dated 1917–1940 verify that Charles E. "Charlie" Perez resided in New York City when he enlisted in the U.S. Army on January 10, 1917, at the age of seventeen.[5] He was assigned to the following units, in this sequence: Headquarters Company, 26th Infantry Regiment; Company D, First Engineers; Company C, 18th Infantry Regiment, 1st Division. He was a corporal when he served as part of the American Expeditionary Forces in France during World War I.[6]

Charlie sailed on the SS *San Jacinto* (a commercial passenger cargo ship chartered by the U.S. Army for the war effort) out of Hoboken, New Jersey, to France in June 1917 to begin his overseas tour of duty as part of the 26th Infantry Regiment.[7] He departed for the front lines before his brother Hector did. His name was found on a passenger list alongside #324 in the first column, third line from the bottom, as "Perez, Charles E. Pvt."

Charlie was slated to return to Hoboken from Brest, France, aboard the SS *Finland* (an American-flagged ocean liner built in 1902 for the Red Star Line), on August 24, 1919. During the war, the SS *Finland* served as a transport ship for the U.S. Navy. However, despite the plan for Charlie to have sailed at this time, we found a handwritten note on the document stating that he did not sail.[8]

His name was also found on a passenger list with the Company D, First Engineers, sailing from Antwerp, Belgium, to Brooklyn, New York. This army transport record showed his sailing date to have been between May 1 and May 31, 1922.[9] Thus he remained overseas an additional three years after his first scheduled departure. His official discharge date was in July 1922.[10]

In the 1920 U.S. Census, Charlie's name was found in two separate schedules for "Military &

Figure 9: Charles E. "Charlie" Perez was the third of Charles and Sarah's four children. He was born September 30, 1899, in Key West, Florida. He had a lifelong affinity with military life and organizations. He was a patriotic young soldier during World War I and was awarded numerous medals for his bravery and gallantry. After the war, Charlie spent most of his early adult life in New York City. He married there and worked for the U.S. Postal Service. He was seriously injured in a taxicab accident in the city during a military parade. His injuries affected his daily life to a large degree. He eventually moved to Florida, divorced, and resided with his younger sister, Dinorah, for a short time. Charlie worked in the hotels managed by his brother-in-law; he suddenly became ill one day while at work and died in 1950. He is buried at Bay Pines National Cemetery in Pinellas County, Florida.

Naval Population Abroad (American Forces in Germany)." In the record taken on April 17, he was listed as a private, while in the record taken on May 1, 1920, he was a corporal, living at the Coblenz Station, Germany, assigned to the 18th Infantry Regiment.[11] The May 1 census record's column 7 ("Color or Race") erroneously described Charlie as mulatto. This mistake was obviously due to his dark complexion. His home address was listed as 1202 Duval Street and 1206 Duval Street in Key West, Florida, respectively, in these documents. The "enumerator" (that is, the individual entering the data) was the same person in both cases, Captain Reinold Melberg. The latter address was corroborated by the 1920 U.S. Census taken in Key West, Florida, which showed his father Charles (widowed) was living with his sister, Lola, and her husband Jose Flores at 1206 Duval Street.[12]

According to Charlie's nephew, William "Bill" C. Atkinson, Sr., Charlie was a machine gunner and an excellent sharpshooter. Bill told us that, when asked about his time in France and whether he killed any enemy soldiers, Charlie stated matter-of-factly that "he had many kills on the battlefield." We will soon learn what those words truly meant.

Battlefield Hero (June–September 1918)

The administrators of the University of Central Florida–National Cemetery Administration's Veterans Legacy Program (UCF-NCA VLP) shared Charlie's military enlistment card with us (figures 10 and 11). Their source for the card was the Florida Memory Program of the State Library and Archives of Florida.[13] UCF's VLP is working with K–12 teachers around the state of Florida who are developing lesson plans related to veterans' history. The National Cemetery Administration's Veterans Legacy Program aims to connect veterans commemorated at national cemeteries to the broader community using innovative technology and approaches. UCF's History Department contracted with the NCA to tell the stories of our nation's veterans memorialized at the Florida National Cemetery in Bushnell, Florida; the St. Augustine National Cemetery in St. Augustine, Florida; the Bay Pines National Cemetery in St. Petersburg, Florida; the Aisne-Marne American Cemetery in Lucy-le-Bocage, France; and the Meuse-Argonne American Cemetery in Romagne-sous-Montfaucon, France.

Charlie Perez is interred at Bay Pines National Cemetery, St. Petersburg, Florida; as noted above, this cemetery is among the locations participating in this project,[14] which harnesses UCF student research efforts to create biographies of veterans buried or memorialized at the cemeteries.

These biographies form the basis for the project's website, which features the veterans' stories, and a mobile application for cemetery visitors, as well as an interactive K–12 curriculum. The project also includes a yearly field trip to one of the cemeteries around Memorial Day. K–12 students join teachers; UCF faculty, staff, and students; government representatives; and the media to share veterans' stories and learn about our nation's history. Charles E. "Charlie" Perez has been chosen as one of the subjects in their project. A UCF-NCA VLP principal investigator and research team member reached out to Lina and Jim because of the information each had in their family tree on Ancestry.com regarding Charlie, asking them to contribute to this project. Lina and Jim immediately agreed. They are creating source packets to honor the service and sacrifice of military veterans. The UCF History Department's Veterans Legacy Program has a website where an online brochure of the project is available. The project conference took place on June 7–16, 2023, in St. Augustine, Florida.[15] Their current grant ended on September 30, 2023.

The date stamped on the reverse of the military enlistment card we received from the UCF-NCA VLP is April 29, 1921, indicating when it was completed.[16] It revealed some remarkable information about Charlie's military service that was previously unknown to us (early in our research, Lina requested Charlie's military records from the National Archives and was told that his records did not survive the great fire at the archives in 1973[17]). Not to detract from the key facts the card provides, the few inaccuracies noted will be covered first.

The front of the card indicates Charlie was referred to as "Charlie" E. Perez, and he was born in Key West, Florida. This is correct. According to the card, he enlisted in the regular army on January 10, 1917, at the age of eighteen years and three months, which we believe is inaccurate. He was born on September 30, 1899, which would make him seventeen years and three months at the time of his enlistment. A review of his application for a military headstone showed the data field on the form for his date of birth was populated as "9/30/1899" but is stricken out in red, and "98" was overwritten next to it, an apparent edit made to his year of birth for reason(s) unknown.[18] There is little doubt that Charlie was born on September 30, 1899. The inaccurate year of birth reported on the enlistment card could also be due to the minimum age for enlistment being eighteen.

The front of the card also indicates that Charlie enlisted at Columbus Barracks, Ohio. We believe this was his first duty station, not the location where he was sworn in. The Columbus Barracks was a recruiting station and a beehive of activity beginning in 1917 when the army increased the number of recruits being trained there.[19]

The section on the card that lists his grade (the hierarchy of military

Five. In the Service of His Country (Charles E. "Charlie" Perez) 47

```
                                                                    1½
      Perez    Charlie E       55,674              white
     (Surname)   (Christian name)   (Army serial number)   (Race: White or colored)

Residence:         Key West                           FLORIDA
         (Street and house number)   (Town or city)   (County)    (State)

*Enlisted in   R.A. Columbus Bks Ohio          Jan 10 /17      –
†Born in       Key West Fla      –             18 3/12 yr      –
Organizations: Hq Co 26 Inf to Feb 5/19; Co C 18 Inf to disch.  –


Grades:        Sgt Sept 20/18;  Pvt Sept 5/19;  Pvt 1cl Sept 12/19;
               Corp Nov 6/19

Engagements:                             –                     –


Wounds or other injuries received in action: None.
‡Served overseas:    June 14/17 to Feb 3/20                    –
§Hon. disch.         Feb 3/20   on demobilization              –
Was reported         0          per cent disabled on date of discharge, in view of occupation.
Remarks:
```

Figure 10: World War I service card for Charles E. "Charlie" Perez (front), dated April 29, 1921, noting details of enlistment location and rank.

rank) and the corresponding dates is also confusing. It indicates he was a sergeant on September 20, 1918, but was a private a year later on September 5, 1919. Then he was a private first class (PFC) a week later on September 12, 1919, and then a corporal on November 6, 1919. The three final entries seem logical, but the date of the initial entry does not. Attempts to clarify these issues have been made and have proven unsuccessful. It may just have been an error, but VLP researchers have informed us that they have found such records often contain conflicting or inconsistent information when compared to data points gleaned from other sources. This is our experience as well. Such discrepancies are often inexplicable and subject to guesswork. They run the gamut from inaccurate dates, places, or names here and there, and they are usually benign in the context of the bigger picture. Mistakes in more obvious areas (such as gender) have also been seen. Quite often one can only make their best efforts to clarify inconsistencies, usually through corroboration with other documents and data points, but often some questions remain unanswered and some issues unresolved.

Charlie served overseas from June 14, 1917, to May 1922. The U.S. Veterans' Administration Master Index reveals his discharge date as July 26, 1922, as we previously discovered. The VLP researchers advised that other sources they found gave his home address at the time of enlistment as 523

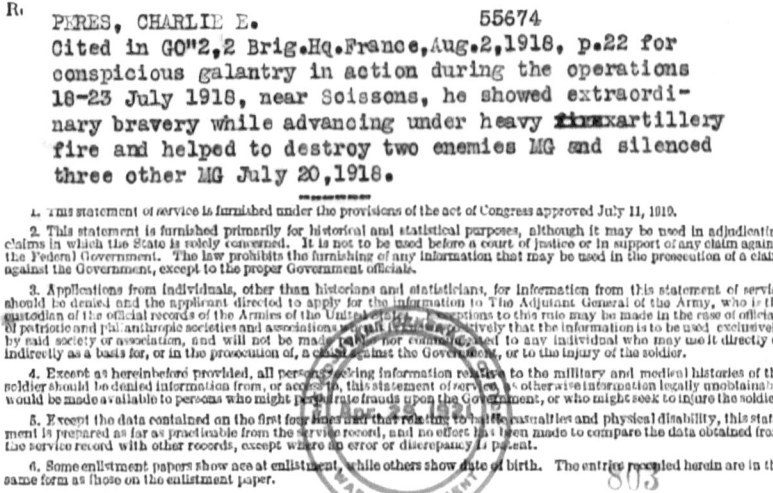

Figure 11: World War I service card (back), noting Charlie's conspicuous gallantry and extraordinary bravery under fire.

West 60th Street in New York City, which was a new discovery for us. This information corroborates the U.S. Veterans Master Index reporting of his residence being New York City at the time of enlistment. The most interesting information would be found on the reverse of the card. We discovered Charlie was cited for conspicuous gallantry and extraordinary bravery more than once.[20]

Incredibly, we learned Charlie was awarded two Silver Stars, which is uncommon.[21] The Silver Star Medal is the U.S. Armed Forces' third-highest military decoration for valor in combat. It is awarded for singular acts of valor or heroism over a brief period, such as one or two days of a battle. These acts must have taken place while in action against an enemy while engaged in military operations involving conflict with an opposing foreign force or while serving with friendly foreign forces engaged in an armed conflict against an opposing armed force. The researchers advised us that in all their years of doing this type of work, they had never come across an individual who was awarded two Silver Stars. Obviously, Charlie's actions on the battlefield were extraordinary, and he performed with consummate bravery.

An inspection of his military enlistment card reveals that Charlie's citations for conspicuous gallantry and extraordinary bravery in action were for the period of July 18–23, 1918, near Soissons as part of the Aisne-Marne offensive. He was also cited for his actions while advancing under heavy artillery fire, and he helped destroy two enemy machine guns and silenced three others on July 20, 1918. Now we understand the meaning of Charlie's statement to his nephew Bill that "he had many kills on the battlefield."

Charlie was a machine gunner. We learned the machine gun was a devastating weapon and a major contributor to World War I casualties.[22] Machine guns were one of the most important weapons of the war. The First World War was primarily a defensive war in that countries established trench systems designed to stop enemy advances. The machine gun was vitally important to this defensive strategy and gave the defending army a large advantage. World War I was such a deadly conflict because the machine gun caused millions of military and civilian casualties. The efficacy of the machine gun during this war cannot be underestimated.

The VLP further advised that information detailed on the reverse side of the card pertains to only one of the two stars awarded to Charlie, designated by the oak leaf cluster on the blue and white bar on one of his many medals. Researchers are attempting to verify information regarding the second Silver Star. It is unlikely they will be able offer additional information until the project and seminar have concluded. By September 2023, their work on Charlie will be partially completed, and we should be able to see the semi-finished product. In turn, the VLP will use the newly updated veteran's information in school programs.

The VLP advised that they received another grant for the 2023–2024 term. Their plans are to create what they call source packets for veterans of Hispanic heritage. One was created for Charlie based on his service record as well as the information we provided to them. The source packet is not a biography per se; rather, it is a list of sources related to the veteran's life. Charlie's is slated to appear at the end of 2023 if budgeting allows. They then plan to have a biography created and translated into Spanish so that teachers can use the bilingual biographies in different ways. Lina was asked for her permission to provide her information in the packet so that she could be put in contact with any teacher in the Tampa area who would use the source packet the VLP creates for a school project. Lina would be asked to speak to the students, and in turn they would demonstrate how they plan to use the source packet containing the information about Charlie in their project. The VLP advised Lina that Charlie's story is one they plan to use for this initiative.

For several years after the war ended, Charlie continued his military service and remained stationed in Europe. He left Antwerp, Belgium, aboard the SS *Chateau Thierry* on May 22, 1922, and arrived in Brooklyn, New York, on May 31, 1922. The U.S. Veterans' Administration's Master

Index records his "Military Date" as July 26, 1922, indicating this was his discharge date. He served five years in the military.

Family heirlooms passed down by Charlie to his nephew, William "Bill" Atkinson, Sr., of whom he was very fond, were displayed in Bill's home for many years (figures 12, 13, and 14).

Bill and, after his passing, his daughter Dinni have the actual service ribbons, the devices, and the Victory Medal that Charlie received for fighting in battles while serving in France during World War I. According to Bill, there were several other medals and awards Charlie received during his military service that have been lost over the years. The battles in which Charlie served and the awards he meritoriously earned remain in the family archives. They are as follows:

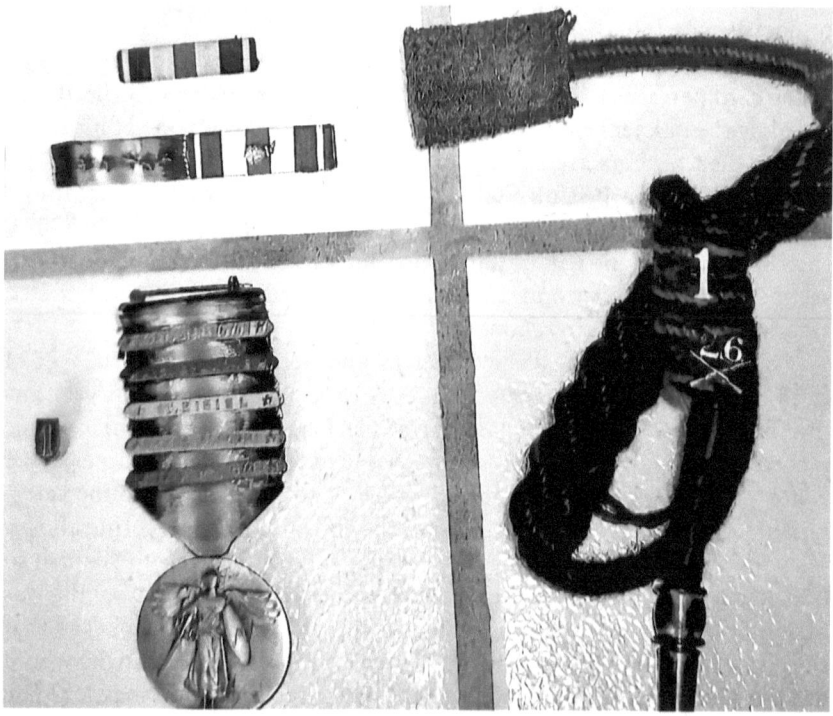

Figure 12: Medals and devices awarded to Charlie after World War I (clockwise from top): Silver Star Medal ribbon: blue, white and red; Fourragere (French Army) lanyard awarded to American units that fought with distinguished service, in the original Croix de Guerre colors of green and red (for units cited 2–3 times) from 1914–1918, with a number "1" pin attached and a pin showing a number "6" with crossed rifles; Victory Medal ribbon with five campaign bars; A number "1" pin; A conjoined Victory Medal ribbon with five battle stars and a Silver Star Medal ribbon with one oak leaf cluster.

Five. In the Service of His Country (Charles E. "Charlie" Perez)

- Victory Medal with five campaign clasps
- Montdidier-Noyon (June 9–12, 1918)
- Aisne-Marne (July 18–20, 1918)
- Saint-Mihiel (September 12–16, 1918)
- Meuse-Argonne (September 26–November 11, 1918)
- Defensive Sector clasps

The Victory Medal itself has an interesting history.[23] It was originally intended to be established by an Act of Congress, but the bill authorizing the medal never passed. This situation left the military department free to establish the medal through its general orders. The Victory Medal was awarded to military personnel for service between April 6, 1917, and November 11, 1918, or with either (a) the American Expeditionary Forces who fought in Russia between November 12, 1918, and August 5, 1919, or (b) the American Expeditionary Forces who fought in Siberia between November 23, 1918, and April 1, 1920. To denote battle participation and campaign credit, the World War I Victory Medal was authorized with a large variety of devices, such as stars and battle clasps, to denote specific accomplishments.

Also in the collection Bill treasured is a faded French fourragere in the original Croix de Guerre colors of green and red (for units cited 2–3 times) dating from 1914–1918, with a number "1" pin (1st Infantry Division) attached and a pin showing a number "6" above crossed rifles.[24] There

Figure 13: Close-up of World War I Victory Medal with five battle clasps: Montdidier-Noyon, Aisne-Marne, Saint-Mihiel, Meuse-Argonne, Defensive Sector.

Figure 14: Close-up of a World War I Silver Star Medal ribbon with oak leaf cluster in center and World War I Victory Medal ribbon with five battle stars.

are also two conjoined ribbon bars consisting of a Victory Medal ribbon with five battle stars and a Silver Star Medal ribbon with one oak leaf cluster, along with a second Silver Star Medal ribbon bar and a loose "1" pin in enamel with a red number "1" and green background worn by the 1st Infantry Division.

Charlie Returns to New York City (May–July 1922)

The records indicate that after Charlie returned home from military service on the Western Front, he lived in New York City beginning in 1922, in the borough of the Bronx. It is also on the record that he was living there at the time of his enlistment in 1917, so in all probability he was returning to the city he left when he joined the military. Something anchored him in New York City. It may have been family or friends. We do not know for certain, and we probably never will. What we do know for certain is that he lived in Tampa with his family up until the time of his mother's death in 1916. As previously mentioned, his army enlistment card stated that he had enlisted at Columbus Barracks, Ohio, but we feel that was more likely his first duty station, as two separate unverified records indicate that his residence was New York City at the time of his enlistment. What could have drawn him there at the age of seventeen, one year after his mother's death? Were the boys (Hector and Charlie) sent to New York City to live with family just as the girls (Evangelina and Dinorah) remained in Tampa to live with family after the unexpected loss of their mother? We found no definitive evidence in the genealogical record of any known extended family members living in New York at that time. The reason for the brothers' presence there remains a mystery.

As we learned from public records, New York City is where Charlie chose to live most of his adult life. According to the 1930 and 1940 U.S. census reports, he lived at 3505 Broadway in the Hamilton Heights section of the Bronx, just off the corner of 143rd Street between Riverside Drive and Upper Manhattan.[25] He worked as a postal clerk. We also found two newspaper stories announcing Charlie's marriage.[26] The first story announced that the bride's parents, Mr. and Mrs. B. van Dyke, reported that their daughter, Emma Louise van Dyke, had married Charles E. Perez in New York on October 2, 1936; he was thirty-seven years old at the time. This first announcement was printed in the *Orlando* (Florida) *Sentinel* on October 4, 1936. It indicated that Charlie had worked for the transportation department of the New York City Post Office since coming home from the war. It also reported that Emma had made her home in Orlando, Florida, for the past seven years after moving there from Marion, Ohio, with her parents. She attended school in Indianapolis, Indiana, and spent one year at Florida State College for Women. The article further reported that Charlie was the son of Mr. Charles Perez of Key West and was a brother to Mrs. William Atkinson of Orlando. The newlyweds were to make New York City their home.

The second newspaper story announcing the marriage was printed in the *Marion* (Ohio) *Star* on October 10, 1936, and repeated the same information that was in the *Orlando Sentinel* but added that Emma had graduated from high school in Miami Beach.[27]

Oddly, there is no mention of the groom's brother, Hector, in either of the two wedding announcements. There is also no reference to his deceased mother Sarah or his other sister, Evangelina, who was then living in Cuba. We believe that if the siblings had had a close relationship, they would have been mentioned. The grandniece, Lina, never thought to ask family history questions of her grandaunt, Dinorah, during a visit to her home in Winter Park, Florida, in the late 1970s.

We learned from the 1930 and 1940 U.S. census reports that Emma van Dyke had been born in Texas on January 6, 1910, and was ten years younger than Charlie. She worked as a doctor's secretary after their marriage. Charlie and Emma were both working in New York City, where they chose to make their home.

One year later, the *Orlando Evening Star* reported on September 27, 1937, that Charlie had sustained serious injuries in a taxicab accident just a year after he married.[28] As a result, he was confined to his apartment. The accident happened during the American Legion parade along Fifth Avenue in New York City. This event was verified in other newspaper reports as well. Charlie was a member of General Bailey Post No. 104, American Legion of New York City.[29] It was evident that Charlie had a deep affinity for the U.S. military. The article went on to state that Charles Perez had visited his sister, Mrs. William Atkinson, in Orlando on several occasions. The photograph (figure 15) of Charlie and his wife shows his left leg curled up due to the injury he sustained during the parade. Displayed in figure 16 is a map of the American Legion Memorial Convention parade route that took place that year.[30]

By early 1942, Charlie and Emma were separated. His World War II draft registration card (dated February 14, 1942) showed Emma residing at her parents' home address of 525 Richmond Avenue in Orlando (figure 17).[31] Charlie and Emma were divorced in Brevard County, Florida, after six years of marriage, in 1942. The exact date of the divorce is unknown. Charlie and Emma had no children. The Florida Divorce Register database (1927–2001) for 1942 in Brevard County was found to be in alphabetical order, making Charlie and his spouse's names easy to find.[32] All the other Perezes listed in that report are unrelated to Charlie. Emma remarried in 1950.[33] She lived another thirty-five years and passed away at the age of seventy-six on August 15, 1985.[34]

It was reported in the *St. Petersburg* (Florida) *Times*

Figure 15: Charlie and wife Veronica circa 1940. His left leg shows the results of an injury sustained from a cab accident during a military parade.

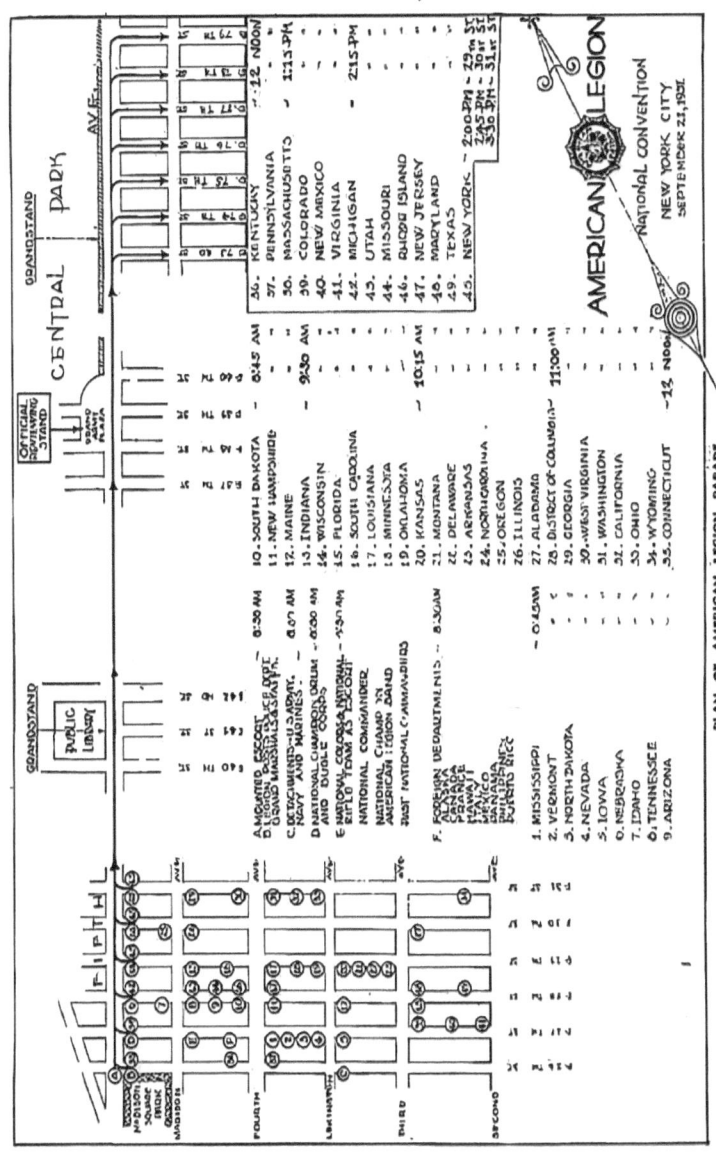

Figure 16: Route map for the American Legion Memorial National Convention parade that took place in New Yok City on September 27, 1937, wherein Charlie was injured.

```
REGISTRATION CARD—(Men born on or after February 17, 1897 and on or before December 31, 1921)
SERIAL NUMBER  1. NAME (Print)                                                    ORDER NUMBER
  T  901        Charles    Ernest    Perez                                         T  10850
                  (First)    (Middle)    (Last)
2. PLACE OF RESIDENCE (Print)
    U.S.V.A. Facility    BayPines    Pinellas    Fla.
    (Number and street)  (Town, township, village, or city)  (County)  (State)
    [THE PLACE OF RESIDENCE GIVEN ON THE LINE ABOVE WILL DETERMINE LOCAL BOARD
     JURISDICTION; LINE 2 OF REGISTRATION CERTIFICATE WILL BE IDENTICAL]
3. MAILING ADDRESS
    Same.
    [Mailing address if other than place indicated on line 2. If same insert word same]
4. TELEPHONE              5. AGE IN YEARS        6. PLACE OF BIRTH
                               42                    Key West
    (Exchange) (Number)   DATE OF BIRTH              (Town or county)
                          Sept. 30 1899              Fla.
                          (Mo.) (Day) (Yr.)          (State or country)
7. NAME AND ADDRESS OF PERSON WHO WILL ALWAYS KNOW YOUR ADDRESS
    Mrs. Chas. E. Perez    525 Richmond Ave Orlando Fla.
8. EMPLOYER'S NAME AND ADDRESS
    Unemployed
9. PLACE OF EMPLOYMENT OR BUSINESS
    (Number and street or R. F. D. number)   (Town)   (County)   (State)
    I AFFIRM THAT I HAVE VERIFIED ABOVE ANSWERS AND THAT THEY ARE TRUE.
D. S. S. Form 1                                   Charles E Perez
(Revised 1-1-42)   (over)   ☆ GPO 16—21630-1      (Registrant's Signature)
```

Figure 17: World War II registration card for Charles E. "Charlie" Perez, showing his residency at the U.S. Veterans Association soldiers' home in Bay Pines, Pinellas County, Florida.

dated March 31, 1941, that Charlie temporarily lived at the U.S. Veterans' Association Center for Soldiers in Bay Pines, Florida. This facility had opened in 1933.[35] In the wake of World War I, on January 5, 1929, Senator Duncan U. Fletcher (the longest-serving U.S. senator in Florida's history, 1914–1936) introduced a bill that would appropriate funds for a Soldiers' Home to be constructed in Florida.[36] We believe Charlie moved in because of the injuries he suffered in the taxicab accident five years earlier, coupled with his separation. The news story went on to state that Charlie was originally from Key West and a veteran of Headquarters Company, 26th Infantry Regiment, First Division, and, as previously stated, a member of General Bailey Post No. 104, American Legion in New York City. The exact nature and extent of his injuries are unknown, though family lore said one leg was affected; at any rate, his injuries were quite serious and protracted until his death.

On her request for information from the Bay Pines facility, Charlie's grandniece Lina was informed by records administrators that if they had any medical records in the archives belonging to Charlie, they would not

Five. In the Service of His Country (Charles E. "Charlie" Perez)

be available to her, as she did not qualify as next of kin. She disagreed with their assessment but was unsuccessful in her appeal. Lina also followed up with the American Legion Post in New York City, which was mentioned in the article, hoping to glean any additional information, to no avail.

As previously mentioned, prior to the time of printing, Bill Atkinson, Sr.—Charlie's last living nephew—passed away on December 20, 2023. Bill recounted that his uncle was married once and had no children. Charlie was described as a quiet man who did not drink alcohol. He lived in the Atkinson home with his sister's family for a short time when Bill and his younger brother Joseph were in their late teenage years. Charlie also kept a room at the Orange Court Hotel, where he worked for his brother-in-law, Bill Atkinson (young Bill's father), who was employed by a company that operated properties in Florida, Texas, and Michigan.

For a brief period, Charlie worked in Michigan at a hotel his brother-in-law managed. Bill Sr. informed us that Charlie was well liked and respected by all the hotel employees, including the bellmen.

In 1943, Charlie lived in Orlando, and in 1945 he lived and worked at the Orange Court Hotel in Orange County, Florida.[37] According to the April 1950 U.S. Census (taken April 4), Charlie lived at 416 Hayer Street in Orlando with his sister, Dinorah, and her two sons, Bill Sr. and Joseph.[38] We learned Charlie was asked to fill in as hotel manager at the North Shore Hotel in Miami Beach. He traveled there after the April 4 census was taken and began his temporary assignment.

Death of a Hero (1950)

In 1950, while filling in at the Miami Beach hotel property, Charlie was admitted to the VA hospital in Coral Gables on April 24 and remained there until his passing on April 30 at 9:00 a.m.[39] We found a brief mention of Charlie's death in the *Miami Herald* from Tuesday, May 2, 1950, on page 26.[40] The *Herald* reported his correct full name, his age, and his residence as the North Shore Hotel, noting that he had passed away on the previous Sunday. He was buried at Bay Pines National Cemetery in Pinellas County, Florida, on May 3, 1950 (figure 18).[41] For such a highly decorated war veteran as Charlie was, we find this brief, nondescript obituary puzzling. There was no mention of his participation in World War I or his numerous decorations for his military service. We found no other obituaries reporting his death in the state of Florida or anywhere else. This is a perfect example of how valued and consequential history fades from memory and is sadly forgotten forever. It is as if the actions and bravery of a man who put his life on the line and served admirably never happened.

A copy of Charlie's death certificate obtained by his grandniece, Lina, in April 2023 revealed that an autopsy was performed, and several coronary issues were the contributing factors to his death. His parents' names are spelled correctly on the certificate. No spouse's name was given, as he was divorced. The informant for the document was the registrar at the VA hospital in Coral Gables, Florida. A few years earlier, this VA hospital was the famed Biltmore Hotel of Coral Gables.[42] Reports suggest the commanding general of the U.S. Armed Forces sent search teams to South Florida to inspect and select hotels that were suitable as hospitals for veterans, with the highest capacity for beds being the main objective. The Biltmore Hotel was selected, as it was a large facility. The War Department converted it into a 1,200-bed hospital in November 1941. The hospital was transferred from the U.S. Army to the Veterans' Administration in July 1947. The newly updated VA hospital consisted of 450 general medical and surgical beds. It was maintained as a VA hospital until the completion of the Bruce W. Carter VA Medical Center, located at 1201 NW 16th Street in Miami, in May 1968.[43]

Charlie was truly an American patriot. He loved his country as well as

Figure 18: The entrance marquee for the Bay Pines National Cemetery, where Charlie is interred.

Five. In the Service of His Country (Charles E. "Charlie" Perez) 59

the military and maintained a close association with U.S. military organizations throughout his life, from his first enlistment at the age of seventeen until the time of his death. The military became and remained his second family. It is not known whether Charlie and his brother Hector communicated often or at all after their military service, nor is it known whether they saw each other during the war. During our research, we learned they both served in the Aisne-Marne/Soissons offensive on July 18–20, 1918. As it was such a gruesome battle, we doubt they would have had the occasion to bump into one other. In the many records we read, there was nothing at all that indicated Hector and Charlie had a relationship after the war. We eventually found evidence to the contrary, as will soon be revealed. There were several instances when we expected to see their relationship verified, such as in newspaper articles, but there was no mention of one or the other stating any emotion of having either lost or found each other, as one might expect close brothers would have.

A Find a Grave memorial (ID #3974667) was created for Charlie by the U.S. Veterans Affairs Office on March 3, 2000. One can enter the ID number into a web browser to view the memorial.[44] The enlistment card (previously cited) for World War I confirms his military service from January 10, 1917, and the U.S. Veterans' Administration Master Index confirms his discharge date.[45] Charlie's actual grave marker provides the following details: "Charles E Perez, Florida, Corporal, 18 Infantry, 1 Division, World War I, SEPT. 30, 1899–APRIL 30, 1950."[46]

Six

In the Service of His Country (Hector Perez)

The Military Career of Hector Perez (1917–1928)

As previously stated and verified, Hector enlisted in the U.S. Army on March 27, 1917, at Fort Slocum, New York, using the name "Hector H. Perry." Fort Slocum was a U.S. military post on Davids Island in the western end of Long Island Sound from 1867 to 1965, in New Rochelle, just outside of New York City.[1] After America's entry into the war, Fort Slocum became one of the busiest recruit training stations in the country, processing 100,000 soldiers per year and serving as the recruit examination station for soldiers from New York, New Jersey, Pennsylvania, and the New England states. Between 1917 and 1919, over 140,000 recruits passed through this post. Interestingly, Recruit Week in December 1917 brought so many recruits to Fort Slocum that the overflow had to be housed in New Rochelle.

It is a mystery why Hector opted to use the name Hector H. Perry and not his birth-given name at the time of his enlistment. No one knows whether it was intentional or whether he was already suffering some sort of mental illness prior to or at the time of his enlistment. As pointed out earlier, one possibility was that he just wanted to "fit in," so he used an anglicized surname. This question remains unanswered.

Another puzzling aspect of this situation is the place where he and his brother chose to enlist. We already know that Hector's younger brother Charlie enlisted two and a half months before Hector. Charlie listed his residence at that time as New York City. (Although his enlistment card reported the location as Columbus Barracks, Ohio, we believe that Columbus Barracks was his first duty station and not the exact location of his enlistment.) It is peculiar that they were both in New York considering that they both lived in Tampa, Florida, a year earlier at the time of their mother's death in January 1916.[2] As we know, the girls (Evangelina and

Six. In the Service of His Country (Hector Perez)

Dinorah) remained in the Tampa area, living with their Velasco aunts, but no one knows for certain what the boys did immediately following their mother's unexpected death at such a young age. We learned from their father Charles' statement, as reported in letters and newspaper stories, that Hector did indeed leave Tampa shortly after his mother's death and was not heard from again. The same does not apply to Charlie, who joined the army in New York City in 1917 and remained in touch with his sister Dinorah and his father. No information concerning their whereabouts at that time could be found. Without documentary evidence, anything would be conjecture. Because both brothers wound up in New York and enlisted there, it is plausible, as we suggested earlier, that they went there to live with family or friends after their mother's death.

Both sons were living with their parents at the time of their mother's death, as records show.[3] In terms of their ages, Sarah Perez was thirty-seven years old when she died. Her husband Charles had just turned forty-three. Hector was nineteen years of age, Evangelina was eighteen, Charlie was sixteen, and Dinorah was not yet thirteen. Traditionally, within Hispanic cultures, men were the providers and women were the glue that kept the home and family together.[4] Without a mother in the house, things would be vastly different for the four Perez children. Catastrophic events often call for drastic measures, sometimes resulting in inexplicable occurrences and situations.

Several theories have been proposed about why the boys were in New York City. One theory is that the boys went there to live with their paternal aunt, Lola Perez, or her children. Lola was their father Charles' only living sibling. As previously reported, she had been born in Havana in 1868, while Charles was born in New York City in 1872. The other two brothers, Ramon and Agusto, were no longer living by the time of the 1900 U.S. Census. Lola was married twice—first to Juan Vasquez in 1886 and later to Jose Flores in 1889. She had six children in total, all of whom were born in Florida. All were within the same age range as Hector and Charlie. Lola's first husband had the surname "Vasquez," and one of her granddaughters married a man with the surname "Sanchez." Most of the Vasquez and Sanchez offspring were within seven to ten years of Hector's age. "Vasquez" is a similar-sounding surname to "Velasquez," one of the names Hector used later. The surname "Sanchez" is an exact match to what Hector adopted while an amnesiac. Vasquez also sounds like "Velasco," which was Hector's mother's birth name. Lola's offspring with her two husbands were first cousins to Hector and Charlie, and they were all close while growing up. However, we cross-referenced their names and places of residence prior to and after the enlistment dates for both Hector and Charlie and found no evidence of any relative known to us residing in New York.

The nagging question remains as to why Hector and Charlie enlisted in New York City. As in most genealogical research, one does not always find answers. Obviously, there is a cost associated with travel and lodging. Traveling from Tampa to New York solely to enlist in the military just does not make sense. They had to go there for another reason. Their father's relatives were the only ones who had any history of being in New York. Our research showed that neither their paternal grandfather, Jose Isabel Perez, nor his wife, Claudia Mora, had family in New York City, so it is still a mystery as to why the boys resided and enlisted there. Could it be that some other relative(s) they were closely associated with lived there? Our research failed to reveal any of their mother's family or extended family members living in New York at that time. Their purpose for traveling to New York City sometime between early 1916 and January 1917 would be nice to know, but, in terms of the bigger picture, it may not be that important.

As to the mode of transportation Hector and Charlie would have used to travel to New York City from Tampa, rail is the obvious choice. In 1917, one would have needed to connect to several trains, as they were independent rail companies, and none ran direct routes to New York City from Tampa.[5] The most common route used from Tampa would be to Jacksonville, Florida; then to Richmond, Virginia; on to Washington, D.C.; up to Philadelphia, Pennsylvania; and ending at New York City.

Earlier, when we researched Hector's record of service form, we verified that he enlisted in the regular army at Fort Slocum, New York, on March 27, 1917, as Hector H. Perry. Although another source showed that his enlistment date was May 27, 1917, that date is incorrect. March is correct, as his age on the form is given in years and months, and, given that Hector was born in December 1896, if he enlisted in March 1917, he would have been 20 years and 3 months, just as the form shows. The March date was corroborated using other documents as well. It is interesting to note that his memory did not fail him in stating his precise age on enlistment.

Hector's given address on the record of service form was recorded as 14 New Chalmers Street in New York, which is perplexing.[6] New Chalmers (or Chalmers) was not an existing street name or address in any of the five boroughs of New York City. Once again, we question where the address shown on this form originated. It was transcribed from another part of Hector's service record. Barring a clerical or communication error, we would have to assume that Hector himself provided the information on the form it was originally taken from. We just do not know when that was. Whether it was documented at the time of his enlistment in 1917 or 11 years later at the time of his general court-martial and imprisonment in 1928, we believe the information about his residential address is incorrect.

Six. In the Service of His Country (Hector Perez)

We are inclined to believe the information was recorded on the record of service form at the time of his enlistment, but we have some reservations. We do not know why the incorrect information exists on the form, but it could be due to memory failure on Hector's part. Regardless of timing, this discrepancy further illustrates an issue with Hector's ability to recall information.

The next data point on the card refers to his birthplace. "Key West, Fla.," was reported. This is incorrect. Of course, one can understand why he might have said that, as he was raised in Key West. We have no other reasonable explanation for this error.

Another data point is "Organizations." The typed response showed "MD," which stands for "Medical Detachment." This is correct. We know he was assigned to the medical detachments of the 15th Field Artillery (FA) and the 4th FA. His grade was listed as private.

The card also noted that Hector was not wounded or otherwise injured in action. The dates given on the card for "Served Overseas" were "Dec 12/17 to July 14/19." This is correct by all reporting. The next data point shows "Deserted" (specifically on June 26, 1920, at Hoff General Hospital, Staten Island, New York). This is also technically correct. This information must have been entered into the card after Hector's separation from the military.

Following this entry, we noticed that the typed words were much darker and bolder in the next space. One can see this information is new due to the dates it reflects. It was entered on the card after Hector's dishonorable discharge from the army. The space for "Remarks" noted that he was apprehended and returned to military control on May 29, 1928, and was dishonorably discharged on September 21, 1928; on the back of the card, the notes go on to indicate that the discharge was due to conviction and the sentence of a general court-martial order.[7] So, all or some of the card's data was clearly typed in after the dishonorable discharge was promulgated on September 21, 1928. We believe the dishonorable discharge is why there is no mention of any commendations Hector received for fighting in many significant battles. We know for certain that whole units were meritoriously awarded medals and ribbons for those battles in which Hector took part while assigned to those units.[8]

We do not believe Hector intentionally fabricated an incorrect address during his enlistment with the intent to deceive or any other devious purpose. We believe he did indeed provide the information, and it is plausible that this mystery could be related to mental health issues or memory lapses manifested from trauma of some sort. We just do not know.

Another record we found added a layer of complexity to Hector's identity issue. The U.S. Veterans' Administration Master Index (1917–1940) revealed a curious record of military service for Hector. It showed his name as "Hector Harrison Perry" with a birth date of December 16, 1895.[9] It also provides a "Military Date" of 1928 and gave his place of residence as Worcester, Massachusetts. The middle name Harrison was unknown to us.

Several data points of this VA record match what we know about Hector. We know he lived in Worcester, Massachusetts, which makes it a direct match. The birth date on the record is a match for the month and day of Hector's actual birth; only the year is off (Hector was born in 1896). The last point to be considered is the "Military Date," which was given as 1928. This date coincides with the year of his return to military control, his general court-martial, and his discharge from the army. So, it seems that rather than resolving the identity issue, this document turns out to be just another proverbial fly in the ointment. Occurrences like this one are common in genealogical research.

This previously unknown middle name of "Harrison" turned out to be another point of confusion for which we tried to find a logical explanation. The connection to this misinformation and other puzzling facts are found in one of the documents Hector's grandniece, Lina, discovered in 2017: an Associated Charities letter dated June 9, 1930, in which the general secretary refers to the War Department's correspondence with her, which included the home addresses of close family members to possibly aid in the efforts to locate Hector's family (the full contents of this letter are detailed later in this chapter). The information contained therein, logically, would most likely have been furnished at the time of his enlistment. Though it is unclear, it is possible that these names and addresses were from his 1928 confinement while being evaluated when he was in custody. However, we seriously doubt the latter was the case. We found the following: "Mr. Perry's father, Charles Perry, was living at 46 Southard St., Key West, in 1918 and that his mother was listed as Clara Harrison, 510 Brown St., Cincinnati, Ohio. There was a sister, Evangeline Perry, whose address was the same as that of the mother. As far as he remembers, his mother's name was Sarah Perry and he tried to locate her on Harrison Street in Cincinnati, Ohio. There is apparently a great deal of confusion in Mr. Perry's mind about these facts and we are anxious to locate these relatives if possible."

We can see that Hector informed the army authorities that his mother was named Clara Harrison. He also claimed his mother's name was Sarah Perry, and "he tried to locate her on Harrison Street in Cincinnati." We looked for other documents from that period to compare the data and found the December 1917 army manifest when he sailed to France, in which his father's name and address were exactly as stated above. If he

Six. In the Service of His Country (Hector Perez)

were then suffering from some sort of manifestation of mental illness back in 1917, he may have been fixated on the name Harrison at that moment for an obscure, unknown reason. Yes, this theory is pure conjecture, but it is plausible and there was no other obvious reason. We know his mother's married name was Sarah Perez, not Harrison. His only niece was named Clara Fernandez, so it is possible that his recollection was a bit skewed, but he did have some of the names right. He recalled the correct name of his sister as Evangeline (Evangelina), but no reference was made to his younger sister Dinorah or to his brother Charlie. As stated in the letter, there clearly was a great deal of confusion in Hector's mind. It must have been a sad thing to see. While he correctly recalled the name of one of his sisters, he did not recall his two other siblings, and he was confused as to whether his mother's name was Sarah or Clara (which was his niece's name). Another still-unresolved issue is where the name and fixation on Harrison came from.

Hector's decision not to use his proper name and address at the time of his enlistment could indeed be an indication that he was suffering from some sort of mental health issue. This condition could have been brought on by the trauma of his mother's death, or there could have been another problem that may have caused some sort of psychological trauma in Hector's life.

Our attempts to ascertain whether Hector used a middle initial or middle name provide another example of how inconsistencies are common during ancestral research. We initially found no evidence that Hector used or had a middle name. Then this enlistment record revealed his middle initial was "H." The only time this initial was seen was in his army records. Then we later found out his true middle name, as you will see. The net result is that genealogical data often gets misunderstood and could easily become warped and misinterpreted. Then, to make matters worse, in an attempt to enlarge their family tree, some users of ancestral programs will eagerly append mistaken details to their family records and present them as facts when they really are not.

The overarching question remains unanswered to this day: Why is some of the information relating to Hector so far off the mark? Could it be that Hector had a reason for willfully providing inaccurate information at the time of his enlistment, or could he have offered it for another reason? As we have seen, a good deal of Hector's personal information given at enlistment is flawed and factually incorrect. It defies explanation, just as his place of enlistment does. Requests for Hector's complete records led us to a dead end due to the fire at the National Personnel Records Administration Building in 1973 (a problem that also affected his brother Charlie's records).

Hector's army record was found detailed in letters dated July 3, 1931, and will be displayed in chapter 7. Besides his enlistment information being Fort Slocum, New York, we learned the following: after enlisting at Fort Slocum in March 1917, he was assigned to duty as a private with the medical detachment at Fort Wadsworth, New York. On June 25, 1917, after approximately ten weeks of basic training, he was transferred to the medical detachment of the 4th Field Artillery Regiment, Fort Wadsworth, on Staten Island, New York.[10] As we learned, the 15th FA was drawn from the transfer of men from the 4th FA. Hector left the United States for service overseas on December 12, 1917, with the medical detachment of the 15th FA, as the passenger manifest revealed.[11] It is difficult to confirm the exact dates when Hector served with specific units, but the surviving record indicates that on March 24, 1918, Hector participated in his first battle; then, on July 4, he was transferred to the Second Regiment of Engineers (2nd Engineers) and remained in battle through November 11, 1918. His numerous battle details will follow later.

In review, we learned the 15th FA was first constituted in 1916.[12] It was organized in Syracuse, New York, on June 1, 1917. The record reflects that Hector was assigned to this unit on June 11, less than two weeks after it was organized. The 15th FA was assigned to the 2nd Infantry Division in September 1917. They sailed for France in December 1917. The unit took part in the heaviest fighting in six major campaigns during the war. The 4th FA was first activated in 1907 from numbered companies of artillery.

The 2nd Engineers was organized in December 1861 in Washington, D.C.[13] They were expanded and reorganized several times over the years, and by the time Hector was transferred on July 4, 1918, they had been redesignated as the 2nd Engineers, assigned to the 2nd Infantry Division. Hector fought in a total of seven battles. Records revealed six of these battles were with the 15th FA and one was with the 2nd Engineers.

The 15th FA and the 2nd Engineers were highly decorated in World War I. By virtue of Hector's battle dates, he should have been awarded medals along with the other soldiers in these units. Sadly, due to the disgrace that had befallen him by no fault of his own, neither Hector nor his family became aware of the medals bestowed on those units during those engagements.

In reviewing this information, we know that Hector, like the other recruits, had to pass the mandatory testing that included physical and psychological aptitude requirements. The army used "Alpha" and "Beta" standardized tests, among others, which would identify those who could serve and classify them into military jobs; these tests were also used to select those who were candidates for leadership positions.[14] The "testing" seems to have found Hector suited for basic medical training because after enlisting he was assigned to Fort Wadsworth as part of the medical detachment. Hector would receive basic specialized training in procedures taught by army physicians in command. Procedures included basic sanitation, stretcher-bearer work and field work, wound packing, and camp infirmary duties. These quickly and minimally trained medical detachments were tasked with gruesome and bloody work.[15]

Major Battles: Eight Months of Hell (March–November 1918)

For most of the time Hector was in France, he was in the thick of seven bloody battles. Over this eight-month span he served with the American Expeditionary Forces (AEF) on the Western Front in France. He spent at least five months engaged in some of the fiercest battles of the war. He was lucky to get out alive. Once back home, the severity of his amnesia and mental state was such that he was not even aware he had served in the war.

Aside from the standard recruit training Hector received, the basic first aid training, and the training conducted during slack time out in the field in the theater of operations, one can easily infer that he was ill prepared for heavy military engagement, as were many new recruits at that time according to numerous army reports. Hector was a high school graduate and classically trained at the piano. He was not the ideal candidate to become a wartime soldier and face the harshest fighting the world had ever seen. We doubt that there was anything in his past that would have even remotely prepared him to face the hardship and ravages of war. His American patriotism likely became his motivation for enlisting. We are convinced that his belief in liberty and freedom, so deeply rooted in his family's past in their native Cuba during its struggles for independence, caused Hector and his brother to enlist. They were not your typical soldier-types. They had no idea what they were about to experience once they arrived overseas. They were in for the shock of their lives.

Hector left the country on the White Star Line's SS *Adriatic*, which was pressed into service for military transport for the U.S. Army. He sailed for foreign service on December 12, 1917, as a private assigned to the medical detachment of the 15th Field Artillery unit.[16] A photograph of the SS *Adriatic* at Southampton in 1907 is displayed in figure 19 and was the best photo of the vessel that we were able to locate.[17]

A portion of the ship's passenger list showed Hector's name on line 15. He was listed as "Hector H. Perry, Pvt." His father's name was listed as Charles Perry, with a residential address at 46 Southard Street in Key West.

Figure 19: A 1907 photograph of the SS *Adriatic*, pressed into service as a U.S. troop transport ship in 1917, delivering soldiers from New Jersey to Europe for engagement in battle on the front lines during World War I.

As verified by the War Department's adjutant general in a letter dated July 3, 1931 (the transcription of which will be displayed later), Hector took part in seven intense defensive and offensive military maneuvers with the American Expeditionary Forces in the French theater of operations between March and November 1918.[18] Hector and his family would not become aware of his battle record until 1931. The battles he took part in consisted of the following:

- The Toulon-Troyon defensive sector took place from March 15 to May 13, 1918. Hector served from March 24 to May 11, 1918.
- The Château-Thierry defensive sector (Ile de France) took place from May 31 to July 22, 1918. Hector served from June 6 to July 16, 1918. He was transferred on July 4, 1918, to the 2nd Engineers unit. This unit was used to perform engineer duties in support of the infantry, to include entrenching (digging trenches) as well as other construction work in the field.[19] The 2nd Engineers went on to the Aisne-Marne offensive on July 18. Château-Thierry was a German spring offensive against the AEF. It was directed at troops from the U.S. Army and Marine Corps units. These units were the newest troops on the front and just barely out of training.
- The Aisne-Marne offensive took place from July 15 to August 6, 1918. Hector served from July 18 to July 20, 1918. Aisne-Marne was

Six. In the Service of His Country (Hector Perez) 69

the last major German offensive on the Western Front during the war. The attack failed when an Allied counterattack, supported by several hundred tanks, overwhelmed the Germans on their right flank, inflicting severe casualties.[20] From all reporting during World War I, we learned that the 2nd Engineers supported, fought, and died alongside the 4th Marine Brigade (known as the Devil Dogs) during enemy attacks.[21] The 2nd Engineers experienced a casualty rate (26.7 percent) ten times greater than the norm for other engineer units (2.65 percent). French military authorities, with the approval of the commander of the AEF, General John Pershing, awarded the 2nd Engineers a Croix de Guerre for the unit's contribution to the Aisne-Marne offensive campaign beginning on 18 July. We suspect Hector was awarded this Croix de Guerre by virtue of the dates he participated in this offensive operation. The German defeat marked the start of the relentless Allied advance that culminated in the armistice with Germany about 100 days later. The Second Battle of the Marne was an important victory. The Allies had taken 29,367 prisoners, 793 guns, and 3,000 machine guns and inflicted 168,000 casualties on the Germans. The primary importance of the battle was its morale aspect. The strategic gains of the Marne marked the end of a string of German victories and the beginning of an Allied victory streak that would end the war in three months.

- The Marbache defensive sector took place from August 6 to August 18, 1918. Hector served from August 6 to August 16, 1918.[22] The Marbache defensive sector happened after a brief rest when the 6th Machine Gun Battalion's companies were again parceled out to the various battalions of the 5th and 6th Marine Regiments. The operation consisted mainly of a series of marches from Carrefour de la Croix to Camp Bois-l'Évêque.[23] The battalion arrived at Camp Bois-l'Évêque on August 18, 1918. Their time at this camp was used to go through intensive training to further familiarize the Marines with their machine guns.
- The final defensive sector took place at Limey on September 9–11, 1918. Hector served for the duration. This was the point at which the Allies launched their offensive assaults at Saint-Mihiel and Meuse-Argonne.[24]
- The Saint-Mihiel offensive took place on September 12–16, 1918.[25] Hector took part in the full length of the engagement. This major battle involved the AEF and 110,000 French troops under the command of General Pershing against German positions. The U.S. Army Air Service (the precursor of the U.S. Air Force) played a

significant role in this action. The attack at Saint-Mihiel was part of a plan by Pershing, hoping the Americans would break through the German lines and capture the fortified city of Metz. The attack caught the Germans in the process of retreating, which meant that their artillery was out of place. The American attack, coming up against disorganized German forces, proved more successful than expected.

- The Saint-Mihiel attack established the stature of the U.S. Army in the eyes of the French and British forces and once again demonstrated the critical role they played during the war. It also showcased the difficulty of supplying massive armies while they were on the move. The U.S. attack faltered as artillery and food supplies were left behind on the muddy roads. The attack on Metz was not realized, as the Supreme Allied Commander Ferdinand Foch ordered the American troops to march toward Sedan and Mézières, which would lead to the Meuse-Argonne offensive.
- The Meuse-Argonne offensive was fought from September 26, 1918, until November 11, 1918, for a total of 47 days, ending with the armistice.[26] Hector served for the duration of this campaign. The Meuse-Argonne offensive was the major part of the final Allied offensive of the war stretched along the entire Western Front. It was the largest offensive engagement in U.S. military history, involving 1.2 million American soldiers. It is also the deadliest battle in the history of the U.S. Army and the largest and bloodiest operation of the war for the AEF, resulting in over 350,000 casualties, including 28,000 German lives, 26,277 American lives and an unknown number of French lives. American losses were worsened by the inexperience of many of the troops, in addition to the tactics used during the early phases of the operation. The widespread onset of the global influenza outbreak called the "Spanish flu" also played a significant role in increasing the casualty rate. The offensive was the principal engagement of the AEF during World War I and was one of a series of Allied attacks, known as the Hundred Days Offensive, which brought the war to an end.

A publication titled "Sector Activities [of the] American Expeditionary Forces on the Western Front and in Italy 1917–1918" is available online and provides four different tables for all the defensive and offensive engagements of the American Expeditionary Forces by province, unit, sector, and periods of occurrence, along with a short instructional page on how to use the publication.[27] The information from this source can be used to verify the dates when Hector served in those defensive and offensive sectors, proving he was truly in the thick of the bloodiest fighting.

A note of importance: Hector and his family had no idea of the battles he took part in until congressional inquiries requested his records from the War Department in July 1931; the letters are displayed later in this book.

Battle Dates Analysis (1918)

Figure 20 provides a comparison of the service record of the two brothers. There were three primary sources from which this data was compiled. The first was the military enlistment record of service of both men—Charlie (Form No. 724–1½ A.G.O.), dated April 29, 1921, and Hector (Form No. 724–5½ A.G.O.), dated after the September 21, 1928, general court-martial.[28] The second source was Bill Atkinson, Sr. (their nephew), who received the information first-hand from Charlie, as well as our interviews with family members and archived documents they have retained; the third source was the July 3, 1931, original copy of the letter to Massachusetts congressman George H. Stobbs from the adjutant general of the War Department, which is also held in the family archives.[29] We will go into greater detail about this letter later in the story. Suffice it to say that this document is the only reference we have been able to locate with details about Hector's active military service. Presently, these are the best records available, according to our knowledge.

An examination of the military/enlistment record of service for the two brothers reveals how starkly differently they were portrayed. It seems as if these records were written with preconceived judgments in mind. While Charlie's card notes meritorious service, it does not mention all the battles he fought in, other than his service at Soissons when he was cited for conspicuous gallantry and extraordinary bravery. The reverse side of his military/enlistment record indicates details are cited in "General Orders GO 2, 2 Brig. Hq. France, August 2, 1918. page, 22."

The most prominent data on Hector's card (figures 21 and 22) deals with desertion and the general court-martial order. There is no mention at all on Hector's card of the theater of operations in which he served. There is no negative or adverse information gleaned regarding his performance in the field of battle. There is no indication of bravery (or the lack thereof) displayed by Hector in the trenches. There is no information whatsoever given regarding these types of issues; therefore, no assumptions should be made one way or the other. The absence of any recognition for his service other than his desertion and dishonorable discharge seems odd to us. The

Campaign	Charles	Hector
Two Silver Stars for gallantry & bravery	July 20, 1918 (*1)	
Victory Medal with campaign clasps	(*2)	
The Toulon-Troyon defensive sector from March 15 - May 13, 1918		March 24 to May 11, 1918 (*3)
Chateau Thierry defensive sector (Ile de France) from May 31 - July 22, 1918		June 6 - July 16, 1918 (*3)
Montdidier-Noyon	June 9-12, 1918 (*2)	
Aisne-Marne/Soissons offensive from July 15 - August 6, 1918.	July 18-20, 1918 (*1, *2)	July 18 - 20, 1918 (*3)
Marbache defensive sector from Aug 6 - 16, 1918		August 6 - 16, 1918 (*3)
Limey defensive sector, September 9 to 11, 1918.		September 9 to 11, 1918 (*3)
Saint Mihiel offensive from September 12 - 16, 1918.	September 12-15, 1918 (*2)	September 12 - 16, 1918 (*3)
The Meuse-Argonne offensive September 29 to October 27 and October 30 to November 11, 1918	September 26, 1918 (*2)	September 29 to October 27 and October 30 to November 11, 1918 (*3)
Defensive Sector clasps	(*2)	

Sources of records
*1 Charles military enlistment/record of service card
*2 Bill Atkinson Sr - there were several other awards
*3 War Department's Adjutant General's letter to Congressman Stobbs (7/3/1931)

Figure 20: Battle campaigns comparison chart for the brothers Hector and Charlie.

card seems to have been written with a predetermined impression of the man in the mind of the writer.

One could easily form the opinion that one card belonged to a saint and the other to a sinner. A review of both cards would cause the uninformed reader to conclude that Charlie served his country with distinction while Hector served in disgrace. This is just one more example of the travesties and biases that Hector was burdened with and the disservice to which he was subjected by the military he fought for and the government he defended.

The official record shows that the military was aware of the engagements Hector participated in by virtue of the detailed information the adjutant general later provided to Representative Stobbs. Of special note would be Hector's service in the Aisne-Marne offensive on July 18–July 20, 1918; it is well documented that the 2nd Engineers unit (to which Hector was assigned) fought valiantly beside the 4th Marine Brigade (known as the Devil Dogs).[30] As mentioned earlier, the men who took part in this battle were awarded the Croix de Guerre by French authorities, a decision approved by General Pershing. Hector and his family had no notion of how bravely he served; yet we know the military did. It is difficult to draw any other conclusion than that the military was intent on supporting one

Six. In the Service of His Country (Hector Perez) 73

of the brothers and holding him up for his valiant service and tearing the other down because of his reported desertion long after the war ended, while he was in a state of crisis.

```
                Perry,    Hector H              16,141        white
                (Surname)  (Christian name)    (Army serial number)  (Race: White or colored)
                          New

Residence: 14 Chalmers St.,   New York                        NEW YORK
           (Street and house number)  (Town or city)  (County)      (State)

*Enlisted in     RA at Ft Slocum NY            Mch 27/17
†Born in         Key West Fla                  20 3/12 yrs
Organizations:   MD to desertion

Grades:          Pvt

Engagements:

Wounds or other injuries received in action: None.
‡Served overseas: Dec 12/17 to July 14/19
§Deserted        June 26/20 at Hoff Gen Hosp Staten Island NY
Remarks:         Apprehended and returned to military control
                 May 29/28; dishonorably discharged Sept 21/28 by *
```

Form No. 724-5½, A. G. O. *Insert "R. A.", "N. G.", "E. R. C.", "N A.", as case may be, followed by place and
March 12, 1920.   date of enlistment.   †Give place of birth and date of birth, or age at enlistment.
‡Give dates of departure from and arrival in the United States. §Give date and place.

Remarks (continued): reason of conviction and sentence of a General Court-martial Order.

1. This statement of service is furnished under the provisions of the act of Congress approved July 11, 1919.
2. This statement is furnished primarily for historical and statistical purposes, although it may be used in adjudicating claims in which the State is solely concerned. It is not to be used before a court of justice or in support of any claim against the Federal Government. The law prohibits the furnishing of any information that may be used in the prosecution of a claim against the Government, except to the proper Government officials.
3. Applications from individuals, other than historians and statisticians, for information from this statement of service should be denied and the applicant directed to apply for the information to The Adjutant General of the Army, who is the custodian of the official records of the Armies of the United States. Exceptions to this rule may be made in the case of officials of patriotic and philanthropic societies and associations when it is known positively that the information is to be used exclusively by said society or association, and will not be made public nor communicated to any individual who may use it directly or indirectly as a basis for, or in the prosecution of, a claim against the Government, or to the injury of the soldier.
4. Except as hereinbefore provided, all persons seeking information relative to the military and medical histories of the soldier should be denied information from, or access to, this statement of service, as otherwise information legally unobtainable would be made available to persons who might perpetrate frauds upon the Government, or who might seek to injure the soldier.
5. Except the data contained on the first four lines and that relating to battle casualties and physical disability, this statement is prepared as far as practicable from the service record, and no effort has been made to compare the data obtained from the service record with other records, except where an error or discrepancy is patent.
6. Some enlistment papers show age at enlistment, while others show date of birth. The entries recorded herein are in the same form as those on the enlistment paper.

WAR DEPARTMENT,   P. C. HARRIS,
THE ADJUTANT GENERAL'S OFFICE,   The Adjutant General.
       WASHINGTON, D. C.

Top: Figure 21: World War I service card for Hector H. Perry (front), dated March 27, 1917. *Bottom:* Figure 22: World War I service card for Hector H. Perry (back).

The military was aware that these reports would follow their subjects after leaving the service and could have negative consequences later in their lives, so the two men would be rewarded and punished as warranted. Again, it bears mentioning that the cards appear to have been written prejudicially, with the purpose of leading the reader to form a judgment of the men. Hector's struggles in life after the war would turn out to be even greater than the battles fought in Europe. Many of the problems he would experience were directly attributable to the effects such military records would have on his perceived standing in general and his inability to get the help he needed because of his service. Denial of military benefits was one of them, particularly the denial of much-needed medical coverage. Psychological care was critical if he were to get "better" so he could function normally and independently in daily life.

To our surprise, a comparison of the military service data for the brothers revealed two interesting points. First, Hector was in the theater of operations for a longer period (eight months versus just over three and a half months for Charlie) and was involved in more battles than his younger brother (seven versus four). According to the document we recovered, Hector served for more than five months out in the theater of operations while Charlie was in battle for 12 days. Because of the unavailability of official military personnel records, we are forced to draw our conclusions based on what we were able to discover through other documentation.

We also found that both brothers participated in the Aisne-Marne offensive from July 18 to July 20, 1918. It would not be surprising that they did not see each other, since it was a bloody, gruesome battle. As previously noted in chapter 5, Charlie was cited for bravery during this period. Meanwhile, Hector was held in contempt by the military brass for his technical desertion during peacetime in 1920 even though they knew he had served in seven of the war's major battles during his service with the 2nd Engineers and 4th Marine Brigade and did so courageously.

Unfortunately, the adjutant general's letter of 1931 did not reveal any information about Hector's demeanor in battle. It made no mention of how he performed under fire. It almost seems as if the adjutant general reluctantly provided information about the battles Hector fought in. Although two Massachusetts congressmen made inquiries, the information was given to one congressman who requested it, but not to the other. The adjutant general was providing the bare minimum of information to the congressional inquiries. One could easily get the impression that, once again, the army leaders believed they had made the right decision. If Hector exhibited behavior that was a serious cause for concern to the army, and nothing was done about it, it may have given rise to unwelcome questioning and scrutiny of the army at a later point in time. If Hector demonstrated valor, then that performance would have been inconsistent with their belief about actions committed by a deserter. In either event, the army's reluctance to reveal the full story is obvious. The army felt it would be counterproductive and not in their best interests to admit mistakes they might have made. Sometimes it is best to let sleeping dogs lie. This may have been seen as a case in which less was better. Ignoring a problem rather than dealing with what might become an even more inconvenient situation may at times appear to be a preferred strategy. However, when doing so, virtue and morality often get abandoned. It becomes unjust. In some circles, such action could be construed as an abuse of power.

Military Tribunal and the Aftermath (1928)

Based on the events that occurred during that chance meeting in Worcester in the spring of 1928 with the "war buddy" who recognized Hector from the time the two had served with the American Expeditionary Forces in France, Hector and Grace hired an attorney, and, on his advice, Hector contacted the army. He was instructed to go to Fort Adams, Rhode Island. He went to the army post as directed, looking for answers that might help him sort through the mystery of his former life and learn his identity. Instead, he was arrested on the spot, charged, and tried for desertion that same day, May 29, 1928. The sentence would then go before the approving body before being promulgated in general court-martial orders. It would be approved, modified, or remitted by this reviewing authority, which was slated for September. During this period, Hector was to be confined until the review.

As we previously mentioned, between June 26 and July 27, 1928, a period of thirty days, the army doctors performed a battery of tests and diagnosed Hector as being in a constitutional psychopathic state with an inadequate personality disorder. Interestingly, within one week of this diagnosis, the members of the general court-martial who sat in Hector's case on May 29 recommended clemency and remission of the dishonorable discharge and six months of the confinement. Their letter was dated August 3, 1928, and addressed to the commanding general, First Corps Area, Army Base, Boston, Massachusetts. The recommendations of the trial officers were unanimous consent by those who heard and deliberated the trial.

While awaiting sentencing, we know that from August 9 through August 12, 1928, the army conducted another battery of psychiatric evaluations on Hector. The diagnosis was determined to be psychoneurosis, hysteria, acute constitutional psychopathic state, and acute inadequate personality disorder. This second diagnosis was even more serious than the initial diagnoses.

To sum it up, Hector was confined for almost four months between May and September 1928. At the general court-martial in May, he was found guilty of being a deserter for a period of almost eight years, from June 26, 1920, through May 29, 1928. In addition to being dishonorably discharged and sentenced to one year in confinement at hard labor, he forfeited all pay and allowances. On September 20, 1928, the sentence was partially approved, and confinement was remitted. The sentence was promulgated in general court-martial orders dated September 20, 1928. Hector was effectively dishonorably discharged the following day, September 21, 1928. The result of the sentence would be Hector's ineligibility for critical medical benefits, which included the psychiatric care he so desperately needed.

His freedom had been taken away while he was confined for those four months, and now he was stripped of the two things that could help him function independently in society when released: his pay and his veterans' benefits. Supported by the determination and dedication of his amazing wife Grace, Hector focused on garnering support and involvement of important individuals and influential organizations so they could help him right this wrong. He and Grace were akin to David facing his Goliath. Because of the couple's irrepressible spirit in the pursuit of identifying and taking every avenue they could to resolve the injustice, many aspects of Hector's military service became known to others, as did additional facts and aspects that are an essential part of his story, which might otherwise never have become known.

A Trail of Clinical Diagnoses (1919–1928)

Military records show Hector was treated for influenza after the war, from January 24 through February 4, 1919, while still stationed overseas. The last battle he participated in was on November 11, 1918, the day when the armistice agreement was signed. On April 17, 1919, five months after the war ended, he was treated for alcoholism. However, there is a great deal of ambiguity and suspicion about the accuracy of this diagnosis of alcoholism since it was changed to a more serious psychological diagnosis on the third day of his 21-day hospital stay. It is not known by any currently living family members whether Hector drank. If he did, no noteworthy reports of it were recorded, and so there was nothing out of the ordinary about it. It is, of course, possible that the atrocities of war led him to drink. Regardless, in all that is recorded about Hector's life, the only time the topic of alcoholism ever came up was in this misdiagnosis, which was quickly changed. There were no reports whatsoever from any sources that he drank excessively or at all. In later years, Hector was drawn to clubs, but it is more likely that he was drawn to them for the music. He loved to entertain and play the piano for others. He often did so at home, in music studios, and mostly (if not exclusively) in alcohol-free environments. We doubt that his attraction to the clubs had anything to do with his own alcohol consumption. Prohibition in the United States lasted from 1920 to 1933 and coincided with the timing of these events.[31] Although possible, we believe it is highly unlikely that alcohol played any role in Hector's life.

As stated earlier, soon after the diagnosis of alcoholism was made, it was changed to "psychoneurosis, type undetermined" three days later on April 20, 1919. Hector remained in treatment from April 17 until May 7, for a total of 21 days. We learned no details about any treatments he might have been receiving during that time. We believe that Hector was transferred to "occupation" duty at Koblenz, Germany, after the fighting ended. The 2nd Engineers movement record shows Koblenz, Germany, as the unit's assigned duty station, and we also find Hector's name on page 217 of that same publication.[32]

We know that during the war, treatment programs consisted of mostly a three-tiered system for shell shock or war neurosis,[33] with treatment to commence as soon as possible after the onset of symptoms. Treatment was ideally applied in or near casualty clearing stations, which were located a few miles behind the front lines. Here, nervous soldiers were given a period of rest, sedation, and adequate food. Through simple forms of supportive psychotherapy imbued with optimism and characterized by persuasion and suggestion, military physicians explained to soldiers that their reactions were normal and would disappear in a few days. Reports from front-line psychiatrists estimated that up to 65 percent of soldiers returned to the fighting lines after four or five days. The second tier consisted of psychiatric and neurological wards in base hospitals, which were located five to fifteen miles behind the front lines. There, soldiers were treated for up to three weeks. The third tier was about fifty miles from the front line, where severe types of shell shock were treated for up to six months. If there was no improvement during this period, soldiers would be repatriated.

Since Hector's record reveals that his diagnosis of psychoneurosis (type undetermined) occurred after the fighting ended, we do not know what, if any, sort of treatment he received to address this concerning diagnosis while hospitalized.

We have no information on his whereabouts between May 7 (the last day of his "hospital stay" due to the mental illness diagnosis) and

July 5, 1919, when Hector boarded a vessel to return to the United States from overseas duty. Such details should have been recorded in his military personnel file; however, as mentioned earlier, his military records were destroyed in the 1973 National Archives fire. His voyage from France back to the United States took nine days. On July 5, 1919, he departed from Brest, France, arriving July 14, 1919, at Hoboken, New Jersey.[34]

During our research, we found a curious passenger list showing Hector's name as Hector H. Perry, army serial no. 16,141, sailing from Brest, France, on July 5, 1919, and arriving at Hoboken nine days later, on July 14, 1919. All these data points were verified to be correct. The vessel was the *Prinz Friederich Wilhelm*. Hector was listed as passenger 27 on a list of fifty-four names. However, this passenger list was titled "Prisoners." Out of the fifty-four listed service members, two were listed as "General Prisoners" and one was listed as "Prisoner for Trial." The rest of the soldiers, including Hector, were "Garrison Prisoners." Hector's emergency contact was given as "Charles Perry" (father), with an address of "510 Broome Street, Lima, Ohio." City street directories failed to reveal a street in Lima named Broome Street.[35] As records show, there is Broome Street in lower Manhattan.[36] Broome Street there runs in an easterly-westerly direction across the full width of Manhattan Island, from Hudson Street in the west to Lewis Street in the east, near the entrance to the Williamsburg Bridge. This never-before-seen Broome Street address for Hector's father is puzzling and appears to be yet another incorrect data point. This discovery leads us to believe that Hector was not well at this time. By comparison, during the trip from the United States to France in 1917 when he was initially deployed, the record reflects that he furnished a different address for his father.[37]

We can surmise from this document that after Hector's diagnosis of a serious mental condition two months earlier, he was released back to his "occupation" duty station, whether in Germany or France, until his return home in July 1919. It is plausible that Hector was acting out in some fashion, as evidenced by him being admitted into an army hospital for twenty days and being diagnosed with a mental condition; then we find him listed as a garrison prisoner on this passenger manifest. We see no mention of this fact anywhere in Hector's army record.

In military vernacular, a "garrison prisoner" is a prisoner at a military post charged with an offense not entailing dismissal or dishonorable discharge.[38] By contrast, a "general prisoner" is a military prisoner who has been sentenced to confinement and to dismissal or discharge.[39] While dismayed, we were a bit relieved when we discovered that Hector was listed as a garrison prisoner, since that tells us his status was due to a minor infraction of some type and not a serious offense.

Six. In the Service of His Country (Hector Perez)

A month after Hector's return stateside that summer, he was transferred to the medical detachment of the 36th Infantry at Hoff U.S. General Hospital #41 at Fox Hills, New York, on August 19, 1919.[40]

The history of Hoff U.S. General Hospital #41 at Fox Hills is interesting.[41] It was constructed in just four months—a record time in 1918—at a cost of two million dollars. This facility became the largest army hospital in the world, with a capacity for 3,000 patients. It consisted of eighty-seven buildings holding sixty-two wards. Each ward contained fifty beds. The one-square-mile area had ninety buildings. It was known as Fox Hills Hospital #41 and operated until 1922. Fox Hills was both a "general" hospital (#41) and a "debarkation" hospital (#2). Debarkation hospitals treated wounded soldiers on disembarking from their overseas tour of duty.[42] This hospital and its grounds were massive and like a small city when Hector arrived. He was part of the medical detachment at the general hospital. Fox Hills was not designated as an army psychiatric hospital.[43] The army could have admitted him to a psychiatric hospital if they felt he required such assistance, but they did not. Then we found there was a brief reference to it in his medical record two months later.

On October 16, 1919, Hector was "under" treatment, but no further details were given and no length of treatment or diagnosis reported. He remained at Hoff General Hospital from March 6 to June 5, 1920, and was treated for a disease not incident to the service.[44] Once again, no other details were given about the nature of the disease or the reason for the treatment. We discovered that from June 11 to June 16, 1920, he was treated for two issues.[45] The first was termed a disease not incident to his military service, and the second was furunculosis, which is a deep infection of the hair follicle leading to abscess formation with an accumulation of pus and necrotic tissue.[46] It is uncertain whether the hospital was his military station for this eight-month span, from October 1919 through June 1920, or if he was there for treatment for an illness or injury of some sort or because he was being treated for a mental disorder.[47] Hector had some medical training because of his initial assignment to the medical detachment of the 15th FA on deployment. We do not know whether that limited medical experience would cause him to be assigned to a hospital for regular duty following his return. We found no evidence that he was particularly skilled at hospital duty other than his first aid training for the field under combat conditions. One would surmise, based on his past diagnosis of psychoneurosis, that he would not be considered a good fit for a hospital assignment. The question of whether Hector was assigned to the hospital as his duty station or if his presence there was because he was being treated for psychological issues remains unanswered. We doubt he was being treated there since Hoff was a general hospital and not a psychiatric facility.

The absence of any mention in the War Department's letter of further diagnoses or psychological treatment being given over this period is a bit surprising. If Hector was being treated for something at the hospital, the duration of the treatment was quite lengthy, in which case it must have been a serious condition. Are we to surmise that the hospital was Hector's regularly assigned duty station? Was he assigned to the medical detachment because he was a patient of some sort? Was he under treatment for the entire time he was there? He was last seen by the military on June 17, 1920, the date he was furloughed and allowed to walk out of the hospital. His record would have shown (and the hospital administrators would have known) he had several profoundly serious diagnoses, and yet he was allowed to leave as any normal, healthy soldier would have.

After he departed the Staten Island hospital on leave, Hector evidently wandered around several New England cities and eventually wound up in Worcester, Massachusetts. It was there that he met the young lady he would eventually marry. Sadly, Hector was suffering from a dissociative disorder of sorts when he and Grace married, but neither of them knew that. Later reports from family stories passed down over decades lead us to believe he suffered from dissociative amnesia with dissociative fugue.[48] Neither condition was temporary, and together they were a rare combination indeed. Certainly, this is why he was unable to provide answers to some elementary questions about his lineage, his family, and his past. He clearly suffered from some form of amnesia, but neither Hector nor Grace would know why he was unable to recall basic information. Grace felt that her husband, who was a gifted piano player, must have learned how to play at an early age due to the complete mastery and expertise he displayed. All he remembered was that he had always played the piano. It was part of his being. It consoled him and gave him comfort. Reports of patients with these dissociative disorders have shown they remember how to play their instrument prior to the onset of amnesia.[49]

As previously stated, requests to obtain Hector's military service records to establish and verify information have proven unsuccessful. On July 12, 1973, a disastrous fire at the National Personnel Records Center (NPRC) in St. Louis, Missouri, destroyed somewhere around 16 to 18 million official military personnel files.[50] Approximately 80 percent of the records of U.S. Army personnel discharged from November 1, 1912, to January 1, 1960, were lost.

To our knowledge, no duplicate copies of these records were ever maintained, nor were microfilm copies produced. There were no indices created prior to the fire, and everything was filed and stored manually. In addition, millions of documents had been lent to the Department of Veterans Affairs before the fire occurred; therefore, a complete listing of the records that were lost is not available. However, in the years following the fire, the NPRC collected numerous alternative records (referred to as auxiliary records) that were used to reconstruct basic service information.

Hector's grandniece Lina requested copies of documents from Hector's service record. A verbatim transcript of the reply from the NPRC to her request follows.

> National Personnel Records Center
> 1 Archive Drive St. Louis, MO 63138-1002
> www.archives.gov

February 14, 2023
EVANGELINA PALMER
XXXXXXXXXXXXXXXXX
XXXXXXXXXXXXXXXXX
RE:Veteran's Name: PEREZ (PERRY), Hector H
SSN/SN: ******942
Request Number: 2-2762366****

Dear Recipient:

Thank you for contacting the National Personnel Records Center. The record needed to answer your inquiry is not in our files. If the record were here on July 12, 1973, it would have been in the area that suffered the most damage in the fire on that date and may have been destroyed. The fire destroyed the major portion of records of army military personnel for the period 1912 through 1959, and records of Air Force personnel with surnames Hubbard through Z for the period 1947 through 1963. Fortunately, there are alternate records sources that often contain information which can be used to reconstruct service record data lost in the fire; however, complete records cannot be reconstructed.

Information may be available in the casualty file maintained by the Department of the Army. We suggest contacting the following office for assistance: U.S. ARMY HUMAN RESOURCES COMMAND, CASUALTY & MEMORIAL AFFAIRS OPERATIONS DIVISION, ATTN: AHRC-PDC, 1600 SPEARHEAD DIVISION AVENUE DEPT 450, FORT KNOX, KY 40122-5405.

Army historical records which contain unit histories may be on file at the U.S. Army Heritage and Education Center, Attn: Patron Services Division, 950 Soldiers Drive, Carlisle, PA 17013-5021, and the New York Public Library, Fifth Avenue and 42nd Street, New York, NY 10018. Although unit histories do not normally include information about specific personnel, they will show the unit's activities and participation during the war. We suggest contacting those addresses, with the specific unit designation, for possible information pertaining to the veteran's unit activities.

If you have any questions or comments regarding this response, you may contact us at 314-801-0800 or by mail at the address shown in the letterhead above. If you contact us, please use the Request Number listed above. If you are a veteran, or a deceased veteran's next of kin, please consider submitting your future requests online by visiting us at http://vetrecs.archives.gov.

Sincerely,
XXXXXXXXXXX
Archives Technician

Additional attempts to uncover Hector's military service record continued through the alternate sources identified in the NPRC response, to no avail. The absence of Hector's medical records cannot be understated in terms of their importance in gaining a better understanding of what his issues truly were and in determining whether appropriate action was taken and, if appropriate, whether treatment (and what type) was given.

While awaiting the outcome of his general court-martial sentencing, as we stated previously, Hector was subjected to intense medical examination at the direction of the army. Hector's involvement with the army picked up right where it had left off eight years earlier—in psychological assessment. Through these examinations, a determination was made of what was behind Hector's behavior. This was done to understand what he was experiencing and what the cause of his condition was. Hector was diagnosed with "constitutional psychopathic state" coupled with an "inadequate personality."

In the late 1920s, in early psychopathology classification according to what researchers then believed, pervasive traits and characteristics were "constitutional," or present at birth.[51] A short publication written by a member of the neuropsychiatric department of the United States Army Medical Corps, Dr. Thomas J. Orbison, MD, in a 1929 issue of *California and Western Medicine* proved extremely useful for us as laypeople.[52] At the time of his publication, Dr. Orbison had already shared this report (dated April 1928) with his peers and stated that he had observed soldiers from World War I for a period of three years. This publication was in line with the date of Hector's return to military control. We felt this article at the very least gave us insight into the thinking of the day. The term *psychopath* was originally a general term unconnected to the egregious moral deprivation it is associated with today. Morally corrupt personalities became known as "psychopathic inferior," which was eventually shortened to "psychopath." It was recognized that psychopaths came in many varieties, and it was important to distinguish their subtypes. There were seven subgroups of constitutional psychopathic inferiors: (1) inferior or inadequate group; (2) paranoid personality group; (3) sex deviates group; (4) emotional instability group; (5) criminal group; (6) pathological liars' group; (7) nomadism group.

Six. In the Service of His Country (Hector Perez) 83

The diagnosis indicates that Hector was in subgroup 1 ("inferior or inadequate"), which a modest dive into the neuropsychiatry publications will confirm covers the ill formed, timid, physically, and psychically impoverished. Their attitudes show plainly their inadequate reaction to life.[53]

Inadequate personality disorder is a term used for a condition without evidence of any mental disorder, characterized by a lack of judgment, ambition, and initiative, leading to failure at everything attempted.[54] Persons with an inadequate personality disorder often have a chronic inability to meet ordinary life's demands. They also have a severe dependency on others. A person with an inadequate personality disorder will tend to become dependent on institutions.[55]

Further examinations conducted on August 9–12, 1928, documented that Hector suffered from "psychoneurosis, hysteria, acute constitutional psychopathic state, and inadequate personality." The last two of these four diagnoses were consistent with the diagnosis offered a few weeks earlier. *Psychoneurosis* is a mental disorder that causes a sense of distress and deficient functioning.[56] *Hysteria* is a term often used to describe emotionally charged behavior that seems excessive or out of control.[57] When someone responds in a way that seems disproportionately emotional for the situation, they are often described as being "hysterical." Hysteria, now called conversion disorder, is a type of mental disorder in which a wide variety of sensory, motor, or psychic disturbances may occur.[58] "Acute" (meaning severe) was added to the "constitutional psychopathic state" diagnosis at this time.

The June 21, 1928, edition of the *New England Journal of Medicine* refers to treatment for psychoneurosis, and wartime trauma is covered in its chapter 10.[59] Again, a quick look at the prevailing thought of the day revealed that "it is a functional disorder," it has "no physical causes," and it "is the result of a series of reactions, constitutional and environmental in nature." Cyclic mood alterations, hysteria, anxiety, neuroses, and involutional depressions are frequently seen among those afflicted. Involutional depression or involutional melancholia is a traditional name for a psychiatric disorder that affects mainly late middle-aged or elderly people, and it is usually accompanied by paranoia. Such was the case with Hector in terms of there being no physical injury; his condition was apparently the result of his reaction to combat trauma. We further gleaned that these patients, with treatment, can adjust sufficiently satisfactorily to enable them to remain in the community.

Keep in mind that all these diagnoses occurred after Hector was taken into custody at Fort Adams in 1928. We do not know what diagnoses were made during his stay at Hoff General Hospital between October 1919 and June 1920, after which he leisurely strolled off the post on furlough. It is hard to believe that no similar diagnoses were made during those eight months, given his prior diagnosis of psychoneurosis on April 20, 1919, during his 21-day stay while still stationed overseas. It is even harder to understand why the army decided to conceal that information. There is no reason for not revealing such information at the general court-martial aside from covering up an act, omission, or culpability. Did the army know something they did not want to become exposed?

Failure to Consider Extenuating Circumstances (1928)

These psychological examinations and diagnoses were made after Hector's general court-martial on May 29, 1928. The members of the general court-martial should have been made aware, at the very least, of his previous diagnoses while serving overseas in 1919. If there was any documented and/or historical evidence of Hector suffering some sort of mental or emotional disorder, disease, or distress, one would think it would have been taken into consideration at his general court-martial. We believe it was not taken into consideration or even known by the officers who heard the case by virtue of their actions. Immediately after the month-long series of psychological examinations of June and July 1928, we see the August 3, 1928, clemency letter was written. It provided their recommendations on the matter. The commanding general of the First Corps Area army post in Boston, Massachusetts, ruled against their unanimous recommendation for remittance of the dishonorable discharge and imprisonment, as evidenced by the general's sentencing.

While Hector's second (four-day) period of psychological examination took place after the date of the clemency letter, the findings of the second set of examinations were consistent with the initial examination, albeit more severe. Based on these findings, the mental disorders Hector exhibited should have been an integral part of the proceedings, covered in depth and taken into consideration for purposes of sentencing. This information was crucial to mounting a proper defense. Since they were not included, one would think the army would at least consider the findings of the reports during the time the sentence was under final review. This is the moment when the commanding officer could have modified the sentence. As we know, normal behaviors in the patient were not fully demonstrated for long stretches of time. The commanding officer did as he thought best, even though he may have been made fully aware of Hector's mental disorder. Hector's defense counsel was appointed by the

Six. In the Service of His Country (Hector Perez)

military, and all the overarching principles and protocols of the armed services would naturally apply. Again, it is worth mentioning that rank was the ultimate determinant in the outcome of the case, deliberations be damned.

We have a suspicion that the tribunal may have believed Hector was technically guilty as charged, but now there were extenuating circumstances, which is why they opted for clemency and remitted the one-year sentence of hard labor. In a non-military legal proceeding, things might have turned out quite differently for Hector. He got a raw deal this time around. In terms of clemency, it appears to have become an issue of hierarchy, with the view of the commanding general taking precedence over the recommendation of all the other members of the court, at which point there would be no further deliberation.

Another aggravating factor was the lack of any clear, substantial knowledge in the field of psychiatry regarding post-traumatic stress disorder. Terms that were used back then are no longer applicable today. In the 1920s, the improved firepower of the recent war had resulted in new and unexpected outcomes stemming from the ravages of combat, the proximity to (and frequency of) bombs exploding, and high-powered munitions going off constantly around soldiers, and the effect of such exposure was widely unknown. The term *shell shock* was used to describe some of the symptoms resulting from intense combat, such as "the 1,000-yard stare" as well as a whole host of other behaviors.[60] This was an unexplored element in the field of psychiatry. A century ago, there was a large degree of uncertainty in many of these areas, as knowledge was still evolving. There was an overall lack of understanding and undefined concepts of the ideologies in the field of psychiatry at the time. Many of the treatments that were accepted back then were untested and unproven and, by today's standards, would be considered barbaric.

We believe Hector's personal history could not have been taken into consideration either. We know he was unable to offer any information of value to the clinicians about his past because of his amnesia. Again, not only could he not recall his name or any of his family members, but he also assumed a whole new identity, on which nothing in his conscious memory was based. He could not recall where he was from or other basic information related to his lineage. Presented with such circumstances, who would not think that something in Hector was mentally off centered? That should not have been too hard to figure out. So, if it were known, then not giving that circumstance the weight it deserved was criminal and not representative of a fair and honest legal system, whether military or civilian. The fundamentals and tenets are alike in both. Justice is the main objective.

Trial Rationale and the Results (1928–1930)

There are many contentious issues surrounding the dishonorable discharge, the forfeiture of allowances, and the hard labor sentence handed down to Hector in September 1928. Technically the criteria are clear cut; however, judging from the outcome, we suspect the underlying circumstances were overlooked throughout the trial. Extenuating circumstances were considered by some and yet disregarded by the ranking officer. The one-year confinement at hard labor was, fortunately, remitted.

The trial was when his mental condition should have been considered. If it had not been considered at that time, then it should have been on the day of promulgating the sentence, which took place four months after the trial. This was when they were armed with all the pertinent and critical facts of Hector's mental state and had been given the results of the initial and subsequent psychological examinations. The difference it would have made in his life could have been monumental and far-reaching. By stripping Hector of the veterans' benefits he had clearly earned, his sentence was like the final nail in his coffin. The ultimate insult to Hector was for the military to use him when they needed him and then discard him like trash when he became a burden. His personal well-being was not taken into consideration. This was paramount to all tenets of fairness. Failure to perform an objective assessment of all the pertinent facts at the time of sentencing is indicative of a severely flawed military justice system. We would not be surprised to find that these critical aspects were purposely glossed over in the final analysis. The military's version of justice left Hector with no way to exist in society. Without help, he would continue to be the lost Hector Perry. He had lost his memory because of the war; now he lost his ability to get treatment, based on flawed judgment by a ranking commanding officer. His was a unique and extraordinary situation, the scope and depth of which were staggering. This sentence was the epitome of injustice.

The single most overarching concept that was not taken into consideration is the absence of *mens rea*.[61] Mens rea as defined stipulates that an act itself does not make one guilty of committing a crime unless the offender's mind is guilty. The concept of mens rea (which is Latin for "guilty mind") allows the criminal justice system to differentiate between someone who sets out with the intent to commit a crime and one who did not mean to commit a crime. Mens rea focuses on what the accused individual was thinking and his intent at the time the crime was committed. There are three key elements of a criminal act: (1) a person's knowledge that something is criminal, (2) the existence of criminal intent, and (3) the presence of a wrongful purpose or guilty knowledge. A guilty mind is often the difference between a crime and an accident or incident.

It should have been argued or considered that Hector's desertion was not desertion in the true sense of the offense. Let us consider these key points of fact:

- Hector did not escape from the hospital. He was allowed to leave on furlough for the purpose of taking accrued time off.
- He had no intent to desert whatsoever. He was merely authorized to leave the hospital on furlough.
- He took no steps to conceal himself. He did not purposely change his name to avoid detection. Rather, his name change was due to his mental impairment. Even though he assumed another name, he plainly had no clue who he was or that he had even served in the war. He did not knowingly try to hide his identity. He did not know his identity. He did not know who he was. At the time he went missing, he did not even recall that he had served in the military, much less during a time of war.
- His memory was so severely affected that he forgot all his family members, including his parents and siblings—people he grew up with and had known his whole life. Such a condition is extremely rare and highly unusual.[62]
- His short-term memory also failed him repeatedly, and not just in a small way. He regularly forgot job assignments and was subsequently fired from multiple positions for failure to carry out all his assigned tasks. Furthermore, he could not adequately explain his actions to the police when he was questioned by them and detained that evening in Newark years before the trial. The personal impacts of his amnesia were extensive.

No evidence whatsoever was found to support the notion that Hector had a guilty mind. In his mind, he did nothing wrong. The absence of mens rea, to us, is proof that he committed no crime. Unfortunately, this was not the opinion of the army. His post-war life and his job history reaffirm that he did not have a guilty mind—he had no recollection in his mind!

While it is debatable whether Hector's mental deficiencies should have been detected through the testing that was in place when he enlisted in 1917, his lack of mental acuity became more than clear on several occasions, notably while serving overseas during the war and during his general court-martial as well. This situation should have been a factor in his trial. Furthermore, it is possible the army would be construed as admitting culpability (or at least negligence) if they considered and disregarded these factors during the general court-martial. This may have been because he suffered mental injury due to the war and the army did little about it other than produce a few diagnoses. The military wanted to make whatever happened to Hector the result of his own actions. The army would share no part in accepting responsibility for his mental breakdown or failing to recognize it.

Without the benefit of reviewing his complete medical records, no one would be able to determine what was or was not done for Hector in terms of psychological treatment. His lack of mental sharpness and his inability to recall basic facts was demonstrated in many forms on numerous occasions over a prolonged period. Given his position as a man of little to no means, were the facts being suppressed in hopes that any problems created by the government's nonfeasance, misfeasance or malfeasance in his case would be rejected, disavowed, and just go away? Why would anyone who had already been through the toughest period of his military service wait 11 months after they get back to the United States to desert during peacetime? It just makes no sense. So where was Hector's advocate? Who would help unravel the mess in which he found himself?

The main result of this unjust trial was the many consequences of Hector's sentence: dishonorable discharge and forfeiture of all pay and benefits. He could not receive mental health treatment through the Veterans' Administration and lost access to financial assistance (of which he had never received a cent up to that point in time)—these losses were essentially a death sentence. There had been an opportunity for the commanding officer to consider and adopt the recommendations from the members of the tribunal in their plea for clemency for Hector, to no avail. Without mental health or financial support, what would become of him? What would become of his family?

The first unexpected result we found of this trial is within records we discovered while researching the period of the aftermath of the sentence from late 1928 through early 1930.

Judging from the U.S. Census of April 1930, Grace and Hector appear to have lived separately for a brief period. In the census, Hector was found to be rooming alone, and Grace was reported as living with her mother, several nieces and a nephew.[63] This was the first time we found evidence of the couple living apart. The city directories showed "Alfred" and Grace listed separately in 1929, and then they were found to be living at the same address again in late 1930.

It is an understatement to say it must not have been an easy period in their life or an easy marriage. But then again, the couple had never experienced an "easy time" in their marriage. Grace's goodness was clearly demonstrated by her actions toward her husband. We can make only educated guesses as to their personal marital challenges after Hector was released from confinement in late September 1928. The record pointed to a brief split, a breather of sorts—a temporary separation.

The next unexpected and yet pleasing result we found, by virtue of the reports and documents we amassed, was that by May 1930 the couple had reunited, and they were seeking assistance from local social agencies, influential organizations, and politicians in their state as they formulated a plan to battle against the bureaucracy of the U.S. Army to right this wrong.

This is the appropriate time to introduce the pivotal letter that would kick things off for the couple and in turn spur others to get involved on their behalf to the extent that they could. This would be just the beginning of good things to come.

The Associated Charities of Worcester Letter (June 9, 1930)

What follows is a verbatim transcription of a detailed, three-page letter dated June 9, 1930, written by the general secretary of the Associated Charities of Worcester, asking the Duval County Welfare Agency in Jacksonville, Florida, for assistance in locating Hector's family. A copy of this letter (as well as all other letters and newspaper stories included in this book) was accessed from the family archives.

As you follow the narrative in subsequent chapters, you will understand that this letter was preceded by inquiries Hector and Grace initiated with the American Red Cross as well as veteran organizations in their attempts to seek aid. This letter offers a glimpse into the type of assistance the organizations had been giving the couple.

The Associated Charities letter was written by its general secretary, Helen Fairbanks, whose address was the Wetherell House in Worcester, Massachusetts. It provides basic military details from Hector's record, including enlistment dates, transfer and assignment dates, the date of his return to the United States from overseas duty, his furlough, and finally his desertion and dishonorable discharge. No information regarding his participation in specific battles is provided. However, the letter does give a timeline of sorts regarding how he arrived at his then-current state. This letter is the most complete description available of Hector's life, as best as it could be pieced together based on the extremely limited information that Hector was able to provide. Grace also gave Ms. Fairbanks first-hand information commencing from her meeting Hector in 1920 that was true and accurate. This letter illustrates the attempts that had been made to assist a veteran and his spouse in their time of desperate need. The thoroughness of the general secretary's letter was key to helping locate Hector's family, as was her engagement with the American Red Cross. It was the single most impactful action taken up to that point in time. The urgency conveyed by her message was palpable. The goodness she embodied is precisely what was needed at that moment.

The main purpose of the correspondence addressed to the Duval County Family Welfare Agency in Jacksonville, Florida, was to lobby for assistance in locating Hector's family. There were many key points laid out in this letter. The general secretary was intent on succeeding in her mission, and she obviously wanted to include as many details as possible since there was really no way for her to determine what parts of Hector's story were accurate prior to his initial meeting with Grace. He had sought help from experts in the field of psychology and from professional organizations that could assist veterans but was rejected due to his dishonorable discharge. The mention of a pending bill being brought before the next session of Congress to revoke the dishonorable discharge and bestow an honorable discharge was welcome news and quite heartening. This was the first time we read any mention of this pending congressional bill.

THE ASSOCIATED CHARITIES
of Worcester, Massachusetts
Wetherell House, 2 State St.
Helen E. Fairbanks, General Secretary.

June 9, 1930

RE: Hector Perry
alias Alfredo Velasquez Sanchez
Miss C. Adelaide Barker
Duval County Family Welfare Agency
700 West 10th Street
Jacksonville, Florida

My dear Miss Barker:

We would like to ask your assistance in locating the relatives of Hector Perry, alias Alfredo Velasquez Sanchez, now of Worcester.

Mr. Perry applied to us April 14 of this year. He had been referred here by the local Red Cross who had been aiding him for a month and were unable to continue with this aid. Mr. Perry was very absent-minded and distracted at the time of his application. He did not give any information about his birthplace, relatives, and other routine questions which are asked new applicants because he said that he was afraid that he did not know any of these facts. Upon further investigation we have found that Mr. Perry is believed to have been born in Tampa, Florida, and he thinks that he was in high school at the time he left to enlist in the army. A copy of the army record, which is in our hands, indicates that he enlisted at Fort Slocum, New York, May 27, 1917, and left for service

Six. In the Service of His Country (Hector Perez)

overseas December 12, 1917. He participated in several battles overseas and during that time was hospitalized. He was returned to the United States July 14, 1919, and was in the United States General Hospital, Fox Hills, New York, at that time remaining until October 16, 1919. He was also under treatment there from March 6 to June 7, 1920, and was then furloughed June 17. He deserted the service June 26, 1920, and returned to military control May 29, 1928. He was found guilty of deserting the service at the trial which took place May 29, 1928, at Fort Adams, Newport, Rhode Island, and he was dishonorably discharged from the service September 21, of that year. Since that time Mr. Perry applied at the Boston branch of the Veteran's Bureau claiming disability and there was some contact with the Social Service department there. Aid was not given because of his ineligibility but various attempts had been made by the Veteran's Bureau and also by the local Soldiers' Relief Department to secure an honorable discharge for Mr. Perry. At present a bill is pending to secure this and is expected to be taken up before the next session of Congress.

In July 1920 Mr. Perry met his present wife and they were married the following year in Worcester. At that time Mr. Perry was using the name of Alfredo Velasquez Sanchez and used that name in the marriage ceremony. Mrs. Sanchez, whom we shall refer to as Mrs. Perry, knew practically nothing about her husband's past. She is a rather reticent lady of about thirty-four years of age. She is physically handicapped as she has worn an artificial right leg ever since she was six years old. She is rather refined and has had a high school and business school education. She comes of average people who are now in rather poor circumstances. Mrs. Perry was apparently very much carried away by Mr. Perry who has a very agreeable and pleasing personality. She made little inquiry into his past and married him without even knowing who his parents were or where they lived. She said that he was always popular. He is an accomplished pianist and is very fond of entertaining people with his talent. Very often, however, he will become very moody and go off by himself or want to play the piano by himself. Shortly after the marriage, the Perrys went to Newark, New Jersey, to live and from then on commenced a period of very irregular employment. Mr. Perry had no regular trade but was able to get jobs very easily. He never stayed at a job more than two or three months because he was extremely absent-minded and would forget to do tasks assigned to him. At the end of two years the Newark police picked up Mr. Perry there and returned him to his home in a confused and dazed condition. The police told his wife that when he had been found he did not seem to know who he was or where he lived. Soon after this the Perrys returned to Worcester where they lived for a short time with Mrs. Perry's mother and then later in a furnished room. Mrs. Perry soon realized that she could not depend upon her husband for support, and she took a job as a telephone operator at Memorial Hospital in this city where she has been employed since then. Her earnings were only $12, and it was difficult for them to manage on this amount.

This past year, Mr. Perry was employed for a short time at a fur shop and also as a helper at the restaurant at Union Station. Both places report that he was well liked but unreliable and undependable because of his absent mindedness. He was dismissed at both of the places.

We found that both Mr. Perry and his wife were anxious for him to get some form of mental treatment and they cooperated very well with us in arranging this. A local psychiatrist, Dr. Jordan, diagnosed Mr. Perry's condition as dementia praecox, remission stage, and he was committed to the Worcester State Hospital for thirty-five days observation. This period would have ended on Thursday, June 11, but Mr. Perry left the hospital last Saturday for an indefinite visit. The doctors had thus far been unable to accomplish anything with him and when they told him it probably would take a year or a year and a half to cure him, he became discouraged and decided to leave. He also felt that there were too many serious mental cases there and was afraid of making his condition worse. He is now extremely anxious to enter some Veterans' Hospital and we are trying to assist him in this. In the meanwhile, we had written to Washington to the adjutant general's office to ascertain names and addresses of relatives which Mr. Perry had registered at the time of his enlistment. I received a reply yesterday indicating that Mr. Perry's father, Charles Perry, was living at 46 Southard St., Key West, in 1918 and that his mother was listed as Clara Harrison, 510 Brown St., Cincinnati, Ohio. There was a sister, Evangeline Perry, whose address was the same as that of the mother. As far as he remembers, his mother's name was Sarah Perry and he tried to locate her on Harrison Street in Cincinnati, Ohio. There is apparently a great deal of confusion in Mr. Perry's mind about these facts and we are anxious to locate these relatives if possible.

Would you kindly see if you can locate his father, Charles Perry? It is possible that the latter has moved from the address given since March a long time has elapsed, but we do hope there will be some means of tracking him or of obtaining some information. We hope to hear from you at your earliest convenience and thank you for your cooperation.

> Very truly yours,
>
> Sgd. Helen E. Fairbanks
> General Secretary
> G.R.T./MIH

As you can see, the Associated Charities letter reveals a great deal about the events in Hector and Grace's lives over a span of a decade. Undoubtedly, there were many steps that took place between the time when Hector and Grace first hired an attorney in 1928 and the time when this letter was written two years later. We can see from Ms. Fairbanks' account that Hector had been seeking and receiving aid from the local Red Cross organization in March 1930 prior to arriving at the Associated Charities office on April 14, 1930. Much of what transpired during that two-year period is unknown, except for his time in the brig in 1928, when he spent four months in confinement, from May through September. We also learned that he and Grace lived apart briefly and then reunited, as mentioned previously. During our investigation we learned the name of the local psychiatrist who evaluated Hector. We researched him and found two possibilities in the Worcester city directory. Both psychiatrists were members of the Worcester District Medical Society. Unfortunately, our attempts to determine which doctor treated Hector were unsuccessful. Whoever it was, we know he diagnosed Hector with "dementia praecox, remission stage." Suffice it to say, there was a lot going on and no stone was being left unturned to find a way to restore Hector's veteran benefits and get him the treatment he so desperately needed and wanted.

At this point, we will mention some of what we discovered during our research. As mentioned in chapter 1, one of Grace's relatives was diagnosed at an early age with dementia praecox, like Hector, though Hector's condition was in the remission stage.[64] This relative's diagnosis took place around 1910, at least a decade before Grace met Hector. This relative was institutionalized at the Worcester State Asylum before or around 1910, as records show.[65] Grace had a close relationship with this family member, and we are certain this experience influenced her thoughts about mental disorders. This family member contracted influenza in 1918 while institutionalized and died from complications. Grace met Hector two years after this relative died. Her relative's death and the accompanying diagnosis would have still been fresh in Grace's mind. Additionally, we learned from public records that Grace lost another close relative during childbirth in 1918.[66] Both the woman and the infant tragically died.[67] It would be safe to assume that Grace was keenly aware of the challenges that mental illness can present to a family. She was also cognizant of the impacts that the unexpected death of a loved one could have on a family.

We also read in the Associated Charities letter that there was a bill pending before the next session of Congress that would address Hector's case. This was the first positive sign that relief might just come Hector's way. However, no specific individual was named by Ms. Fairbanks as being connected to this bill.

Known Events

From two letters (provided later) written by the adjutant general of the War Department, Major General Charles W. Bridges, in response to congressional inquiries, we learned a great deal about Hector's army record and medical record.

Hector's first battle began in March 1918 at Toulon-Troyon; he served in six other engagements through November 11, 1918. We are uncertain whether his unit was transferred to occupation duty in Koblenz, Germany, after the war ended or whether they remained in France. He was treated for influenza (which may have been the "Spanish flu") in January–February

1919, while still stationed overseas. He was next treated for a 21-day span, from April through May 1919, and diagnosed with "psychoneurosis, type undetermined." On July 5, 1919, he was shipped back home aboard the SS *Prinz Friederich Wilhelm* from Brest, France, and arrived in Hoboken, New Jersey, on July 14, 1919. A month later, he was transferred to the 36th Infantry Medical Detachment at Hoff General Hospital #41 at Fox Hills in Staten Island, New York. His record does not reveal where he was stationed between July 14 and August 19, 1919. On October 16, 1919, he was apparently under treatment at Hoff. We have no clues or records that can inform us as to what transpired during this three-month period, from July 14 to October 16, 1919, and we do not know what he was being treated for.

Then, five months later, from March 6 to June 7, 1920, the record indicates that he was "under treatment not incident to service." One can only speculate that a hospital stay of close to 90 days would not be necessary for treatment of a minor ailment. From June 11 to June 16, 1920, he was again treated, this time for two medical issues. One was not incident to his military service (again), and the second was for furunculosis (previously mentioned), which is a deep infection of the hair follicle. On June 17, 1920, he was furloughed. When he failed to return by June 26, he was considered AWOL (Absent Without Leave) for a period of 30 days; afterward, his status was changed to "deserter," as is customary.[68]

Regarding the disease for which he was treated twice, all we know is that it was unrelated to his military service. Whatever it was, it must have been serious enough to have required a three-month period of treatment. It may well have been a psychological condition; we do not know. Perhaps he was being treated for "trench disease," of which there were several types, including trench foot, trench fever, trench mouth, typhoid or typhus fever, influenza, "la grippe," malaria, tuberculosis and shell shock.[69] Those were extremely common maladies but were considered incidental to service. Additionally, reports of the day revealed that venereal diseases of various types were prevalent.[70] We just do not know what treatment he received over those ten months (August 1919 through to the furlough date of June 1920) because it was not addressed in the War Department's correspondence. Some believe this information may have been purposely omitted.

The known record reflects that Hector was not medically treated for anything until October 1919, three months after his return stateside in July 1919. We can only speculate about this point given the vagueness of the record. Considering the serious mental diagnosis given to him overseas in April 1919, it is baffling that no follow-up treatment or investigation was provided. Was the army willing to keep such a soldier on active duty without attempting to address his deeply rooted psychological illness? They had a responsibility for their soldiers' well-being. Was the unofficial position of the army brass on issues of this nature to stay mum and let sleeping dogs lie? Was there no effort made to determine the army's culpability and/or responsibility for Hector's condition? That might be hard to believe for some. The prevailing thought may have been that it was best not to mention everything that was known on the record. In any event, the army still had to contend with him.

We do not know anything about what happened outside the given dates for which Hector was officially treated, and we never will, seeing that the records were destroyed in the 1973 fire at the National Archives.

The day after his final treatment for an abscess on June 16, 1920, Hector was furloughed. He left the army hospital at Fox Hills, Staten Island, on June 17 and was due to return to active duty on June 26, which he failed to do. Therefore, the official dates of his status as a deserter ran from June 26, 1920, through May 26, 1928, that fateful day when he eagerly and innocently arrived at Fort Adams with hopes of getting answers about his forgotten past.

Starting on that fateful day in May, which led to the dishonorable discharge sentence being promulgated in September 1928, Hector and Grace were working hard to make ends meet and at the same time find a way to get Hector the help he needed in order to function normally in society.

The Associated Charities letter confirms that they sought assistance from local social services and charities around March 1930, to include the Soldiers' Relief Department, the Veterans Bureau, the American Red Cross, and the Associated Charities of Worcester. Many of these agencies arose out of necessity and altruism during hard times. There were many people during that time who needed help for various reasons, some related to these types of military discharges, and others brought about by the Great Depression, which lasted from 1929 to 1939.[71] These agencies were critically needed by many people who could not function on their own. For some, it was their hope of last resort. However, as we know, the Veterans Bureau and Soldiers' Relief Department could not assist Hector due to his military status—namely, the dishonorable discharge the army so unfairly bestowed on him. We wondered whether anyone in the military involved with Hector's case ever considered the sentencing's aftereffects and the stigma they cast over him, which would be the very thing that would prevent him from getting the help he needed. Since the young couple could not access treatment at the veterans' hospital, they were relegated to relying on the good nature of social services and civilian agencies. Think of how draining that process must have been, to be forced to retell a convoluted story repeatedly, a tale you could not relate in twenty words or less. One thing was certain, and that was the couple's commitment to getting treatment for Hector. They were left to advocate for themselves and, on their own, had to develop a strategy and implement it. They were heavily reliant on others, and they needed someone influential who would listen, who was empathetic and would feel compelled to get on board, and who had the resources and right connections. We learned they identified several potential movers and shakers of the day. Think for a moment of the enormity of it all. It is staggering.

By 1930, the young couple, now disillusioned and exhausted, regrouped and formulated an adjusted plan. The overarching goal would be to reverse the dishonorable discharge and, in its place, obtain an honorable discharge with back pay and benefits. Unfortunately, they could not get back the time Hector spent in prison. Only one way forward existed for them. It was a monumental aspiration that pitted them against a most formidable foe—the bureaucracy of the U.S. Army. Their lives were not easy before the dishonorable discharge, but now things must have seemed truly hopeless. They had nothing more to lose after having just lost everything.

Up to this point, the couple still believed Hector's name was "Hector H. Perry," the name he had used in the army. And Hector and Grace had no idea of his participation in battle during the war, let alone in seven of the bloodiest battles known to humanity. This was all about to change.

Seven

Public Sentiment

A Rally of Powerful Supporters

There were many things happening to aid Hector on several fronts and on many levels, led by his wife, who stuck by him in his darkest hour. What they went through took place over several years, with Grace advocating for her husband while she remained his main supporter the entire time. It would have been easier for Grace to file for divorce and put that part of her life behind her, like a bad dream. We know from the record, as previously mentioned, that they did live apart for a brief time, and we feel, given their circumstances, they found this arrangement too costly; it is also plausible that Grace might have noticed a change in Hector's behavior or spirit and decided to stay by his side. We know she loved him deeply, and reuniting, it seems, was her only real choice. This aspect of Grace's role in handling this challenge intrigued us. What she did took fortitude, determination, empathy, love and intelligence. It almost seemed as if her very existence during this protracted period and arduous journey was to be her husband's champion. In this regard, Hector was a very blessed and lucky man.

As you will soon see, many individuals, along with military, civilian, governmental, political, and professional organizations, rallied in support of Hector. However, the process was not easy, and it was not quick. Progress was being made ever so slowly. A clock cannot tick any slower than it does for an innocent person who has been incarcerated with no access to advocacy when their very life depended on it.

In our view, Grace and Hector's relationship would turn out to be the key to their success. If they were to get through this mess, it would be together. This period must have been an extremely challenging time for Hector and Grace. Many people in a similar predicament may have just given up and resigned themselves to their feelings of hopelessness. There seemed to be no way out at that moment in time. Many war veterans have chosen a dark path and sought to end it all. Fortunately, Hector did not.

However, try as he and Grace might, prospects for the desired outcome were looking dim and distant. The pending bill had yet to be introduced to Congress, so they had a long, steep hill yet to climb.

There is so much still to be revealed that will provide a more complete picture of their predicament. Take a moment to think about how you might face your existence on a day-to-day basis if you were in this situation. What would be on your mind the first moment you woke up? What would be your most prevalent thoughts as you proceeded throughout the day? What would be on your mind at the end of the day when you laid your head down on your pillow to sleep? When faced with what they had to contend with, Hector and Grace could not have had a pleasant existence. Very little could bring them joy. Every day must have been a challenge. Surely anyone with an ounce of compassion could not help but feel empathetic about the arduous journey the couple faced, what was yet in store for them and all they had to overcome. Anyone who witnessed and was privy to what Hector and Grace were enduring would have to be moved deeply. It turned out that many were. Thanks to the goodness in the hearts of the numerous people this story touched, Hector and Grace came to acquire powerful and influential supporters in their quest to reverse the dishonorable discharge so he could gain access to the veterans benefits he desperately needed. As awareness of their story was increasing in the right circles, support began to come from many fronts.

As noted in the previous chapter, many agencies and individuals were working on behalf of the couple in their attempt to locate Hector's family. A portion of his military record was in the hands of Helen Fairbanks, the general secretary of the Associated Charities of Worcester. In her efforts to elicit support for the couple, she had spread the word in a steady stream to a network of people whom she thought could help. Her diligence and hard work made all the difference.

Following the unjust general court-martial in 1928, when they first learned the name that Hector had used with the army, Hector and Grace commenced their efforts in seeking his family under that name. Three years later, somehow, their quest proved successful. Hector's family in Key West was located. His father was identified as Charles "Perez" rather than Charles "Perry." It was understandable that attempts to locate him had been difficult, as the wrong name was being sought. We see no mention of correcting or addressing the surname discrepancy in the letter that Charles wrote to them following the discovery. This would not be the place to do so. Indeed, this was a joyous moment for all.

Again, we see the goodness of many people working on behalf of strangers to help remedy a grievous situation. There was elation, joy, and happiness. It must have been a very emotional experience.

Seven. Public Sentiment

Letter from Charles to Hector and Grace (June 20, 1931)

What follows is the verbatim transcription of Charles' letter to his son and daughter-in-law after being notified that his long-lost son, Hector, was alive and well, married and living in Worcester. The letter is dated June 20, 1931. A few weeks later, both Charles' letter and his daughter Dinorah's letter, addressed to the young couple in Worcester, were published in newspaper accounts. Clearly the private letters between family members were shared with the media by Hector and Grace to help garner public support for their case.

Key West, Fla.,

June 20, 1931

My dear son and daughter:

You do not know how happy I am to know that you are alive. I have just learned of your whereabouts from the American Red Cross who have had correspondence with the Associated Charities relative to you in an effort to locate me. I am happy to know you are married to a refined girl and that she has been faithful to you.

I find that he has lost his memory and wants to give you the following information about his family: Hector was born in West Tampa, Fla., Dec. 16, 1897. His mother, Sarah Velasco, by birth, married in 1896 in West Tampa, Fla., she died in 1916. He left Tampa in 1916 shortly after his mother's death and has not been heard of since. He has one brother, Charles E., at present working in the general post office, transportation department, New York City. You can contact him at this address. He has two sisters, Mrs. William C. Atkinson, nee Dinorah Perez, who now lives at Orlando, Fla., and Mrs. Esteban Fernandez of Havana, Cuba.

I am sorry I have not the means to go and see you at once, but I hope to go to New York in the very near future, and if I do, you may be sure that I will do all possible to see you both.

You do not know how much I have worried about you and the efforts I have made to locate you in every way I could think of. I am glad that it is all over now. I have notified his brother and sisters. Please let me hear from you soon and tell me all about yourselves. God bless you both and you have my very best wishes.

Your father,

CHARLES PEREZ

What we learned definitively from Charles' letter is that Hector did indeed leave Tampa shortly after his mother's death in January 1916, after which time his family neither saw nor heard from him. No other mention is made about this fact. We do not know when the younger son, Charlie, went to reside in New York City (as his January 1917 military enlistment card revealed). This letter also confirms that Charles had ongoing contact with his younger son, as he shared with Hector and Grace where Charlie was employed and his home address in New York. It is clear that Hector's father loved him very much and had looked for him all these years and worried about him the entire time. Not knowing whether a child is alive or dead is incredibly stressful, to say the least.

The day that so many had hoped for had finally arrived. Grace and Hector's persistent hard work brought them to one of their two goals: finding Hector's lost family. The second and most critical goal was to reverse the unjust charges and grant him a dishonorable discharge with benefits.

Letter from Grace (June 24, 1931)

What follows is the verbatim transcription of a letter written on June 24, 1931, from Grace to her father-in-law Charles, whom, up to that point, she had never met.[1] She wrote the letter after receiving Charles' initial letter written on June 20, in which he detailed how he first learned his son was alive. Mail delivery was certainly swift during those years. From our perspective, this letter gave Grace an identity. She was now a real person to us. She came across as a concerned, sweet, loving wife and daughter-in-law. This letter breathed life into her as a special human. Her empathy is visible for all to see, and her devotion to her husband was immeasurable. It turned out that Grace was exactly what Hector needed. We note that in her letter Grace advised Charles that her husband's mind was not always so bad. This gives us hope he was getting better.

General Delivery,
June 24, 1931
Worcester, Mass.

Dear Father:-

I was so happy to hear from you and to know that you are also alive, for I knew he must have had a father somewhere and as you say, I'm glad it is all over with, I have found you.

I am writing all the details about his war record to his brother in New York.

Mrs. Fairbanks of the Associated Charities will write you the number of his bill which is going to be introduced in Congress next December.

I was surprised to know he had a brother and two sisters. His mind is not bad all the time, it is only at intervals, and he apparently got that way in the army.

Senator Walsh of Massachusetts thought his war record was splendid. Of course, I believe Senator Walsh will try and do his best; nevertheless, any other influence would help a great deal.

I have tried to do my best taking care of him for eight years and I will always try to help him. He is a splendid fellow; he is so good. It is a shame the way he was treated after being through the thickest of fighting during the war. He was in all the big battles in France, this alone should merit an honorable discharge.

Senator Walsh said his record was commendable. I think you have a very brave son and one to be proud of. He should be getting compensation for the service he rendered to his country, but he is not getting anything, and it is a shame. Everybody thinks so.

I hope your health is good. I will write to you later and I want to hear from you real soon again. I thank you for your blessing for us and hope God will be good to you. We will both be glad to see you.

With much love,

Your daughter

Despite all that Hector and Grace had gone through, things finally appeared to be working out for them. What an uplifting letter this must have been for Charles, as a father, to read.

While events seemed to be heading in the right direction, there were still so many unanswered questions. Some of these questions were as evident to the casual observer as they were to any senator or congressman who might be reviewing the matter and considering sponsorship of a bill to remedy the unjust events perpetrated by the U.S. Army and its bureaucracy. It seemed this option was the only way to remedy the injustice.

Up until June 1931, the Perez family had no idea as to what the details of Hector's war experiences were. In this letter we learn of Senator Walsh's involvement, by name, for the first time. All Hector and Grace knew about his army service was that the senator said he found Hector's war record "commendable," and Grace stated in her letter that Hector had been in "all the big battles in France." This comment shows that the couple, by this time, had been informed (we suspect by the senator) of the battles Hector participated in. Armed with this knowledge, the young couple forged ahead to get Hector's story out into the public sphere and help garner additional support for the upcoming congressional bill being introduced by the senator.

The historical record reflects that Senator David I. Walsh of Massachusetts joined the crusade by at least June 9, 1930, as evidenced by the letter written on that date by Ms. Fairbanks of Associated Charities of Worcester to the Duval County Welfare Agency in Jacksonville, Florida, sharing the good news that a bill was being introduced to Congress to aid Hector. Senator Walsh was a politically powerful man and well liked in Massachusetts, having been born there in 1872.[2] He was educated at Holy Cross College in 1893, earned his law degree from Boston University in 1897, and practiced law in Boston. He entered politics as a member of the Massachusetts House of Representatives from 1900 to 1901 and was lieutenant governor from 1913 to 1914. Walsh secured the Democratic gubernatorial nomination and went on to win the election to the governorship in 1913. He was reelected for a second term before he served as U.S. senator from 1918 to 1925 and again from 1926 to 1947. He was the first Irish Catholic senator elected in Massachusetts. He was a well-connected man and a force to be reckoned with. He believed in Hector's cause and proposed a solution to remedy the injustice perpetrated against him. Introducing the bill for Hector's relief was just the beginning.

Congressional Inquiries to the War Department (1931)

The record also reflects that Hector had garnered support from two Massachusetts congressmen by at least June 1931. They had each written to the War Department requesting information on Hector's military and medical records by that date. These two congressional representatives were George H. Stobbs and Pehr G. Holmes, both of whom became powerful allies.

Representative George R. Stobbs was born in 1877.[3] He was the successful Republican nominee for a seat in the U.S. House of Representatives in 1924. He was reelected twice and served for six years in the 69th, 70th, and 71st Congresses (March 4, 1925–March 3, 1931). Representative Stobbs attended public schools in his hometown of Worcester and then headed off to Phillips Exeter Academy in New Hampshire. He later attended Harvard, received his law degree, and began working as a lawyer in Worcester.

U.S. Representative Pehr Holmes, a Swedish immigrant and city industrialist, was born in 1881.[4] He was councilman, alderman and mayor, serving as mayor from 1917 through 1919 before serving as the Republican congressman from Massachusetts for 16 years (March 4, 1931–January 3, 1947). Holmes was chosen by his party to run for Congressman Stobbs' position after Stobbs chose not to run for another term. Congressman Holmes was also well known in Worcester, having lived there since he was five years old. He had a reputation for being involved in his community and with his constituents. He was personally aware of and involved with Associated Charities in Worcester. Mr. Holmes was also responsible, in part, for a major ruling in the 1940s that helped Syrians in Massachusetts be classified as Whites and not Asians, thus permitting them to apply for citizenship.[5] His record of accomplishment was well respected, and he was now in Hector's corner.

Things were heating up, and Hector's predicament was resonating with many who could make a difference. Congressmen Holmes and Stobbs represented the 4th Congressional District, in which Grace and Hector resided.[6] Both of these politically powerful men were known for helping the underdog, and they were ready to take on the bureaucracy of the U.S. Army until Hector received justice.

On July 3, 1931, responses were sent from Major General C.W. Bridges, the adjutant general of the War Department in Washington, D.C., to inquiries from Representatives Holmes and Stobbs (mentioned in previous chapter).

So, by this date in 1931, we know three of the most powerful politicians in the state of Massachusetts were advocating for Hector. Think about what an accomplishment this was and what it meant for the couple and their family. Even by today's standards, when most citizens know they can go to their elected representatives and seek assistance for a myriad of matters, they infrequently go through all the motions required to bring those officials on board. To us, what Hector and Grace accomplished up to this point was truly impressive.

Letter from War Department to Holmes (July 3, 1931)

A verbatim transcription follows. This was the first time that Hector's military record became known.

In the general's reply to Congressman Holmes' previous inquiry, dated June 30, 1931 (as noted on letter), the dates and places of Hector's field deployments are listed prominently. The response cited his enlistment and briefly mentioned that he sailed for foreign service. It also advised that Hector returned stateside and had an eleven-month assignment at the Fox Hills hospital on Staten Island, from which he deserted. The letter fails to mention that his desertion occurred when Hector was furloughed and neglected to return when his allotted leave was up. It also fictitiously reported that Hector surrendered to military authorities at Fort Adams. We know he was not aware that he was "surrendering" since he had no idea he had served in the army. He went to Fort Adams to find out who he really was. Surrender is a mischaracterization. Aside from what he was told by a former war buddy whom he had not even recognized, he had no knowledge of his army service, much less any idea that he had done anything wrong or that he was being sought. He was being surreptitiously instructed to go to Fort Adams so the army could exact its revenge. In hindsight, we see he was like a sheep being enticed to slaughter.

Detailed information regarding Hector's medical and psychological treatment and the dates when they took place are included in the response.

Although it was a fact-based, emotionless reply, this letter provided our first glimpse into what Hector was medically and psychologically treated for. It can be safely assumed that this information may never have become exposed or been subject to unbiased scrutiny if not for these congressional inquiries, initiated through the efforts of Grace and Hector. The army already had a chance to consider Hector's psychological condition as part of the equation at the general court-martial, and it was vetoed. The inclusion of this latest information concerning Hector's medical record was very revealing. Unquestionably, these details should have been presented in granularity at his general court-martial. They were provided, seemingly, after the fact and were rejected.

A word-for-word transcript of the adjutant general's letter of July 3, 1931, follows:

WAR DEPARTMENT
The Adjutant General's Office
Washington

July 3, 1931

In reply refer to
AG 201- Perry, Hector H. (6–30–31) WW
Honorable Pehr G. Holmes,
Representative in Congress,
167 Commercial Street,
Worcester, Mass.

My dear Mr. Holmes:

I have your letter of June 30, 1931, requesting that you be furnished with the military and medical record of Hector H. Perry, Army serial number 16,141.

The records show that Hector H. Perry, Army serial number 16,141, enlisted March 27, 1917, at Fort Slocum, New York, and was assigned to duty as a private, Medical Detachment, Fort Wadsworth, New York. He was transferred to the Medical Detachment, 4th Field Artillery June 25, 1917, sailed for foreign service December 12, 1917; returned to the United States July 14, 1919, and deserted June 26, 1920, at Hoff General Hospital, Staten Island, New York, and remained in desertion until May 29, 1928, when he surrendered to military control at Fort Adams, Rhode Island. He was tried by General Court Martial and pursuant to the sentence thereof was dishonorably discharged September 21, 1928, at Fort Adams, Rhode Island, a private, Medical Detachment.

The medical records show him treated from April 3, to 17, 1917, for German measles; January 24, to February 4, 1919, influenza, April 17, to May 7, 1919, alcoholism, acute, with change of diagnosis April 20, 1919, to psychoneurosis, type undetermined; March 6, to June 5, 1920, for a disease not incident to the service; June 11, to 16, 1920, (1) a disease not incident to the service, (2) furunculosis; June 26 to July 27, 1928, constitutional psychopathic state, inadequate personality and August 9, to 12, 1928, psychoneurosis, hysteria, acute, (constitutional psychopathic state, inadequate personality).

Very respectfully,

C.W. Bridges (signed)
Major General,
The Adjutant General

This was when the couple first learned of Hector's past medical record within his service dates (mentioned previously). There is nothing in his record to indicate that he was medically treated for anything other than German measles prior to going overseas. He was given a clean bill of health and cleared for military service. After the war was over, however, it became a vastly different story, as an extended period of medical visits and unknown treatment would begin.

What we learned from the adjutant general's letter was that while serving overseas, as we have previously reported, Hector was treated for influenza between January 24 and February 4, 1919. We believe this illness was a bout with the "Spanish flu." Between April 17 and May 7, 1919, he was treated for what was initially diagnosed as alcoholism; a change in diagnosis was made on April 20 to "psychoneurosis, type undetermined." The basic definition for "psychosis" and "neurosis" was detailed previously, and we revisit it here. Thought of as a break from reality, *psychosis* is characterized as disruptions to a person's thoughts and perceptions that make it difficult for them to recognize what is real and what is not. These disruptions are often experienced as seeing, hearing, and believing things that are not real or having strange, persistent thoughts, behaviors, and emotions. While everyone's experience is different, most people agree that psychosis is frightening and confusing. *Neuroses* are characterized by anxiety, depression, or other feelings of unhappiness or distress that are out of proportion to the circumstances. They may impair a person's functioning in any area of his life, relationships, or external affairs, but they are not severe enough to incapacitate the person. Patients with neurosis do not suffer from the loss of the sense of reality seen in persons with psychoses.

Within three months of this official diagnosis (which was made while he was still stationed overseas), Hector would be returned stateside. As we previously mentioned, discovering Hector's name on a list of garrison prisoners during his return to the United States on July 14, 1919, was eye-opening for us. For Hector to be a garrison prisoner, he would have had to commit a minor infraction while on duty and still serving out his military commitment overseas after the war. Logic points us to the possible explanation that he "acted out" in some inappropriate manner after being released from the hospital and was charged with a minor offense. Garrison prisoners are not generally confined.

A mental disorder was first identified in Hector in April 1919, five months after the war ended. Hector's initial diagnosis of alcoholism was clearly flawed, as it was changed three days later to a diagnosis indicating an even more serious underlying mental disorder. He was not a known drinker, according to family lore. For the rest of his life, no issues regarding the use of alcohol arose, even remotely. This may be why the diagnosis was changed so quickly to psychoneurosis (type undetermined). Alcoholism was not the root of Hector's mental illness.

The military's failure to disclose Hector's true and complete diagnoses was critical, considering the final general court-martial adjudication. The psychological diagnoses that were made while Hector was serving overseas should have been illuminated and highlighted during the trial. Someone of rank needed to see the big picture and advocate for him. Instead, it seemed that everything and everyone was lined up against him. More appropriately, all the psychological evaluations Hector was subjected to should have been presented when the commanding officer chose to approve, modify, or remit the sentence in September 1928. All the facts were known by then. Three separate mental illness diagnoses by the army proved Hector was not well and needed treatment.

There was a second letter sent by the War Department, also dated July 3, 1931, to former Congressman George H. Stobbs under separate cover in response to Stobbs' recent inquiry (for which no date was noted). We have examined the limited, but pertinent, medical information about Hector's mental condition in the general's letter to Congressman Holmes on the same date, but the letter to Congressman Stobbs failed to mention any medical or psychological treatment Hector received overseas. Instead, the letter to Stobbs detailed information not previously mentioned regarding the battles Hector in which fought during his foreign service. We found some minor discrepancies between the two letters, but none of great significance. Things were about to change, as all the battles Hector fought in had finally been revealed.

The war record of Hector H. Perry was taken from one of Major General Bridge's letters and later published in the *Worcester Evening Post* on Monday, July 13, 1931. Again, we believe Grace and Hector, having been given a copy of the letter by the congressman, shared it with the newspapers in their attempt to further garner support for the pending bill about to be introduced before the December 1 session of the 72nd Congress.

Seven. Public Sentiment

War record taken from letter written by
Major General Charles W. Bridges, Adjutant
General, War Department. (published in
"The Worcester Evening Post," Monday, July 13, 1931.)

> July 3, 1931.
> Hon. George R. Stobbs,
> Representative in Congress,
> Worcester, Mass.

My dear Mr. Stobbs:

Reference is made to your recent personal request for information regarding the military service of Hector H. Perry, Army serial number 16, 141.

The records of this office show that he enlisted May 27, 1917, at Fort Slocum, N.Y., and on June 11, 1917, was assigned to duty as a private, medical detachment of the 15th Field Artillery; left the U.S. Dec. 12, 1917, for service overseas; was transferred July 4, 1918, to the Second Engineers, served in the Toulon-Tryon [sic] defensive sector, March 24 to May 11, 1918, and in the Chateau Thierry defensive sector (Ile de France) June 6 to July 16, 1918; participated in the Aisne-Marne offensive, July 18 to July 20, 1918; served in the Marbache defensive sector, Aug. 6 to Aug. 18, 1918; in the Limey defensive sector, Sept. 9 to 11, 1918; and participated in the St. Mihiel offensive, Sept. 12 to Sept. 16, 1918, and the Meuse-Argonne offensive, Sept. 29 to Oct. 27 and Oct. 30 to Nov. 11, 1918.

The records also show that he returned to the U.S., July 14, 1919, and was transferred to the medical detachment, 36th Infantry, Aug. 19, 1919, U.S.A. General Hospital, 41, Fox Hills, N.Y., October 16, 1919; was under treated in that hospital, March 6 to June 7, 1920, and June 12 to June 16, 1920; was furloughed June 17, 1920, and deserted the service June 26, 1920, returning to military control, May 29, 1928. He was found guilty by a general court-martial of having deserted the service of the U.S. on or about June 26, 1920, and of remaining absent in desertion until he surrendered May 29, 1928, at Fort Adams, R.I. The court sentenced him to be dishonorably discharged from the service, to forfeit all pay and allowance due or become due and to be confined at hard labor for one year. The sentence was approved by the reviewing authority, but the confinement was remitted and as thus modified, the sentence was promulgated in general court-martial orders dated September 20, 1928.

The original copy is retained in the family archives.

One minor discrepancy we noticed in the War Department letters concerns Hector's date of enlistment. In the letter to Congressman Holmes, it is given as March 27, 1917. In the reply to Congressman Stobbs, Hector's enlistment date is given as May 27, 1917. The correct enlistment date is March 27. This discrepancy appears to have been a clerical error in the second instance.

As hard as it may be to believe, despite the adverse impact that fighting in the war had on Hector from a military perspective (e.g., dishonorable discharge, the loss of benefits, and being sentenced to hard labor in prison), the life-altering impacts were far greater. The consequences permeated every aspect of his life from that point on. In the end, one might hope the adverse aftereffects of war on an individual would be identified and addressed as soon as possible after they become known, but, in Hector's case, the direct impact of fighting under such traumatic conditions would take more than ten years to begin to be addressed. Eight years later, in 1928, when he was arrested and taken into military control, there was no mention of treatment—only of assessment. Any therapy Hector might have received on his return to the United States in July 1919 was not found in the limited reporting we see from the War Department. From a treatment perspective, nothing was done about the previous psychological diagnoses that were made overseas. These facts are puzzling, to say the least, and demonstrate a total lack of individualized care given to a soldier in crisis.

Contradictory Words and Actions by the Government

World War I taught the United States many lessons. One of the most profound was how the government treated its veterans. This war was the first in which more than half of those who served were drafted. More important, there was no prevailing knowledge of how to deal with the mental ailments seen in so many returning veterans. Those veterans, however, soon learned that their peers who did not serve or who avoided the draft were earning more money, enjoying better health, and owning more property than they did. To make matters worse, many veterans found themselves out of work following the start of the Great Depression.

The World War Adjusted Compensation Act in 1924 (commonly referred to as the Bonus Act) promised veterans additional bonus pay of a dollar a day for stateside service and $1.25 a day for service overseas, for service rendered from April 5, 1917, to July 1, 1919.[7] Payouts were capped at $500 for stateside veterans and $625 for overseas veterans. In 1926, $625 equated to roughly $8,600 in 2016 dollars. Distributed among 4.7 million veterans, the total payout would have been around $2.4 billion in 1926, equal to roughly $33 billion in 2016 dollars. Although this act was vetoed by President Calvin Coolidge, the veto was overridden by Congress in 1926, but there was a catch: Veterans who were owed more than $50 would have to wait until each veteran's birthday in 1945, which would be 26 years after the war ended. Veterans were allowed to borrow against the bonus certificates beginning in 1927, but by 1932, thanks to the Great Depression, banks were short on credit to give.

In 1930, President Herbert Hoover established the Veterans' Administration, and yet he fought Congress' efforts to release the funds early.[8] Veterans desperately needed the money they had been promised, but the funds set aside for the bonuses were not growing sufficiently to meet the anticipated claims.

Suffice it to say that the public was well aware of the flip-flopping happening with politicians for and against the Bonus Act, to include presidents, the House and the Senate, since the act had been passed in 1924.

By the spring of 1932, veterans organized a march across the country to Washington, D.C., from Portland, Oregon, with four hundred unemployed men.[9] Their goal was to get the bonus payout as quickly as possible because they really needed the money. Along the way, the marchers were offered food, shelter, and transportation from sympathizers. Their ranks grew, and the press followed them during their journey. They arrived in Washington in late May, at which time their numbers swelled. There were 17,000 veterans, family members, and affiliated groups that had amassed.

In mid–June 1932, the House passed a veterans' relief bill for an immediate payment of $2.4 billion, but the Senate rejected it.[10] Some legislators were opposed to the bill because it required the government to spend money it did not have in the treasury. Even if the Senate had not rejected it, President Hoover would have vetoed the bill, just as it had been vetoed by President Coolidge and by President Warren G. Harding in the preceding years. Many veterans returned home while others remained at the camp originally set up for them across from the Capitol, aptly named "Hooverville."[11] By the end of July, conditions in the general area had deteriorated, so protestors set up tents in the streets of Washington, D.C. It was estimated that between 20,000 and 40,000 people had joined the camps. Organizers called the demonstrators the Bonus Expeditionary Force (B.E.F.), to echo the name of the American Expeditionary Forces, while the media referred to them as the "Bonus Army" or "Bonus Marchers."[12] The demonstrators were led by Walter W. Waters, a former sergeant. Hoover asserted (and rumors circulated) that Communists, hoodlums and ex-convicts were responsible for raising public disturbance. A deflection? Perhaps.

On orders from the attorney general of the United States to clear out the camp, the police sent in one hundred officers; they were met with resistance, which led to a riot. During the melee, police shot and killed two protesters. The chief of police, himself a retired World War I brigadier general, would later resign over the incident. President Hoover had the secretary of war intervene, and Army Chief of Staff Douglas MacArthur led six hundred troops of the 3rd Cavalry (Brave Rifles) to the scene.[13] They were joined by six tanks commanded by General George S. Patton. The cavalry, using tear gas and threats of bayonets, began to disperse the crowd.

According to his aide, Dwight D. Eisenhower, MacArthur twice ignored orders from the secretary of war and crossed over the Anacostia River via the Anacostia drawbridge, which led to the original camp. The infantry followed, and within hours the camp, which was estimated to still be inhabited by 10,000 people, was set afire.[14] An infant died, and hundreds were wounded. The rest went home. Almost thirteen years after World War I ended, the capital of the United States itself looked like a war zone.

Once again, the army prevailed and considered the operation a success. The press saw it differently. It was described as "a pitiful spectacle" to see the mightiest government in the world chasing unarmed, starving, ragged veterans, women, and children with army tanks. As the *Washington Daily News* put it, "If the army must be called out to make war on unarmed citizens, this is no longer America."[15] The incident destroyed President Hoover politically, as he did not win reelection.

Today, the Bonus Expeditionary Force and the drama of that period are mostly forgotten. You can still visit the same field where the shantytown briefly stood. Now used as playing fields, the site hosts groups playing flag football and soccer.[16] Picnickers enjoy summer afternoons along the river. Residents walk, jog, and bike the Anacostia River Trail. This land is also home to the U.S. Park Police and National Capital Parks–East headquarters. There is little to no evidence remaining of the tragedy that took place there. Yet think of the numbers of veterans who felt betrayed by their own government and the impact on their families, who were denied what they felt their loved ones had fought so valiantly for. Yes, sometimes memories fade and events once important are gone from memory.

The entire incident was another example of how contradictory the government was and how the army was ill equipped to care for the returning soldiers who suffered from combat-induced PTSD due to a general lack of knowledge in the field of mental illnesses caused by war.[17] Even worse, it further exemplifies the absence of goodness in the hearts of some people when in power.

With regard to Hector's situation, by virtue of the record up to this time, which included the reports of Senator Walsh's pending bill and the introduction of the facts contained within the two letters written by the adjutant general of the War Department in July 1931 to the two congressmen who represented Hector and Grace's district in Worcester, we know the couple's plan to reverse the dishonorable discharge was inching closer to fruition.

The young couple understood the power of the media and how it could help spread Hector's story. The newspaper accounts and letters to be shared in the following pages date from early to mid–July 1931 through September 1931. They disclose the extent to which the couple struggled and how they shared their story wherever they could. Highlights of the events that took place during this period illustrate the lengths to which many people and agencies went to help right the wrongs that Hector fell victim to by a bureaucracy that refused to admit any wrongdoing.

Once again, we cannot stress the point enough that we feel the army did not fully consider Hector's mental condition and the extenuating circumstances. It began with his questionable furlough, which led to his technical desertion during peacetime, his incarceration, general court-martial, and subsequent dishonorable discharge with ultimate forfeiture of pay and benefits. In the end, he was treated like a traitor to his country. He was abandoned and discarded like useless trash. It was the moral equivalent of being kicked while down. Did the army really believe Hector and Grace would accept this situation? How could the army have permitted this injustice to happen? It really was not the simple issue the army was making it out to be. This matter was much more complicated, but revealing the complexities of how Hector was treated would not be to the army's benefit, so they sought to keep those points hidden. This turned out to be a serious miscalculation on their part, as Hector and Grace would find a way to reveal the complexities for all to see.

Analogous to defensive battles becoming offensive engagements during the war, Hector and Grace went on the offensive. Their noble battle continued.

Initial Newspaper Articles (July 1931)

A series of newspapers in several cities and towns in Florida and Massachusetts reported the story about Hector's unimaginable predicament. It was not an easy story to tell, as it included numerous twists and turns. Several distinct aspects of the matter were highlighted in these articles, and while there were a few errors in some of the reporting, the essence of Hector's story in general was captured in detail. Reading these accounts must have been heartening for those knowledgeable of Hector's story as well as for the public. The story of his predicament and all that he had innocently suffered at the hands of the army was very moving. These newspaper stories gained Hector and Grace new supporters who rallied for his dishonorable discharge to be rescinded and his benefits restored.

Faith in the goodness of humanity was being relied on to right the wrongs perpetrated against him by the army. So far, goodness was playing catch-up. These initial articles revealed detailed information of the salient points and who the key players were.

Key West Citizen (July 6, 1931)[18]

The headline of the *Key West Citizen* article read, "Father Visits Son Missing 14 Years," accompanied by the following subheading: "Local Lad Located by Red Cross Aid, Lost Since War." We believe this was the first article written about Hector's predicament. It was clipped out from the original newspaper and lovingly kept in a folder by Hector's family and handed down to his niece, "Bibi." The article reported that Charles Perez left Key West to see his son Hector in Worcester, Massachusetts, on Independence Day. It informed readers that Hector joined the war effort in 1917 and had not been seen or heard from by his family for almost 15 years. Hector's family had been located through the efforts of the American Red Cross, at which time it was confirmed that Hector H. Perry was indeed Hector Perez. Finally, their efforts were paying off. The veteran known as "Hector H. Perry" was now known to be "Hector Perez," the missing son of Charles Perez of Key West. The family was elated to get some good news about Hector after such a long time of not knowing anything of his whereabouts, with all their previous efforts failing to locate him for over a decade. The article ended by reporting that "Hector Perez is well known here and is a brother of Miss Dinorah Perez formerly of this city."

The newspaper reports that were published regarding the matter were not simply good news and uplifting for the family but were a great human-interest story as well. An army of many volunteers had joined forces and engaged in sustained efforts along several fronts that succeeded in achieving one of their two main objectives: the reunification of a family with their long-lost son and brother. The second objective was the bill then pending in Congress. (More on this topic will follow shortly.)

Several other articles of particular interest were published on July 13, and 14, 1931, in newspapers from Worcester, Massachusetts; Daytona Beach, Florida; Tampa, Florida; and Boston, Massachusetts, recounting Hector's predicament and the successful outcome of having found his family. Notably, the *Boston Herald*'s story was the most complete; among other things, it revealed that the ex-congressman who represented the district where the young couple lived in Worcester, George R. Stobbs, had played a role in remitting the sentence of 12 months' hard labor (we found mention of this point twice in our research with no hard evidence to verify that it is factual; to our knowledge, the two congressmen became involved in Hector's case after the fact).

Worcester Telegram (July 13, 1931)[19]

The *Worcester Telegram* published an article detailing what we had learned and verified—essentially that Hector Perez "served during the World War under the name Hector Perry." The story went on to report that he had been living under the assumed name of Alfred Sanchez in Worcester, Massachusetts, after leaving the military. This was true but not 100 percent accurate in that the assumed name he was living under was Alfredo Velasquez Sanchez. Another partially inaccurate statement in this article was that he married Grace in 1928. They were married in 1921, a year after they met, which was two years after Hector's return from the war. A record of the 1921 Massachusetts marriage registers, previously mentioned, verified this fact.

Hector had no known connection to Worcester prior to his arrival there. From all reports, he roamed through several towns and cities after he left the Fox Hills hospital on furlough in June 1920. Interestingly, Hector stopped and remained in Worcester after meeting Grace. We believe that Grace was why he chose to stay in Worcester. He connected with her and she with him. Had these events not happened as they did, one can only imagine the result would probably not have been favorable for Hector.

The *Telegram* article was titled "World War Veteran Comes to Himself," and it reported that "Hector J. Perez disappeared from his home in West Tampa in 1916 and had 'found himself' through a chance meeting with a former army buddy" while walking down Main Street in Worcester.

The reference to Hector disappearing from Tampa in 1916 was true. Other reports corroborated this date, and the sequence of events was further confirmed by his father, Charles, in his letter dated June 20, 1931. We know Hector's mother died in 1916 when he was 19 years old, and he left home without further communication with his family.

Articles from the *Worcester Evening Gazette*, *Daytona Beach Journal*, *Tampa Tribune*, and *Boston Herald*, which are discussed in subsequent pages, followed a similar pattern. They all reported the known facts with minor errors, but the gist was correct. The story pulled at readers' heartstrings, moving them to stop everything they were doing in that moment and read the details, albeit with incredulity. The articles explained how Hector's mind was a blank, and amnesia may or may not have taken hold at that time. Hector's service in World War I was covered, along with his treatment in Fox Hills, New York, his furlough, his eventual marriage, the chance meeting with a war buddy, and the general court-martial and dishonorable discharge. The congressional bill that was being introduced the following winter to revoke the dishonorable discharge and bestow an honorable discharge to Hector was the best news anyone could have wished for.

Multiple articles note claims made by Hector's friends that he was not conscious of what he did, referring to his act of desertion. As previously postulated, he did not have a guilty mind (mens rea); therefore, he had not committed a crime. He had amnesia, and there was evidence of extenuating circumstances as to why he should not have been dishonorably discharged. He should never have been found guilty of desertion at the general court-martial. He should never have been sentenced to prison. There should not have been forfeiture of all pay and benefits. This last penalty was the most profound, as it denied Hector access to much-needed mental health treatment that he desperately sought through the Veterans' Administration's network. Professional help was unquestionably necessary to restoring Hector so he could lead a normal, productive life.

Worcester Evening Gazette (July 13, 1931)[20]

Titled "Establish Identity of Wounded War Veteran," this article stated that "war department officials have established the identity of Alfred Sanchez" as "Hector J. Perez." It went on to report that "since leaving a N.Y. army hospital in 1920 Perez's mind has been blank and he was unable to account for his activities before or since the hospital treatment." (Many of the articles published throughout July 1931 incorrectly assigned Hector the middle initial "J.") This article also reported that Hector "himself did not know how he got out of the army."

The details provided in the *Gazette* article mention most of the facts we know to be correct—namely, Hector's various ailments during his military service, his deserter status, and the eventual general court-martial in 1928. His loss of memory is also mentioned. Here we see, for the first time, a more complete list of the many agencies and politicians who assisted Hector in recovering his identity and finding his family (mainly the Associated Charities of Worcester and the Red Cross).

Daytona Beach Journal (July 13, 1931)[21]

The *Journal* dedicated a fair amount of print to this news item on its front page and provided a comprehensive, thorough, and fluid chronology of Hector's life from 1916 through July 1931. The title of the article was "Tampan, Dazed 15 Years, Finds Out Who He Is," subtitled "War Victim Had Married, Settled Down in Massachusetts."

The article reported that Hector "disappeared from his home in West Tampa in 1916 and served during the world war under the name of Hector Perry." It correctly mentioned his current residence as being in Worcester and noted that he "has been living in this city under the name of Alfred

Sanchez." It went on to report the "chance meeting with a buddy" in the spring of 1928, when he bumped into the man "who addressed him by the name of Perry." This encounter allegedly "revived the slumbering mind of the veteran," at which time he and his wife hired an attorney. On the advice of the attorney, "he wrote to the War Department in Washington" to see whether he could be identified. "He was ordered to report to Fort Adams, R.I., where he was tried by general court martial, convicted of the charge of desertion, dishonorably discharged, and sentenced to serve a year of confinement at hard labor." Interestingly, the article informed readers that the prison sentence was remitted "through the efforts of ex-congressmen George Stobbs." (As we stated previously, there must be some explanation for this claim since we know sentencing took place in 1928, and the congressmen did not get involved until three years after Hector's conviction. We were unable to verify the statement.)

This article also reported that the "Red Cross has been trying to find Perez's family and finally succeeded in locating his father a short time ago."

Tampa Tribune (July 14, 1931)[22]

The *Tampa Tribune*'s lead-in on July 14, 1931, was "Relatives Find Former Tampan After 15 Years," followed by the subtitle "War Veteran Regains Memory and Identity." It provided all the known facts that had been reported up to this point. However, this story mistakenly characterized Hector's departure from Fox Hills hospital as an "escape." In fact, he left with permission, on accrued furlough.

We can see that many of the initial newspaper stories went into granular detail recounting Hector's predicament. Most errors in the reporting were of no consequence, as previously mentioned.

Overall, the reporters did an excellent job of conveying how unjust and unimaginable Hector's story was. It moved people. Public sentiment at the time was highly attuned to the plight of World War I veterans since many were being treated inhumanely by the ill-equipped U.S. Army bureaucracy that was entrusted with the lives of these young men. Thanks to detailed reporting in daily newspapers throughout the country, the public became aware of the bloody, gruesome battles in which these soldiers had bravely fought, as well as the mistreatment many received when they needed medical, psychological and financial assistance after returning home.

Hector and Grace, by this point, were well aware of the power the media held. In Grace's letter to Charles Perez from the previous month (June 1931), we see how she did not fail to let her newly found father-in-law know that "any ... influence would help a great deal." Grace understood that for Hector's relief bill to be passed into law, they needed public support to put pressure on the politicians voting on it in the upcoming December session of Congress. Thus, she was always working toward the goal of heightening public awareness of her husband's plight and getting support from whomever she could. Moving into the mid- to latter part of July 1931, we find that the couple had skillfully shared their recent correspondence with family members, social service agencies, the Red Cross, the War Department, and politicians with various newspapers, knowing full well that readers were hanging on to every word being reported about Hector, since theirs was truly an unusual story and now on the verge of a happy ending if all went according to the plan. This was something everyone with awareness of the matter wanted to see happen.

Boston Herald (July 14, 1931)[23]

The *Herald*'s story titled "Amnesia Victims Record Defended" was factual, albeit with minor errors, and it touched on all the main points of importance in the sequence of unfortunate events that befell Hector. Once again it was reported that the ex-congressman who had represented the 4th District, George R. Stobbs, had played a role in remitting the 12 months' hard labor sentence (as mentioned, we have not been able to verify this claim). The story went on to say that Senator David I. Walsh and Congressman Pehr G. Holmes were collaborating to have the dishonorable discharge upgraded to an honorable discharge the following winter. Toward that end, they would be introducing a congressional bill to remedy the injustice perpetrated against Hector. The report further stated that Hector suffered from "amnesia or aphasia or some mental trouble" when he left the army hospital in New York. This article highlighted the fact that Grace and Hector had married under the name he used when he did not "know who he was." This aspect is yet another example of the legal complications that the couple would need to address at some later date. One can only surmise from one's own experiences in obtaining state identification cards and the like how convoluted the process of straightening out their marriage records would be.

Overwhelming Support for Hector Goes National (1931)

While several organizations and individuals played important roles in the resurrection of Hector Perez from the ashes of Alfredo Velasquez

Sanchez and Hector H. Perry, their involvement was interconnected. Their participation spanned separate and diverse agendas. The list is not inclusive of all who took part in this odyssey.

The War Department's interest centered solely on apprehending Hector to mete out military justice; they were not at all concerned about his well-being or reuniting him with his family. The Associated Charities in Massachusetts; the American Red Cross in three states (Massachusetts, New York, Florida); the Duval County Family Welfare Agency in Florida; the American Disabled Veterans in three states (Ohio, Massachusetts, Florida) and the District of Columbia; the U.S. Marine Hospital at Key West; the Soldier's Services in Boston; and social services in Worcester had all focused on helping Hector find the family that had been lost to him for more than 14 years, as did many journalists and people they connected with along the way. Additionally, Congressman Holmes and ex–Congressman Stobbs, joined by Senator David Walsh, were seeking to have Hector's dishonorable discharge revoked and, in its place, award him an honorable discharge so that he could gain access to critical mental health care. It finally seemed that the next hurdle, rescinding the dishonorable discharge and the award of an honorable discharge with pay and benefits, was on the horizon.

For two neophytes tasked with mastering strategic planning, community organizing, and media relations, we find that Hector and Grace worked their way skillfully through this complex maze in the struggle to achieve their goals. His life depended on it. They remained committed through the toughest of times and in the darkest of places to finally arrive at a spot where they could rest a moment and take a breath. They were near the finish line, and they were still together. This was their strong suit, their irrepressible unified spirit. They just wanted this ordeal to be over so Hector could start treatment and live his life normally.

After Hector's father was finally located in early June 1931, and the story broke with the initial newspaper stories dated July 6 through July 14, lengthier stories appeared in the press, which included reports of senatorial involvement. National attention was now focused on this story. From the record, we know that Senator Walsh was already initiating motions to introduce a bill for the relief of Hector H. Perry (the name on his army record) in the December 9, 1931, first session of the 72nd Congress.[24] The public also learned for the first time, shared by a reporter sourced from family letters, the locations of the battles Hector participated in and the dates they took place. As one newspaper editor said after learning of the matter, "This man Perez has an impressive war record."

As detailed in chapter 6, Hector served in seven of the bloodiest battles that took place in France. However, he had no memory of being in the trenches or even in the war. Due to his dishonorable discharge, Hector had not been informed by the army of the medals of distinction awarded to the soldiers of the 2nd Engineers unit that served with the 4th Marine Brigade during the Aisne-Marne offensive.[25] The 4th Marine Brigade, with close to 10,000 men, was the largest Marine unit to see major action in World War I. They were allegedly dubbed "Devil Dogs" (*teufel hunden*) by the Germans; the 4th was part of the 2nd Division of the American Expeditionary Forces, nicknamed the "Race Horse Division" for its rapid and devastating pursuit of the enemy.[26] Hector was assigned to that unit on July 4–20, 1918. The soldiers who survived the Aisne-Marne battle were awarded the Croix de Guerre by French authorities (with approval by General Pershing). As previously noted, the average casualty rate for engineer units in World War I was 2.65 percent while Hector's 2nd Engineers unit had a 26.7 percent casualty rate. If he was not awarded the Croix de Guerre during his lifetime, we believe Hector is entitled to the Croix de Guerre posthumously. We have also learned that the entire 2nd Infantry Division (to which he was assigned) was awarded several medals for notable service during combat. Posthumously bestowing on Hector all the medals he was entitled to receive would be another step in the direction of addressing the injustices perpetrated against him, as he should be remembered for what he did and who he was, not for how he was portrayed, especially by some who lacked objectivity. How can the army award medals to a deserter? It seems almost counterintuitive.

D.C., Florida, Massachusetts, Ohio—Letter, American Disabled Veterans of the World War to Captain Daniel, Executive Officer in Florida of the U.S. Marine Hospital, Key West (July 17, 1931)

A copy of the letter from Ralph L. Chambers dated July 17, 1931, and retained in the family archives, disclosed that Mr. Chambers was the chairman of Washington, D.C.'s National Rehabilitation Department of the American Disabled Veterans of the World War. He was assigned to their national headquarters in Cincinnati, Ohio. They also had offices in D.C., Florida, and Massachusetts, and they all participated in Hector's case one way or another.

In the aftermath of World War I, disabled veterans in the United States found themselves seriously disadvantaged and lacking governmental support. Many of these veterans were blind, deaf, or mentally ill when they returned from the front lines. An astonishing 204,000 Americans in uniform were wounded during the war.[27]

The idea to form the American Disabled Veterans arose at a

Christmas party in 1919 hosted by Cincinnati Superior Court Judge Robert Marx, a U.S. Army captain who had been injured in the Meuse-Argonne offensive in November 1918.[28] Although the organization had already been functional for some months, the American Disabled Veterans of the World War was officially created on September 25, 1920, for the benefit of disabled military veterans of the U.S. Armed Forces. Issued as a federal charter by Congress in 1932, it had over one million members; today, it is a 501(c)(4) social welfare organization. The American Disabled Veterans is now universally known as the Disabled American Veterans.

Mr. Chambers was responding to questions asked by Captain Richard Curd Daniel in a letter he had received thirteen days earlier. Captain Daniel was the department executive officer of the U.S. Marine Hospital at Key West. Central to the matter was the issue of eligibility for compensation due to disability as it applied specifically in cases of desertion and dishonorable discharge. Mr. Chambers incorrectly assumed Hector had two enlistments, with the first during the period of World War I, followed by a later reenlistment from which he deserted. However, Mr. Chambers also stated that he believed even if there was one single period of service, if it could be shown that the veteran was of unsound mind at the time of his desertion, it might be possible to obtain benefits. Specifically, he wrote that if the veteran did have a period of honorable war service, and if he received disabilities during that period of service either "by presumption or by direct evidence, compensation may be paid to him notwithstanding the fact that he later re-enlisted and deserted."

The letter closed with a suggestion that those interested in the claim could secure valuable assistance from the Boston office, since the case would likely be managed in the Boston area. Mr. Chambers referred the captain to the organization's rehabilitation officer in Boston, T. James Gallagher.

The main purpose of this correspondence should not be overlooked or underestimated. It was intended to grant Hector eligibility for benefits so he could secure medical and psychological support. It was reassuring and heartening to us to see the work of good men and women who had joined forces to attempt to rectify the injustice Hector had suffered.

The American Disabled Veterans were paving the way in uncharted territory in their effort to provide much-needed support for veterans who were injured in service to their country. Assistance with a claim was being sought. There was obviously a lot more going on in the background to correct the inequity the army had created. These documents show just a portion of the flurry of behind-the-scenes activities that were taking place to make things right.

The mere fact that this letter had been written to Mr. Chambers, we believe, was solely due to Captain Daniel learning of Hector's case from a relative of Hector's, Miss Margarita Lacedonia. She was the stenographer for the U.S. Marine Hospital in Key West, and Captain Daniel was her superior. We also know from family history that she was very active in spreading the word to "anyone of influence" about Hector's case. These were the exact words Grace wrote in her letters to family members when asking them to take action.

A verbatim transcription of the letter follows:

NATIONAL HEADQUARTERS
2940 Melrose Ave.
Cincinnati, Ohio.
AMERICAN DISABLED VETERANS
OF THE WORLD WAR
NATIONAL REHABILITATION DEPARTMENT
MUNSEY BUILDING
WASHINGTON, D.C.
Ralph L. Chambers
Chairman

July 17, 1931

Mr. Richard Curd Daniel
Capt. U.S.A. & E.C.R. Perez, Hector
U.S. Marine Hospital
Key West, Florida.

My dear Comrades

Statements contained in your letter of July 4, 1931, indicate that this veteran probably had two enlistments; the first during the period of the World War with a later re-enlistment from which he deserted.

If the veteran did have a period of honorable World War service and if he did receive disabilities during that period of service which may be held due to service, by presumption or by direct evidence, compensation may be paid to him notwithstanding the fact that he later re-enlisted and deserted.

The above statement is based upon the assumption that this veteran had an honorable period of World War service and was honorably discharged from his World War Service and upon the assumption that he deserted from an enlistment after his discharge from this period of service.

Even though there was one single period of service, if it can be shown that the veteran was of unsound mind at the time of his desertion it may be possible to secure benefits for him.

It is suggested that those interested in the claim may secure valuable assistance from Comrade T. James Gallagher, D.A.V. Rehabilitation Officer, 600

Washington Street, Boston, Mass., as it is quite probable that the case will be handled in the Boston area.

> Cordially yours,
>
> Sgd. Ralph L. Chambers
> RLC:GF

Notes: Capt. Richard Curd Daniel is Dept. Executive Officer in Florida.

This letter helps to demonstrate the overwhelming support Hector was receiving from influential people who could make a difference in his specific case. He and Grace were slowly garnering support from many sources.

Maine—La Justice de Biddeford, News Report, French Language (July 17, 1931)

News of Hector's predicament was also published in a French-language newspaper from Biddeford, Maine—*La Justice de Biddeford*—on July 17, 1931.[29] The translation of the text from French to English was provided courtesy of Drake P. Starling (Hector's great-grandnephew and coauthor Lina Palmer's son).

The title of the article was "Ex-Soldier Was a Victim of Amnesia," subtitled "Hector J. Perez was ignorant of his own identity for more than eight years. Wants Congress to revoke the dishonorable discharge given to him."

It started out by reporting that Hector J. Perez had been "a victim of amnesia" and "did not know his own identity." There was due mention of the effort of the congressmen and the state senator to introduce a bill in Congress that would rescind the dishonorable discharge given to Hector. This story erroneously informs readers that Hector reported to Fort Adams in 1928 after learning his true name; as detailed in earlier chapters, Hector did not learn of his identity until after his arrival at Fort Adams. His trip there was not because he had learned his identity; instead, he went there seeking it. At that time he was still not aware of who he really was. He was Hector Perez, not Alfred Velasquez Sanchez nor Hector Perry. This fact would not become known for another three years.

The article went on to inform readers that Hector, "after distinguishing himself on the battlefields in France, was discharged from the army hospital in New York on June 26, 1920, while suffering from amnesia, or other mental disorders. He wandered through several cities in New England and finally arrived in Worcester." It then reported the marriage being registered under the assumed name, as Hector was not aware of his true identity. It also detailed his difficulty holding down jobs due to memory issues, forgetting the roles assigned to him.

Florida—Miami Herald, News Report, "Perez Identifies Long Lost Son" (July 19, 1931)[30]

The *Miami Herald* article titled as above and subtitled "Key West Father to Return After Massachusetts Trip" reported that "Charles Perez of 1117 Duval Street in Key West went to Worcester" to meet his son Hector, "who had been missing from his family for 15 years." It went on to say that Charles' visit would be more than "two weeks" long and he was to return to Key West shortly, and Hector planned to visit Key West later that autumn. According to this article, Hector "remembered nothing of the past." It also stated, "Young Perez, enlisted in the army and served overseas during the World war, disappeared from an army hospital in Fox Hills, N.Y., in 1920 while mentally impaired."

Florida—Key West Citizen, News Report, "Amnesia Victim Returns Home" (July 20, 1931)[31]

The *Key West Citizen* reported on Friday, July 20, that Hector had met with his father Charles Perez and the two would soon return to Worcester after spending the past two days in a New York hotel room getting reacquainted.

While reading this story, we truly hoped this gathering had included Hector's brother, Charlie, since he lived in New York City, though there is no mention of him. Like other newspaper articles, this story recounted events that precipitated Hector's disappearance and how his memory was jogged by a chance meeting with a fellow soldier with whom he had served overseas, who recognized and remembered him.

Charles was reportedly "overjoyed to see his son again and to know" his fourteen-plus-year search for Hector was finally over. Just imagine the overwhelming sense of relief Charles must have felt in knowing his son was alive and safe. The elation he must have felt at that time surely gave him peace of mind now that he no longer feared the worst for his son. In this article, for the first time, Hector was described as "happy." Events were finally heading in the right direction for him. One month earlier, for the first time in over a decade, father and son had communicated, as was reported in the previously mentioned letter of June 20, 1931.

As with the other articles, there were a few minor errors in the reporting here. However, the focus was on Hector's powerful story. According to this article, during all the years he was lost, "his relatives," including "his father, brother, and sisters searched the country for news of him," all the while not knowing whether he was alive or dead.

The newspaper reported that earlier Hector had sat "with his father whom he had completely forgotten." As his father mentioned names and places that should have been familiar to him, "dim recollections filtered through Hector's mind." "He wrote a short note to his wife," who remained in Worcester, "saying that he and his father had sat up all night recalling days and hours long since gone." He wrote that he and his father would come to Worcester in a day or two, so Grace could meet her father-in-law for the first time.

Florida and Massachusetts—Key West Citizen, News Report, Family Reunification and Senatorial Involvement (July 23, 1931)[32]

A lengthy newspaper article, taking up over one-third of an entire page and published on July 23, 1931, in the *Key West Citizen* primarily addressed the issue of the family's reunification, senatorial involvement, and the plans to reverse the charges against Hector. It was written by William J. Belleville of the *Worcester Evening Post* and was by far the most comprehensive account of Hector's predicament up to this date. It included his military service dates as well as family correspondence and provided more detail than any of the other published reports. Without question, this was the newspaper's feature article of the day, due to its length and the depth of reporting. It was chock full of facts about Hector's life over a fifteen-year period, from 1916 to 1931. Coverage of a news item with greater detail is hard to find.

The headline read, "Senator David I. Walsh Wants Congress to Lift Perez Discharge Stigma," followed by the subheading "Sees Facts Clearly Establish Lack of Mental Responsibility, Excellent War Record Shown."

Belleville wrote of the U.S. senator's efforts to remove the stigma of Hector's dishonorable discharge, as Hector lacked the mental capacity to be held accountable. According to this article, "Senator Walsh planned to introduce a bill in the next congress designed to obliterate the dishonorable discharge given to Hector J. Perez of Key West, an amnesia victim who became lost to himself as well as to his family here for 14 years following the World War." He was "only located by his father, Charles Perez, last week through the assistance of the American Red Cross and the Associated Charities."

The story went on to report in granular detail all the known facts about Hector's case. It explained that everything changed during a chance meeting in the spring of 1928 while Hector was walking down Main Street. The reporter told how he had consulted with an attorney, who "in turn directed the befuddled soldier to contact the War Department," and how this outreach prompted the army's eventual response to Hector that he should report to Fort Adams. With optimism and "curiosity of learning his identity still moving his spirit, he did." The story then reported the facts of the general court-martial, the clemency letter written by the members of the tribunal to the commanding officer, and how the commanding officer rejected their recommendations.

From this article, we learned the attorney had made an appointment to visit Senator Walsh, and, with Hector in tow, he went to the senator's Clinton suburb home. "The senator was deeply moved by the situation and was especially impressed with the man's war record."

In addition to stating what was covered in previous articles, this story displayed correspondence to Hector and Grace from both his father Charles Perez and his youngest sister, Dinorah Perez Atkinson (both letters are retained in the family archives). We suspect that Hector and Grace gave the newspapers copies of these and other letters—another example of the young couple skillfully managing the media. We believe this was Grace's forte.

The letter written on June 20, 1931, from Charles Perez in Key West to his long-lost son and his daughter-in-law in Worcester (which we displayed previously) was published in its entirety. Also provided was a letter from Mrs. Dinorah Atkinson of Orlando, Florida, dated June 22, 1931. In it, she wrote that she understood "Hector was under medical supervision, as an aftermath of war," which tells us he was receiving some sort of medical care, solely psychological in nature. If true, this would have been a good thing. The efforts of many were finally producing positive results in meaningful ways for Hector.

Next, the article displayed a copy of the letter from Major General Charles W. Bridges, adjutant general of the War Department, written to former congressman George Stobbs on July 3, 1931, regarding Perez's war record. This letter was previously displayed in detail, and the original is preserved in the family archives.

A verbatim recollection of the conversation that took place in May 1928 when Hector met his former army buddy was also included in the *Key West Citizen* story. In addition, this article reported Hector meeting his younger brother Charlie in the attorney's office in Worcester, noting that the brother (who was then employed by the New York City post office) was unfamiliar to him and Hector had some doubts that Charlie was truly his brother. Hector did not know he had any siblings. He did not recall his mother, and the picture he had in his mind of his father did not match his father's physical appearance on meeting him for the first time in 15 years. The article further mentioned the many military engagements in which Hector had fought and the medical treatment he received. Unfortunately, it did not specify what the nature of Hector's treatment was.

Massachusetts and Florida—Letter from News Editor W. J. Belleville to Captain Daniel, Executive Officer in Florida of the U.S. Marine Hospital, Key West (July 27, 1931)[33]

A letter from W. J. Belleville of the *Worcester Evening Post* dated July 27, 1931, was written in response to Captain Daniel's previous inquiry. Captain Daniel was the executive officer of the U.S. Marine Hospital in Key West. Mr. Belleville was fulfilling a request for materials and had promised to deliver additional papers to the captain from the newspaper's circulation department. We believe Captain Daniel was requesting newspaper stories that had been published about Hector's case. We have no evidence other than logical assumptions of the facts.

This correspondence showed, once again, that many efforts were made to assist Hector. Belleville wrote of being impressed with Hector and believed his case to be sincere. He thought "it certainly does not seem such a weird situation could be imagined by an ex-soldier."

Grace's support for her husband and her declaration of his kindness to her are noted, as is her physical handicap, requiring the use of a wooden leg and crutches, which we first learned of earlier from the 1930 letter written by the general secretary of the Associated Charities of Worcester to the Duval County Family Welfare Agency. Belleville referred to Grace as a "fine woman" and said that "she really worked to support [her husband]." Belleville's compassion for Hector and all that he had endured was evident. He wrote of his hope that assistance could be rendered in Hector's case and announced that he had himself joined the effort to assist in correcting this injustice.

Belleville ended his letter by stating, "The whole thing is filled with situations that stir up any red-blooded man and I hope that you and others who are trying to help may be successful." He informed Captain Daniel that he would be glad to hear from the captain in the future as to whether he received the papers and materials, and he also hoped Captain Daniel would do anything he could to assist Hector Perez. It was encouraging and impressive to see another significant person join Hector's cause, and Mr. Belleville was no doubt an influential newsman. (As with all the other important documents, the original copy of this letter is kept in the family archives.)

Massachusetts—Worcester Telegram–USA Today Network, News Report, "Death Gives Up Soldier Son" (August 2, 1931)[34]

Another article was published in the August 2, 1931, edition of the *Worcester Telegram–USA Today Network*. Several headings and subheadings were used in the presentation of the article, including "Death Gives Up Soldier Son—Charles Perez of Key West and Boy, Hector, Are Reunited. Lost Since War—Memory Gone 14 Years Army Now Calls Him Deserter."

This article led with an image of Hector and his father Charles that had been taken by a *Telegram* staff photographer the previous day. Hector and his father were seated next to each other in what looked to be an attorney's office and were dressed in business attire, as was customary at the time. The photo was captioned "Father and Son Reunited."

This story restated all the facts known up until this date. Here we found the first mention of any report questioning the legality of the charges brought against Hector by the army: "The Worcester attorney was consulted, and he made legal motions as to the legitimacy of the dishonorable discharge."

The Worcester newspaper went on to report that the father and son had been reunited two weeks earlier for the first time in 14 years. "Hector insisted his father come to Worcester to meet his wife Grace, the 'newly found' daughter-in-law Charles had never seen." Remember, this was not a father and son who chose to separate and not see one another for an extended period. This story was about a man who had no clue whether his son was dead or alive. It was about a man who went through painstaking efforts to find his firstborn child, the son from whom he had not heard for nearly 15 years. Charles had believed his son was quite likely dead when in reality his son had suffered amnesia and lost all memory of his past.

In our opinion, the fact that Hector insisted that his father meet his wife illustrates the core values of Hector's character and how family oriented he was. In the few letters written between father and son, there was always an apparent warm regard. Hector was also an integral part of his wife's close-knit family, as they were the only family he knew. We believe that his birth relatives understood and were grateful for this closeness.

The *Telegram* reported that in the "afternoon the day earlier, in the front room of the Perez house at 9 King Street, Grace met her father-in-law for the first time." "She had just returned from work and the meeting between the father and daughter-in-law was one of joy."

The article mentioned the medical treatment Hector had received for nervous disorders after returning from the war. It accurately describes that he was deemed a deserter when he failed to return to the Fox Hills hospital on Staten Island once his scheduled furlough was up.

In this newspaper report, we again see how the trial court recommended clemency for Hector, as well as remission of the hard-labor prison sentence that was still hanging over him. The report stated that, according to Hector, "General Preston Brown of the First Army Corps returned the papers with a veto." Hector was "at a loss" to understand the commanding officer's reasoning for the veto. We are certain the commanding officer clearly understood the ramifications of his decision.

According to Hector's attorney, there was a question about the lapsed medical insurance for veterans. This was a new aspect that bubbled up in this report, and apparently the attorney had sued in Boston regarding Hector's medical insurance, which was being "held in abeyance." It seemed as if the Veterans Bureau claimed his insurance had lapsed, as Hector had failed to pay his premiums. The meaning of this statement is not fully understood, but clearly someone dropped the ball, once again, to Hector's detriment. No one took any action to ensure that a man with amnesia would follow through on all the prerequisites to maintain medical insurance in a matter of such grave importance.

The involvement of Senator David I. Walsh of Massachusetts was once again reported. This article detailed much of what was included in the previous newspaper reports and noted that, after reading Hector's war record, the senator announced that he would introduce congressional legislation to have Hector's dishonorable discharge changed to an honorable discharge so that he would be eligible for the psychological and medical treatment he sorely needed. This treatment would help Hector become a self-supporting citizen and care for himself and his family.

Senator Walsh also declared that "he would introduce legislation" to grant honorable discharges to other soldiers suffering from memory loss produced by war neuroses. During our research, we learned no senator introduced more bills at that time for the relief of soldiers than Senator Walsh.[35] Two things were clear: his heart was in the right place, and these dishonorable discharges were an emerging and prevailing issue that needed to be corrected. The senator took it on himself to champion the veterans' cause.

Senator Walsh was another example of the good-hearted people who came to Hector's aid once they became aware of his predicament. The overwhelming support for Hector that had been building up over many months finally found its way to a national platform. David Walsh served in the Senate from December 6, 1926, through January 3, 1947. He was one of the longest-serving senators from the state of Massachusetts, and we can understand why.

This was the only report in which we saw mention of "physicians" who handled Hector's case. From this article, we learned they had all agreed that treatment was necessary to bring him back to being a normal, self-supporting citizen. According to these medical professionals, if

Hector's papers were in order, he would be eligible for treatment at any government hospital. In this case, one could say the military (synonymous with the government) had turned its collective back on Hector when he needed them the most, even though he put his life on the line for his country during a time of war and was there for his government when they needed him the most. The need for volunteers in World War I had been great, and the country had instituted the draft for the first time since the Civil War.[36] However, Hector had volunteered for military service prior to that date. When his country called, he answered that call. Sadly, the reverse was not true. This discrepancy was what the senator wanted to rectify.

The article ended by reporting that Hector's main objective was "to secure an honorable discharge." It further informed readers that at the time of publication, Hector was an outpatient at Worcester State Hospital, reporting for treatment each month. We were of course very pleased to see that. It is worth noting that this was the very same institution in which Grace's relative had received treatment for a variety of illnesses and later died from influenza complications in 1918.

Unquestionably, this newspaper article was the single most comprehensive account of Hector's saga that was ever reported, accurately covering all the prominent points of the matter.

Florida—Letter from Miss Margarita Lacedonia, Employee at U.S. Marine Hospital, Seeking Congressional Support (September 12, 1931)

Miss Margarita Lacedonia (figure 23), an employee of the U.S. Marine Hospital at Key West, wrote a letter dated September 12, 1931, to Representative Ruth Bryan Owen through the Key West Chamber of Commerce. Ruth Baird Leavitt Owen Rohde, also known as Ruth Bryan Owen (October 2, 1885–July 26, 1954), was the first woman elected to Congress from the state of Florida. She represented Florida's 4th Congressional District in the U.S. House of Representatives from 1929 to 1933, after which she served as U.S. envoy to Denmark from 1933 to 1936.[37]

Margarita was Hector's first cousin once removed. Coauthor Lina and her mother "Bibi" visited Margarita during the 1980s, at which time contemporaneous notes were taken.

At the time Margarita wrote this letter in 1931, she was employed at the U.S. Marine Hospital in Key West (see appendix). Since 1928, she had worked as a stenographer and clerk in the Office of the Marine Hospital. She was a bright young woman and by 1936 owned her own home on Eaton Street in Key West. She had an entrepreneurial spirit and later in life owned a small motel in Key West. Her grandmother, Dolores "Lola" Perez, and Hector's father, Charles Perez, were siblings. Her letter is maintained in the family archives.

Margarita informed Congresswoman Owen that Hector had been born in Tampa and raised in Key West. She introduced his very commendable war record, a copy of which she promised to send to Ms. Owen shortly. She added that the congresswoman might be interested to know that the young man's father, who was a resident of Key West, went to see him shortly after learning of his whereabouts.

Margarita's letter referenced the congressional bill sponsored by Senator Walsh of Massachusetts that would grant Hector an honorable discharge. Margarita was anxiously seeking political support and additional assistance from the Key West Chamber of Commerce. If Hector's disability were deemed to be service connected, it would thereby make him officially eligible for coverage of health benefits. He would then be able to get help with the hope of relieving his amnesia and restoring his life to normal. She enclosed correspondence regarding the bill, which was slated to be introduced at the next session of Congress in December of that year. Margarita concluded her letter by stating that nothing could be done other than expediting Hector's request for admission to a veterans' hospital and having his disability considered service connected. She advised that Hector was residing in Worcester and, therefore, would be referred to and assisted by the Regional Office of the Veterans Bureau in Boston.

Figure 23: Margarita Lacedonia, Hector's paternal first cousin once removed. Her grandmother (Dolores "Lola" Perez) and Hector's father (Charles Perez) were siblings. She was a stenographer and clerk at the U.S. Marine Hospital in Key West, Florida. She was the reason why the U.S. Marine Hospital executive director, Captain Daniel, became involved in aiding Hector by seeking advice from the American Disabled Veterans of the World War regarding the case and contacting newspaper editors to ensure that Hector's story would be circulated.

A review of the facts in this case reveals an impressive collection of influential persons, politicians, and organizations (civilian and military) that were contacted by or joined Hector's cause—networking at its finest in 1931.

Eight

Bill S. 851—A Partial Victory

The Senate Bill (1931)

On December 6, 1931, during the first session of the 72nd Congress in Washington, D.C., Bill S. 851 was among more than one hundred bills introduced by Senator Walsh, who sponsored more bills than any other legislator during that session. The bill was read twice and referred to the Committee on Military Affairs, dated December 9, 1931.[1]

The purpose of Bill S. 851 was to grant relief to Hector H. Perry (the name under which Hector had served in the military). Many of the relief bills were aimed at upgrading the dishonorable discharges of ex-servicemen who had served under extreme conditions. Their extenuating circumstances were not considered when they should have been, usually at the time of their general court-martial. Such remedial action was necessary to deal with the phenomenon now known as *post-traumatic stress disorder* (PTSD).[2] As previously mentioned, PTSD is a mental health condition triggered by a terrifying event—either experiencing it or witnessing it. Symptoms may include flashbacks, nightmares, and severe anxiety, as well as uncontrollable thoughts about the event. Most people who go through traumatic events may experience temporary difficulty adjusting and coping. They often require professional help. Over time and with good self-care, those afflicted usually get better.

Unfortunately, in some cases, PTSD symptoms may get worse, lasting for months or even years, and could interfere with day-to-day functioning.[3] Getting effective treatment after PTSD symptoms develop can be critical to reducing symptoms and improving function. PTSD symptoms may start within one month of a traumatic event, but sometimes symptoms may not appear until years later. These symptoms often cause significant problems in social or work situations and in relationships. They can also interfere with one's ability to go about their normal daily routine. PTSD symptoms are grouped into four types: intrusive memories, avoidance, negative changes in thinking and mood, and changes in physical and emotional reactions.

Symptoms can vary over time and from person to person. Every case is unique. In many or most cases, people affected by PTSD will need years of therapy and professional help. It was truly fortunate that in the 1920s and 1930s, some of the power brokers of the day recognized the seriousness of the problem and took action to deal with this terrible by-product of war. Those afflicted with PTSD were also casualties of war, although it may not have been obvious due to the lack of information about this disorder.

The government also needed to do its part in assisting afflicted veterans by removing dishonorable discharges from their records, in addition to alleviating stigma where possible. Once they received honorable discharges, veterans could access the resources needed to restore their lives. Professional mental health care was paramount to the healing process. Even if the veterans did recognize their own affliction, most did not have the means to pay for their own psychological care. This is why access to veteran health benefits was critical at this juncture in their lives. Being denied the help they needed was like a death sentence considering that the onset of their PTSD was a result of their service to their country.

The passage of these "relief bills" was of the utmost importance to Senator Walsh, as we can see by the number of bills that he sponsored and brought before Congress. It would make a world of difference in the lives of many who had served their country in its time of need.

Bill S. 851, titled a "Bill for the Relief of Hector H. Perry," ordered that Congress bestow rights, privileges, and benefits on Hector H. Perry, hereinafter to be considered honorably discharged from military service on September 21, 1928. It is interesting to note that on the copy of the actual bill, the name "Hector H. Perez" is handwritten above the type-written name "Hector H. Perry." A verbatim representation of the bill is presented next. A copy of the original is retained in the family archives.

72d CONGRESS
**1st SESSION   S. 851

IN THE SENATE OF THE UNITED STATES
DECEMBER 9, 1931
MR. WALSH OF MASSACHUSETTS INTRODUCED THE FOLLOWING BILL: WHICH WAS READ TWICE AND REFERRED TO THE COMMITTEE ON MILITARY AFFAIRS

A BILL
FOR THE RELIEF OF HECTOR H. PERRY
[CORRECTED BY HAND TO PEREZ]
BE IT ENACTED BY THE SENATE AND HOUSE OF REPRESENTATIVES OF THE UNITED STATES OF AMERICA IN CONGRESS

ASSEMBLED, THAT IN THE ADMINISTRATION OF ANY LAWS CONFERRING RIGHTS, PRIVILEGES, AND BENEFITS UPON HONORABLY DISCHARGED SOLDIER HECTOR H. PERRY WHO WAS A MEMBER OF THE MEDICAL DETACHMENT, SECOND REGIMENT UNITED STATES ENGINEERS, SHALL HEREAFTER BE HELD AND CONSIDERED TO HAVE BEEN HONORABLY DISCHARGED FROM THE MILITARY SERVICE OF THE UNITED STATES AS A MEMBER OF THAT ORGANIZATION ON THE 21ST DAY OF SEPTEMBER, 1928: PROVIDED, THAT NO BOUNTY, BACK PAY, PENSION, OR ALLOWANCE SHALL BE HELD TO HAVE ACCRUED PRIOR TO THE PASSAGE OF THIS ACT.

The Results of the Rally to Support Hector

Changing Hector's dishonorable discharge to an honorable discharge would make him eligible for the veterans' benefits he had fought so long and hard for. Most important, Hector could now have access to treatment for his war-induced amnesia and PTSD. The best outcome would be his restoration to his prior self (or as close to it as possible). That was the main intent of the legislation, and it had always been Grace's primary goal. All would agree that getting the proper treatment was an exceptionally good thing and had the potential to change Hector's quality of life drastically so he could be as self-supporting as possible.

It is Congress' responsibility to enact laws that influence the daily lives of all Americans.[4] Congress is intended to serve as the voice of the people. Be it the legislative, judiciary or executive branch, as President Abraham Lincoln so eloquently stated in his Gettysburg Address in 1863, the essence of the American system of government is "of the people, by the people and for the people."[5] This has always been the hallmark of the system of American governance.

For the government to do nothing would be unfair, immoral, unjust, and plain wrong. A man who fought for his country with valor for such an extended period should be fully embraced by the country he served and defended. Hector had fought while his own life was put in jeopardy. With the help and support of Grace and the many others whom she mustered to come to his aid, Hector was finally served some degree of justice. It was not quick, and it was not easy. He and Grace endured years of hardship that could never be undone. Those years could never be recaptured or fully restored. Half-measures would not do.

Disappointingly, the bill stipulated that no "bounty, back pay, pension or allowance shall be held to have accrued prior to the passage of this act," meaning that Hector would not be eligible for any form of monetary benefit prior to the bill passing. While it is true that the bill had the potential to provide what Hector needed most in this matter—namely, the resumption of medical coverage and benefits—it did not address monetary compensation. If conditions were such that they needed to be remedied, they should have been addressed part and parcel, not piecemeal. Compensation should most definitely have been included, and damages should have been awarded in the bill. While not meaning to sound unappreciative for what was championed and achieved, it is hard to see the distinction between medical and monetary remediation in this matter. They go hand in hand. It is difficult to understand the principles that were applied to reach such a conclusion. Nevertheless, what the bill did was a good thing, and it restored some degree of faith in our country's ability to right the wrongs that our military bureaucracy perpetrated against many disabled veterans. In this case, it worked—to a certain degree. However, it would still take time to pass the bill and see the full results.

Report on the Senate Bill S. 851 Passing (February 27, 1935)

In the February 27, 1935, edition of the *Worcester Evening Gazette*, the newspaper's Washington correspondent reported that Senate Bill S. 851 had passed, along with many others.[6] The newspaper article's headline was "Senate Passes Walsh's Bills," with the tagline "Ten Private Relief Measures Filed by Massachusetts' Senior Senator Have Received Approval." The Senate passed more private bills introduced by Senator David I. Walsh than it did for any other member during that session. There were more than one hundred private relief bills in total sponsored by Senator Walsh that were subsequently passed. Senator Walsh became involved in the effort to right the wrongs committed by the army and its bureaucracy against many veterans. The sentences the army handed down too often did not consider extenuating circumstances. The private relief bills that were passed along with Hector's were wide ranging, and the circumstances and reasons for the dishonorable discharges that were being overturned by these bills varied. Several veterans were specifically named in separate bills, such as a former captain who was subsequently allowed to claim all the benefits and privileges of the Emergency Officers' Retirement Act (the captain had been "gassed" while in France and was now disabled). Another bill that passed was for the relief of a soldier who had enlisted while underage to fight in the Sioux Indian campaign of 1876 and was later dishonorably discharged for desertion.

The article further stated, "The bill that passed pertaining to Hector H. Perry was that his army record would be changed to reflect an honorable discharge." It went on to report the details of Hector's case up to that point, including how he had received treatment from "various doctors" at the state hospital. This section of the story was very heartening, as this treatment was critical for Hector's well-being. He and Grace had fought a long, hard battle to achieve this goal. We were very impressed by their determination and grit to see this mission through until the desired result was achieved.

Government Accountability

How do you put a price tag on 14 years of someone's life? If Hector had no serious issues with his mental health and memory prior to the war and acquired amnesia because of his wartime service, one might argue that he was abandoned by the government he served. The punishment to which he was subjected and the way the government went about exacting justice on him was undeniably harsh and unfair. Was it appropriate that he not only be abandoned by the country in whose service he acquired these deficiencies but also be subjected to punishment because of what transpired in its wake? To a large degree, his country was responsible for Hector's mental condition, whether it was acquired in combat or already existed at the time of his enlistment.

If Hector became stricken because of his wartime service, the issue of responsibility is a clear-cut case. He was obviously mentally ill while still serving overseas, as the War Department's letters attest. He was treated for mental issues while still stationed in Europe, based on the best information available. However, the truth is that no one knows when Hector first became mentally ill. It may have been the day he was treated, or it could have happened during the first battle he participated in. An educated guess leads us to believe the months he spent in the trenches surrounded by violence and death caused such trauma to his mind that it triggered a defense mechanism to bring about amnesia.

Of course, it is possible that he had already acquired some sort of mental or emotional condition prior to his enlistment; in this case, his problems would have been exacerbated by his wartime service, and the government would have been complicit in his deterioration. The government and military bureaucracy became liable when they failed to recognize his disorder and permitted him to enlist for military service, thus exposing him to a very dangerous environment that would surely invoke an intense emotional response in any normal person. Additionally,

Hector did not get the help he needed when he served in the military even though his illnesses were clearly diagnosed. His condition should have been identified, scrutinized, and properly dealt with. Instead, he was later punished for his symptoms and actions, which were not entirely of his own making.

Had Hector lost an eye or a limb or was otherwise physically wounded, the military would have sought to adequately address his medical needs and do their best to make him whole. They would have wanted to restore him as close as possible to his former self. However, in terms of the medical treatment Hector received for his condition while in the service of his country, there is no evidence to support the notion that anything was done for him psychologically or emotionally other than making a few diagnoses. Because the military records were destroyed by the great fire at the National Archives in 1973, it is impossible to learn exactly what sort of treatment Hector was given. We do believe that at the time all these events occurred, the military was fully aware of Hector's condition. The adjutant general of the War Department would have had access to all the information, as it was decades before the fire in which the records were destroyed. If all the protocols related to administration of military personnel records were enforced, and they were, the adjutant general would have had the ability to get the most complete picture of this troubled soldier.

Even if he was given the most appropriate treatment and therapy available at that time, Hector's struggles in his own bizarre world may have still existed and continued over an extended period. It is our contention that the government could have taken an approach more conducive to helping Hector rather than making him the scapegoat in this situation. Instead, they focused on blaming him for his condition. We believe the authorities at that time chose to deny their culpability for the conditions Hector developed under their command. They may have felt better served by shifting all responsibility for his problems on him and him alone. They made him out to be the guilty party, but the bottom line is that he was not solely responsible for his condition. The government needed him at the onset of U.S. involvement in the war and allowed him to engage in the most brutal battles in human history, but he did not have the mental or emotional capacity to serve by the end of his tour. Hector's overall condition was created by a series of events; it did not occur all at once. There was no single point in time that anyone could put their finger on and say this was the moment when he went over the edge. By not giving Hector timely treatment for the emotional and psychological injuries that he acquired on the field of battle, while still allowing him to serve, the military kept him exposed to the conditions that were causing his disability. At this point, the government became complicit in what Hector experienced and was responsible for his welfare. They acted in their own self-interest without considering what was in Hector's best interest.

The economic burden all of this turmoil inflicted on Hector was immeasurable. There is no question that the adverse effects of over three decades were intensified and compounded by circumstances that should have been addressed much earlier. There may have been an awareness among some people that there was an issue with this soldier, but little was done by the army to take proper remedial action or at least minimize his exposure to the source of his condition. Failure to treat this soldier in crisis was a travesty. The military identified the issue, and the news was not good. Once they observed the psychoses and neuroses in Hector, further measures should have been put in place to ensure that he did not create problems for or inflict harm on others or himself. Being permitted to leave the hospital in 1920 on furlough without supervision and allowed to roam loose on his own was a recipe for disaster. While it is understood that under normal conditions a soldier cannot be denied furlough, special consideration should have been given to someone whose thinking processes were not normal. An unsupervised furlough in this case was akin to a petri dish of problems from which issues, benign and minor at first, were allowed to multiply and fester into graver issues, resulting in confinement and hard labor in prison.

From a medical perspective, aside from being treated for influenza in January 1919 (two and a half months after the war ended), Hector received no psychological treatment for mental disorders as far as we could find. Then, in April 1919, he was diagnosed with alcoholism. The initial diagnosis was changed to psychoneurosis (type undetermined) three days later. Did his superiors or the doctors not see a change in him after the fighting concluded in November 1918, especially given the prevalence of this newly coined mental disorder they called shell shock? What was behind the initial misdiagnosis of alcoholism and why was it changed? Therein lies the key to responsibility in Hector's case. With a corrected diagnosis of psychoses and neuroses, what measures were then implemented on his behalf? Were his individualized needs not taken into consideration? Why wasn't he given the attention he so desperately needed? His record in 1919 shows he was treated for twenty days. Was someone not paying attention, or did the army have bigger issues to address? What would have been at stake from the army's perspective? Would it have been in their best interest to admit Hector's illness was mishandled? Is it possible that it would be best for the army to manage such matters as isolated incidents? Without reviewing his medical records, there is no way to tell how Hector was treated or whether he received the proper treatment. It bears repeating that while we cannot ascertain how Hector's mental illness initially manifested, the adjutant general of the War Department was privy to those records. It seems that the officers who presided over the general court-martial at Fort Adams, Rhode Island, in 1928 learned of his diagnoses from when he was stationed overseas in 1919, which, combined with the evaluations made by the army psychiatrists during this imprisonment period, led them to their swift recommendation of clemency one week after the psychiatric evaluations. The officers wasted no time in making sure their recommendation to the commanding general was clear and represented a unified front for clemency. As we know, they were overruled.

Mental health disorders continued to plague Hector when he arrived stateside, as evidenced by the medical information that was mentioned in the War Department's letters to the congressmen in 1931, which separately provided details of the medical treatment Hector received and a list of the battles he fought in, as well as his time served in each military campaign. No indication whatsoever was found in any record to demonstrate that the psychological prognosis and subsequent treatment that Hector received was adequate.

Steps should have been taken to find Hector after he left the Fox Hills hospital and determine why he did not return from leave. Of course, he should not have been allowed to leave in the first place. We wondered whether his amnesia was present at that time. The answer would appear to be yes, by virtue of the facts we have uncovered. He did not know his name. He did not remember his family.

Did a light bulb not go off in anyone's head to determine whether appropriate individualized measures were being taken? That is the nature of medical treatment—it is always individualized. Did the army really think Hector fled, or did anyone consider that his absence might be due to his numerous mental illness diagnoses? Even after the point when he disappeared, did anyone ever question the rationale they applied when they allowed him out on his own volition? In hindsight, did anyone not think the decision might have been a poor judgment? Did anyone consider the potential consequences to the patient and the public? Did anyone even care? It seemed as if Hector's case fell through the cracks, and he was gone.

Obviously, mental patients require individualized and situational treatment, guidance, and (if needed) continued observation, surveillance, and ongoing assessment. Individual cases have specific needs. At times, these individuals may need to be protected from themselves. In Hector's case, we never saw any mention of self-harm or violence aimed at others. In the case of others with mental health difficulties, their exposure to the public may pose a risk. Such is human nature.

The net result of the army's failure to act appropriately was that a

Eight. Bill S. 851—A Partial Victory

soldier with memory failure and mental illness was wandering around New England towns with no connection to anybody or anything.

The army, their posts, their hospitals, and other institutions all have rigid requirements in terms of procedures, processes and protocols that must be met. At times, deviation from the norm may be the best or even most logical course of action to take, and yet it would not even be considered by most military personnel. Such action would be discouraged as a rule because deviation from duty may be construed as dereliction of duty. The success of the military is rooted in discipline. Yet, when Hector failed to return from furlough, did it dawn on anybody that he might have been absent due to his mental illness?

Once outside of the army's control, dealing with a sick soldier became someone else's problem, not the military's. This was the moral equivalent of kicking the proverbial can down the road. As far as we were able to discover, nothing was done to help Hector on an individual level.

Much of Hector's confused state could have been avoided or better managed, and Hector's well-being dramatically altered for the better, had someone thought outside the immediate scope of their job, including what they did and how they did it. Sometimes conventional wisdom should be challenged, and assumptions should be questioned. It could easily be argued that these factors were among the responsibilities of the army's medical institutions. However, they were more interested in controlling Hector than helping him. Rather than giving him the help he needed, something else happened. Hector's tenure in the military was managed by the army in several ways. The recruitment branch saw to his enlistment. The battle command saw to his assignments in the theater of operations on the Western Front. The medical institutions saw to his medical and psychological care (arguably poorly). The judicial branch saw to his castigation and punishment. By all measures, Hector did not have a positive experience with the army.

In a military or paramilitary organization, a large emphasis is given to duty, protocol, and the chain of command. While an organization may still focus on solving problems, sometimes success can get mired down in process and procedure. Those who treated Hector medically probably had a checklist of items they could or should do. We doubt that there was any intention on the army's part to harm Hector, but their decisions may not have been the right ones from Hector's perspective. We know the army does not have a reputation for readily admitting mistakes. (Just ask the Bonus Army.) The army leaders dealt with Hector as best they knew how. It seems natural that the army would prefer to fulfill its obligation, but it would be easier to no longer have to deal with him. In 1920, the army had more than just Hector to contend with. There were large numbers of combat-related symptoms being reported at that time, many of which appeared in veterans without physically visible injuries. The sheer number of relief bills brought before Congress to rectify the harm done by wrongful discharges served as proof of that fact. As stated earlier, in the session of Congress during which Hector's bill was enacted, there were over one hundred similar personal relief bills introduced. It is reasonable to think that other sessions of Congress presented more of these bills around that time. A cursory review of the congressional record supports this assumption. And it is probable that not all cases deserving such political action as Hector's were fortunate enough to be brought before Congress or influencers who could make that happen. That speaks to the enormity of the problem.

In our view, the greatest travesty in Hector's case was the general court-martial itself. It was the big-time trouble two-step, a dance with the devil. The second greatest travesty that would befall Hector was that his mental condition was not considered when he was permitted to go on leave. These two actions—the failure to apply common sense before Hector's furlough coupled with his general court-martial eight years later—were tantamount to setting him up for failure. And when he did fail, the army let him have it with both barrels. They would arrest, charge, incarcerate, and strip all benefits from him, making this his death sentence. Then they threw him out.

The consequences of dishonorable discharges often resulted in veterans becoming homeless or getting arrested by the police for acting out in public and not being able to adequately explain themselves or their actions. These were all distinct possibilities, as was suicide. The army must have felt they had no obligation, accountability, or liability, but if that was the case, they were grossly mistaken. They had an obligation to protect Hector. They certainly should have been held accountable if their action or inaction caused an adverse event to occur. The army created this situation. It might not have been required protocol on some checklists back then, but someone should have asked Hector what his plans were when he went out on leave. Not doing so defies logic.

It seems rather than helping him, they created conditions that had a deleterious effect on him. It was the perfect storm, an amalgamation of doing nothing, failing to make the right decisions, and then doing the wrong thing—a decade's worth of governmental nonfeasance, misfeasance, and malfeasance. This is the U.S. Army bureaucracy at its worst.

While there might be some who believe this congressional bill was a total success, there are others who have different thoughts. It was not the do-all, end-all, be-all remedy it was made out to be. Many people familiar with this situation believe that the personal relief bill did not go far enough. In their view, Hector was short-changed and should have received back pay and financial compensation for the suffering to which he was subjected. Many accompanying bills for others were specifically designed to grant pensions. Hector should have at least been awarded his back pay and allowances for the misery the war and general court-martial exposed him to, the inadequate treatment he received, and his mistreatment by his superiors in the chain of command. In total, the fight at home against the Goliath that was the bureaucracy of the army left Hector drained and helpless. The army could have and should have done a better job dealing with him.

Financial and Economic Impacts

Hector was unemployable for at least eight years, from 1920 through 1928. Had he not been taken into custody by the army in 1928 and incarcerated until his trial, he might have remained unemployable for the rest of his life and unable to receive treatment for his mental health problems. He was denied the opportunity to make a decent living because of his impairment, which was a result of fighting in World War I. If you believe, like we do, that his affliction was due to his military service, then you must conclude that this rough patch was not the result of anything Hector did or did not personally do. While he was able to find work, he could not hold onto jobs for very long due to his absentmindedness (PTSD) stemming from his military service. Despite his good nature, his employers had to let him go. His wife was forced to support him, despite her physical disability. There came a point in time when the couple had to move back in with Grace's mother. This was around the time Grace's father died. It was not a pleasant period, and things must have been getting desperate. Yet, if not for the benevolence and goodness of his wife and her family, Hector's life could have taken a darker, downward spiral into the abyss of a hopeless and homeless existence—or worse.

In addition to being mentally incapacitated, job prospects were not particularly good in general during that era. Hector was adversely affected by the convergence of his mental condition and the prevailing economic circumstances. Conditions were such that there was no room for errors. We saw the reports of his employers doing their best to keep him on their payrolls, but their businesses were suffering due to his chronic condition. This had become Hector's way of life. This was the path he had been on for eight years, and there were no off-ramps in sight.

Sharp deflationary recession set off the 1920–1921 depression.[7] The "forgotten depression," as it later became known, saw "the U.S. stock market fall by 50%, corporate profits declined by over 75%," and there was a sharp rise in unemployment, followed by unprecedented currency deflation. The "Roaring Twenties" ushered in robust growth when the American public discovered the stock market and dove in headfirst.[8] Unfortunately, the Great Depression of 1929 was much worse than its predecessor nearly a decade earlier.[9] "The stock market would eventually drop almost 90% from its peak."

By the end of 1929, the Great Depression became a worldwide phenomenon. The economic calamity hit America and Europe with full force. By 1933, 25 percent of all workers and 37 percent of all nonfarm workers in the United States were completely out of work. The economy began to recover in 1933 but stalled for most of the following two years. The American economy had yet to fully recover from the depression when the United States was drawn into World War II in December 1941.

Economists and historians agree that the Great Depression was one of the country's largest and most catastrophic events. It is often called a "defining moment" in twentieth-century history. Its most lasting effect was a transformation of the role of the federal government in the economy. Simply put, inactivity followed by overreaction contributed to the Great Depression. The long contraction and painfully slow recovery changed economic thinking and led many to accept and even call for a vastly expanded role for government, although most businesses resented the growing federal control of their activities.

The federal government assumed responsibility for many of its most vulnerable citizens with the creation of the Social Security Act for those who had been employed, giving the unemployed compensation for a brief period.[10] The Social Security Act of August 14, 1935 (H.R. 7260), was passed to provide for the general welfare of citizens by establishing a system of federal old-age benefits and enabling the country to make more adequate provision for elderly persons, blind persons, dependent and disabled children, maternal and child welfare, public health, and the administration of unemployment compensation laws. The act also established a Social Security Board, raised revenue, and had other purposes specified within it.

The job creation of Franklin Delano Roosevelt's "New Deal," combined with a flood of government investment in the private sector in preparation for World War II, jolted the country out of the depression.[11] However, there is disagreement among economists regarding whether the depression would have ended sooner with less government intervention, and some also felt the protections put in place for citizens were very much needed. While there may have been conflicting views on this period, the fact remains that it was a very trying time in American history.

Regardless, the emergence of all these factors, coupled with then-present economic and personal influences, could just as well have been called Hector's "Raw Deal." However, now that he was on the road to recovery and in a better state of mind, things were improving. He continued to be gainfully employed over the next three decades and maintained membership in several professional organizations. His network of professional contacts was expanding, and his career was on an upward trajectory.

The Aftereffects of Psychological Help

As time passed, Hector was finally able to get the psychological help that he needed at the Worcester State Hospital because his military dishonorable discharge was upgraded to an honorable discharge.

Once known as the Worcester State Asylum, the Worcester Lunatic Asylum and the Bloomingdale Asylum, the hospital dates to January 12, 1833, when it opened as the Worcester Insane Asylum. It is nice to know that some of our nomenclature for these types of treatment centers has improved. Most people understand the concept behind a state hospital (a public psychiatric hospital) and prefer to use this term over lunatic or insane asylum, which many find offensive for several reasons. We learned Hector would have weekly sessions there, and we surmise that the treatment was helping him, as he was holding steady employment and he improved his engagement in society in general. He was increasingly becoming more socially and financially independent.

As we mentioned previously, Grace had a close relative who was institutionalized before 1910 at the Worcester State Asylum. The name of the institution had evolved slightly over the years, with "Insane" being removed from its formal name by 1910. This fact regarding her family member corroborated our previous belief that Grace seemed more empathetic than most people when confronted with accepting mentally challenged individuals and understanding their situation. She and her family had experienced it first-hand. Hector was indeed blessed when he met his amazing Grace!

Whether Hector would have gotten the professional help he needed had the congressional bill not been enacted is debatable. We can see his life became more even keeled after its passage. Anyone who participated in these extraordinary efforts must have been happy and considered the endeavor a remarkable success. Hector's case was the epitome of what social service agencies in Worcester should look like. The American Red Cross could likewise call his story one of their great successes.

NINE

The Final Three Decades

Works Progress Administration and World War II Draft Card (1937–1942)

A local newspaper article dated April 24, 1937, in the *Worcester Evening Gazette*, reported that Hector was employed at that time by the Works Progress Administration (WPA),[1] as were many other Americans. He worked as a piano player for a tap-dancing class the WPA sponsored at a local Union Canadian Center in Worcester.[2] During our research, we found this type of "class" was instituted by the Federal Music Project, a part of the New Deal program "Federal Project Number One," which was formed in September 1935 to provide employment for qualified artists, musicians, actors, and authors.[3] The primary objective of the Federal Music Project (1935–1939) and the subsequent WPA Music Program (1939–1943) was to employ professional musicians registered on the relief rolls.[4] The project employed these musicians as instrumentalists, singers, concert performers, and teachers. The general purpose of the Federal Music Project was to establish exacting standards of musicianship, to rehabilitate musicians by assisting them to become self-supporting, to retrain musicians, and to educate the public in the appreciation of musical opportunities. This report was encouraging, as we could see Hector working and taking steps to become a responsible, productive citizen. He was also able to use his love for (and mastery of) the piano as a tool of his rehabilitation, leading him to financial independence.

Professionals from the private sector were often recruited to head these programs. Dr. Nikolai Sokoloff, former conductor of the Cleveland Orchestra, was appointed director of the Federal Music Project.[5]

The Works Progress Administration was an ambitious employment and infrastructure program created by President Franklin Delano Roosevelt in 1935, during the bleakest days of the Great Depression. Over its eight years of existence, the WPA put 8.5 million Americans to work

Nine. The Final Three Decades

through a variety of projects. Best known for its public works projects, the WPA also sponsored projects in the arts, as the agency employed tens of thousands of actors, musicians, writers, and other artists. The WPA was renamed the Work Projects Administration in 1939 and employed mostly unskilled men to carry out public works infrastructure projects. They built more than 4,000 new school buildings, erected 130 new hospitals, laid 9,000 miles of storm drains and sewer lines, built 29,000 new bridges, constructed 150 new airfields, paved or repaired 280,000 miles of roads and planted twenty-four million trees to alleviate loss of topsoil during the Dust Bowl.[6] (The Dust Bowl was the result of a period of severe dust storms that damaged the ecology and agriculture of the American and Canadian prairies during the 1930s.)

Discussed next is Hector's World War II draft registration card (figure 24). At this time, Hector was 45 years old, as he indicated when this registration card was completed on April 26, 1942. It is peculiar that the card is filled out in the name of Hector H. Perry. One would think that by this time, he would be using his birth name. It could be assumed that he registered under this name, instead of Hector Perez, because it was the name he had used during his military service, allowing him to avoid any complications that might arise from administrative sources if he used his birth name.

Another understandable decision can be observed in his response to a subsequent data point—namely, "the person who will always know your

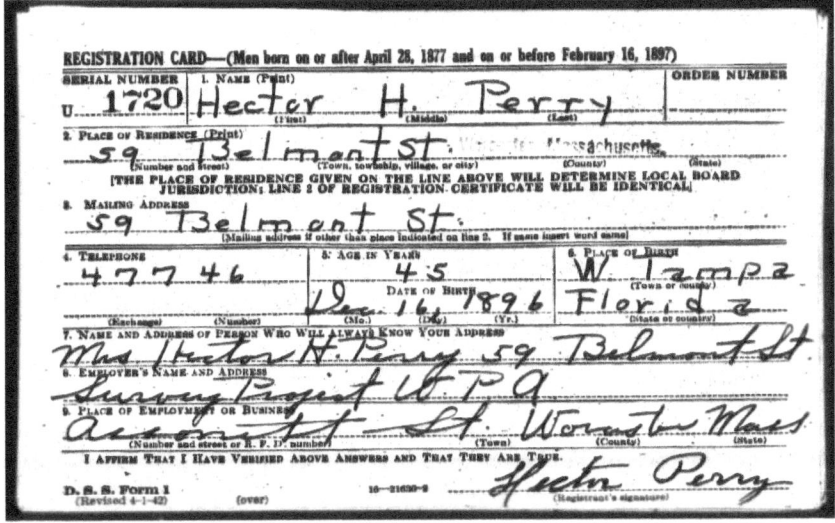

Figure 24: Hector H. Perry's (Hector F. Perez) World War II registration card.

address"—for which he put down "Mrs. Hector H. Perry." We know that he was referring to his wife, Grace Perez. It was common practice for married women to use their husband's first name, as done here. Hector may have applied the same thought process to this section that he did when asked for his name. That is the only reasonable explanation. At that time, he reported that he lived at 59 Belmont Street in Worcester with his wife. He also said he was employed by the WPA Survey Project. So, in review, we see Hector working as a piano player for the WPA in 1937, while in 1942 he was working for the WPA "Survey" Project. Regarding which "Survey" Project he worked on, we find there were two Survey Projects: (1) Survey of Federal Archives, terminated in June 1942, and (2) Historical Records Survey Project, terminated in February 1943.[7] One can only hope that he had been employed continuously for these five years.

Family Trips to Cuba and the United States (1937–1956)

Circling back for a moment, among the documents that we reviewed during our research was a September 3–4, 1937, ship's manifest for the SS *Cuba*, which sailed from Havana to Tampa. This route was exceedingly popular in the 1930s and was operated by the P & O (Peninsular and Occidental) Steamship Company, which also owned another vessel, the SS *Florida* (built in 1931 and capable of accommodating more than six hundred passengers), that followed the same route.[8] Hector's name is located directly in the center of the document, fourteen lines from the top and fourteen lines from the bottom.[9] We believe his wife Grace did not go with him, as her name did not appear on the manifest. This passenger list documents the first time that Hector traveled to Cuba, as far as available records show.

His father Charles moved to Cuba after the death of his second wife in 1932, and he stayed there for the remainder of his life, though he was known to visit family in Key West and Tampa occasionally. Charles died in late 1937, but the exact date of his passing is unknown due to our inability to obtain vital statistic records (or even church or cemetery records) from Cuba, as well as the absence of personal family knowledge about the exact date of the event from still-living relatives. We know only that it was after late 1937. We believe the reason for Hector's trip to Cuba was likely to visit his father, who had become ill. Charles was living with his daughter Evangelina, her husband Esteban Silvestre Fernandez Quintanal Barroso, their three children, and Esteban's extended family members in Cuba. Hector learned about having siblings in 1931, as reported earlier, and there must have been some form of communication between the family members that was not previously highlighted in any of the news articles after their reunification in 1931. Otherwise, how would Hector have known his father and sister Evangelina were in Cuba? Our folder contained no data that revealed travel to or from Cuba. Family lore has it that Hector did in fact stay connected with his sister and father in Cuba. Hector had to have become aware of the fact that his father was not well at some point in time.

The next piece of the record we will discuss is a group family photograph that was in the possession of coauthor Lina Palmer's mother, "Bibi." It was in the documents folder discovered in 2017 after her passing. This photograph verifies the visit that Evangelina paid to Hector and Grace in Worcester prior to her death in 1952.

Figure 28 shows eight adults and two children. Six adult women are standing in the back row, one holding a young child in her arms. Three of the women are older, and three are visibly younger. The front row shows two gentlemen kneeling, one younger than the other. The younger man is holding a small girl in his arms. We know that Hector was the older of the two men kneeling. We believe the younger man was a nephew of Grace's, holding his young daughter. It is also possible this younger man was married to one of the nieces. In the back row, we find Grace and one sister, along with three younger-looking women, who we believe were Grace's nieces. The final adult female in the picture is Hector's sister, Evangelina, who was visiting from Cuba.

Among the photographs contained in this folder, we found another also taken during this visit, showing, from left to right, Grace, Hector, and Evangelina (figure 25). Here we see them smiling, a simple act that meant the world to us as relatives and researchers. The worst was behind them by the time this photo was taken. Imagine the relief Hector and his family must have felt after clearing up the legal mess created by the U.S. Army, with his healthcare benefits finally in order. By all appearances he was living a meaningful existence, earning a living teaching music, and was content. In addition, learning that his sister made the long trek from Havana to Worcester was a sign to us that they had reconnected and that this was a joyful occasion.

We know that Evangelina died in Havana, Cuba, in 1952. We also know that Hector died in 1963. Therefore, it is a given that these family photographs were taken prior to Evangelina's death in 1952. We researched records for any trips Evangelina made between Cuba and the United States. The only passenger manifests with her name were for October and December 1945. We found her name included on each of the two passenger lists as Evangelina Fernandez, age forty-seven, born in Key West. We interpreted these family photographs as another heartwarming sign that Hector was leading a normal existence and was deeply connected with family on an ongoing basis. It must have been difficult for all the Perez children to attempt to return to the childhood relationships they had enjoyed in the past, given how much had transpired since then. When Hector was reacquainted with his brother in 1931, he questioned whether his brother was truly related to him. He also had no recollection of having sisters. He had even questioned whether his father was really his father because he had no recollection of him and felt no sense of familiarity around him. Unfortunately, there is no known information regarding what the father and son spoke of when they rekindled their relationship. We have no sense of whether there was anything that Charles might have discussed with his son that resonated with anything in his memory.

Figure 25: Grace, Hector, and Hector's sister, Evangelina, late 1940s in Worcester, Massachusetts.

We also found Hector's name on a passenger manifest of a Compañia Cubana de Aviacion Flight 461 departing Havana and arriving in Miami, Florida, on March 31, 1956.[10] The reason for this visit to Cuba is unknown, and he traveled without his wife once again, only this time by air. Our records indicate, as previously mentioned, that his sister Evangelina's husband, Esteban, had died in 1944 and she had died in 1952. Their daughter Clara (Bibi), who was Hector's only niece, was married and lived in Havana. Personal family knowledge indicates that Bibi was experiencing marital troubles during that period, and, in an effort to rally around her and show familial support, her aunt Dinorah called up all the family members she could muster to come to Bibi's side in Havana during her time of crisis. As both her parents were deceased, and her two brothers resided in the United States, Bibi had no immediate family to whom she could turn. The possibility that Hector flew to Havana to offer support is not too far-fetched. With his father, brother and one sister deceased, it would not be unreasonable for Hector and his remaining living sister, Dinorah, to come to the aid of their only niece. We do not know for certain the reason for Hector's visit, but we feel this may be why.

A Man and His Music

Taught to him from an early age, the piano was Hector's favorite thing. He had been attracted to it since he could walk, and it would prove to be part of the key to his success. Family lore tells us that both Hector and his sister Evangelina were playing the piano by the age of four and five, respectively. They were the only two out of Sarah and Charles Perez's four children who showed promise and naturally gravitated to the instrument. Since Sarah taught the piano to her students mainly from home, the children grew up hearing music of all types. We know that complete mastery of any instrument requires rigorous daily practice, and up until Hector left home, he practiced and played enthusiastically. We know from Grace's comments in her letters that after they met in 1920, she noticed he would seek out the piano and play for hours on end. Although they could not afford one early in their life together, we know he attended a local Catholic church not far from his home and feel access to a piano there was a major factor in his almost daily attendance. We also learned from Grace's comments that Hector played for others frequently and found solace when playing the piano. To calculate his years of training, we know that from 1900 to 1916 he received the proper foundation from his mother. He then joined the army and did not have access to a piano until at least December 1918. However, music was in the trenches during World War I, and General John J. Pershing once remarked, "Music is as necessary to the boys as sleep and food."[11] So Hector most likely started playing again in late 1918 after the war ended and then returned home in 1919. We know he was stationed in New York and later furloughed in 1920, at which time he met Grace in Worcester. From her accounts, we learn he practiced and played until his general court-martial in May 1928. On release, he began playing again, finding solace in his music. So far that is roughly 25 years of piano playing.

It is unknown what Hector did for work between 1932 and 1937, but, as discussed earlier, we found him employed in 1937. This discovery revealed that Hector was no longer a hired hand performing menial tasks and mundane jobs. Rather, he was a music teacher, playing piano for WPA-sponsored tap-dancing classes. It is uncertain how long Hector was involved in WPA work. It may have been continuous from 1937 (when the article was printed), or even earlier, through April 1942, when he filled out his World War II draft registration card. We found evidence in Worcester city directories between 1941 and 1961 that he worked as a music teacher specializing in piano and harmony and had a studio in which he taught. He was listed in the business directory under "Music Teachers."[12] This revelation that Hector used his love of the piano as a source of gainful employment was again very uplifting.

From all the reporting we have read and all the documentation we have seen, we can safely presume that in the latter part of Hector's life, the Perez household was filled with music, just as it had been when he was growing up with his parents and siblings.

From 1954 to 1956, Hector taught music at St. Gabriel's School of Music on High Street in Worcester.[13] The music center was one mile from his home. St. Gabriel's was owned and operated by the Sisters of Mercy order, founded by Catherine McAuley in Ireland in 1832. The Sisters of Mercy arrived in Worcester in 1854 and opened the first hospital in the city, St. Elizabeth's, located on Shrewsbury Street (it closed in 1871 when Worcester opened City Hospital). In addition, "they opened St. Gabriel's School for Girls and, in 1901 opened the Nazareth Home for Boys." The sisters remained busy and opened several parochial schools in the area for some years. "They also opened the St. Gabriel School of Music where young people could learn to play musical instruments." This is where Hector landed, from an occupational standpoint. He was now teaching young students to play the piano or sing. This work must have been very gratifying for Hector. He was fulfilling his destiny. Piano playing was not just a pastime for Hector; it was a way of life and a source of income. He was available as a resource for students needing private lessons.

Grace also must have felt a sense of relief and much satisfaction, happiness, and joy. She stood by her man through thick and thin, but she was not a passive partner. She advocated for him and was an integral part of his restoration and recovery. She, too, had been through a lot and was now seeing the payoff from their hard work together. Imagine what it would be like to see one's partner succeed and flourish after the ravages of war and the resulting injustice almost finished him off. Without Grace at his side and her efforts on his behalf, it is quite likely that Hector would not have been able to function successfully or independently in society. He may not have even survived for very long without Grace being there for him.

In our continued search for evidence of Hector's sources of

employment, we found him listed in the 1955 edition of the "National Directory of Piano Teachers, United States of America"[14] (figures 26 and 27). The upper portion of the page provided information about the resource itself, and the bottom portion displayed the list of members located in Worcester. On the fifth line, the name "Hector Perez" appears. His surname is followed by the initials "F.M.," which is the designation of membership in the Federation of Musicians. His home address was given as 59 Belmont Street, which is the same address he used when he filled out his World War II draft registration card in 1942. This discovery told us that he most probably lived at the same address for at least 15 years. Joining professional organizations illustrates his sense of civic engagement and his ongoing participation in his chosen field.

Music is certainly as unique as the human psyche. Hector is an example of how a formally trained pianist, who, after being exposed to the ordeals of war, may have forgotten his family, where he was from, and even his own identity, but he never forgot how to play music. Think of how profound that is. Piano playing was such an inherent part of his being and so naturally soothing that he also turned to it when times were tough. He used it like someone thirsty needs water, seeking a release from the difficulties he experienced daily and relief from things he did not understand. Music was a source of peace for him and gave him comfort when he was brooding and melancholy. We knew Hector had a small music studio where he would tutor students, and this space was probably where he would go to get away. Many of the letters that we found reported how much he loved to play the piano, make music, and entertain others with his talent. How is it that he remembered his music but not his own family, much less his own identity? During our research, we discovered examples of documented cases of musicians who suffered from amnesia and yet still

NATIONAL DIRECTORY OF PIANO TEACHERS
UNITED STATES OF AMERICA

DIRECTORY OF MEMBERS OF THE NATIONAL GUILD and the
AMERICAN COLLEGE OF MUSICIANS

The following list includes the names of all members who were affiliated with the Guild by July 1, 1955. See New Member Division for those who joined later.

Figure 26: Page heading of the 1955 National Directory of Piano Teachers, which lists Hector as a member.

WORCESTER, MASSACHUSETTS

Desplaines, Florence L., 141 Grand St.
Johnson, Mrs. Mildred E., 332 Day Bldg.
LeClerc, Mrs. Philippe, 69 Hamilton
Levenson, Mrs. Madelyn Sadick, 21 S. Lenox St.
Perez, Hector, 59 Belmont St. (F.M.)
Powers, Mr. Augustine (Gus), 306 Main St., Room 445
Rawling, Miss Norma Lucille, 58 Briarcliff Rd.
Roberts, Doris M., 225 Fairmont Avenue
Sinclair, Anna L., 42 Circuit Avenue
Splane, Gertrude Brodeur, 17 Ashmont Ave. (F.M.)
Walker, Benjamin G., 63 Mason
Weiner, Mrs. Dorothy H., 5 Dudley Pl.

Figure 27: 1955 directory listing for the Federation of Musicians (F.M.) revealing Hector's membership.

remembered how to play their instrument of choice.[15] The part of the brain that stores musical abilities is in a separate area from the part that retains episodic memories. In this regard, Hector would be considered "normal."

From 1956 to 1958, Hector was reportedly affiliated with the music department at Catholic University (CUA) in Washington, D.C. We also found mention of this connection later in Hector's obituary. To date we have had no success in finding archived records to corroborate this affiliation via email communications with CUA's archivists, who searched but produced no results. In 1950, a music department was established at Catholic University of America.[16] By 1956 the final addition was made to the music department building, and by 1967 it was named "Ward Hall," after Dr. Justine Ward. Its first chairman, John Paul, was a musician and scholar at the College of William and Mary and was recruited to head the newly formed music department. Under Dean Paul's leadership, the department became the School of Music in 1965. Nearly twenty years later, in spring 1984, the school was named the Benjamin T. Rome School of Music, in honor of alumnus, trustee emeritus, and longtime friend and benefactor Benjamin T. Rome. Today there is a recital hall named "John Paul Hall" (or JPH, as it is more commonly known).

We learned that Hector had a music studio from the 1940s through the 1960s, and the studio contained a piano. We also learned from Dale relatives that he had a piano at home. We are uncertain as to when he obtained either of the pianos. This development revealed to us that his economic situation had improved, and he could afford the luxury of owning two pianos. Upright pianos in the 1940s came in many price ranges,

Nine. The Final Three Decades   153

from low-end models of a few hundred dollars to high-end models costing a few thousand dollars.[17] Used pianos were another option for those on a budget. Regardless of whether the pianos were new or used, this was a major leap forward from his previous situation of being a low-income earner and clearly indicates how things had been progressing, slowly but surely. His life condition was much improved, and he was earning higher wages, heading in the right direction. Hector had been performing meaningful work doing something he enjoyed since at least 1937. As the mysterious elixir, music had helped restore Hector to a state of equilibrium. His life finally appeared to have reached a return to normalcy. The catalyst was the gift of music, a blessing from his mother and Creator. However, his health and success in later years was due primarily to the unwavering support of Grace.

There now seemed to be a steadiness about Hector and the way he lived. He was a creature of habit and stuck to a routine. He embraced the status quo. He lived in the same place for well over a decade. He enjoyed sustained professional affiliations in professional organizations and attended a Men's Prayer Group at Our Lady of Fatima Church, his neighborhood Catholic church, rarely missing a meeting.[18]

He dressed in a conservative fashion and continued to get along well with others. The uncertainty of the past was finally over. It was not immediately noticeable, and it had not happened swiftly or easily, but Hector had finally turned the corner. If one were to pass him in the street in the 1940s, 1950s, or 1960s, no one could ever imagine all he had been through. We learned he did not talk about his war experiences because he had no recollection of them. Aside from his musical talents, he had become totally unremarkable. This was a most welcome change for all involved.

From 1961 up until a few months prior to his death in August 1963, we know Hector only tutored students at home.

Not many photos of Hector are known to exist. Once Grace entered his life, he was aligned with her family more than his own birth family. With his mother gone and no children of his own, it is understandable why so few pictures of him exist. Aside from the one displayed in figure 28, and one printed with his obituary, there are only a handful of others we know exist.

We know that musical talent ran deep within the Velasco line, especially in Hector's immediate family. Like him, his mother Sarah and his sister Evangelina were highly accomplished pianists. As previously mentioned, there were several other Velasco family members who were also musically talented.

According to family lore, and as you will read in his obituary, Hector was credited with composing the popular song "Dardanella."[19] Following

Figure 28: Hector (cropped) in a photograph taken in the late 1940s in Worcester, Massachusetts.

this YouTube link will take you to the 1919 recording of "Dardanella": https://www.youtube.com/watch?v=cgLeNIfgFuY.

Published by McCarthy and Fisher, Inc., "Dardanella" was successful right from the start. The first recording was made by bandleader Ben Selvin at Victor Studios, which was owned by the RCA-Victor Company, which merged from two earlier companies—the Victor Talking Machine Company (founded in 1901 after the development of the cylinder phonograph) and the Radio Corporation of America (better known as RCA, which was formed in 1919 by the General Electric Company). It went into the business of producing phonographs, providing consumers with recorded music and sounds and the means of playing them, which at the time was a new concept. The Radio Corporation of America spawned several supporting businesses, like RCA-Victor, to better manage its growing interests.

"Dardanella" was recorded in New York City on November 20, 1919, and released in December 1919. The single reached number one status the following month and held that position for 13 weeks. It also topped the charts and ranked number one for the year 1920. It became the second-highest-selling single of the 1920s. The recording by Selvin broke records by becoming the first record to sell more than three million copies.

Nine. The Final Three Decades

It would go on to sell more than five million copies. It appeared as if "Dardanella" was not your ordinary run-of-the-mill catchy tune, as it established and set numerous industry benchmarks. We can only make an educated guess that Hector could have composed the tune and the music and then sold the rights. However, we were not able to find any evidence that he had indeed composed and sold the rights to the song. We were never optimistic that we would.

As with all recordings, there was a warning placed on the front-page ad in the January 2, 1920, edition of *Variety* magazine that warned "thieves and pirates" not to "imitate, copy, or steal any part of 'Dardanella.'" At that time, the market was rife with unauthorized copies, and knockoffs in general were a hot commodity. The warning served as a safeguard to protect against this type of piracy.

Over the decades, there have been several recordings of "Dardanella," starting in 1920, and later including one by Bing Crosby and Louis Armstrong on their 1960 album *Bing & Satchmo*.[20] This was three years before Hector's death. What a thrill it must have been to know that iconic entertainers like Bing and Satchmo were recording his work and that it was so well received by the public, even after 40 years. "Dardanella" was later performed by Geoff and Maria Muldaur (of "Midnight at the Oasis" fame) in 1974.[21] Lawrence Welk also played it.[22] The song was receiving airtime for over five and a half decades.

As previously mentioned, Hector is not credited as the official composer of record for "Dardanella," but we need to ask the question: Is it possible that he could have been? We wondered how this story originated. From a timeline perspective, it easily fits that Hector could have composed the music and even written the lyrics to it. Could he have entered into an agreement that he did not fully understand if he had in fact sold the rights to it? As a young man in his early twenties, how well versed could he have been in these matters? It is also possible that he sold the rights knowingly. He may have needed money. This was during the period before he was furloughed, when he was stationed in New York. One thing is for certain: Hector would gravitate toward locations where music was played, such as nightclubs and churches. No one knows what his frame of mind was except that it was lacking in clarity, to say the least. Between his return from France in July and the recording date of November 1919, there was an opportunity for this transaction to take place. Although the war was officially over, Hector was experiencing war fog and was not in a good mental state at all during that period. Nothing was found to indicate he was under any sort of military confinement at that time. It is more than likely that his mental issues existed around the time he sold the rights to "Dardanella" (if he indeed had).

There may be no record of a transaction even if one did take place. In this case, it likely would have been a private transaction, so there would be nothing publicly available about it. Naturally, there must be some reason behind how this bit of family folklore started, but we cannot explain it. Since Hector did not meet his birth family again until 12 years after the composition went public, one would think the story had to have started with him. He would have shared this information first with his wife Grace, and later she would have included this story in his obituary. We believe that while he was forgetful, he was not a liar. There must be some basis of truth to the story. Facts are sometimes embellished, but families usually do not make things up. Unfortunately, our efforts to find evidence to support this story have proved fruitless. The answers to these questions are speculative.

Lost Potential

Suppose for one minute that Hector did in fact compose "Dardanella." He most likely composed it sometime prior to or following his return to the United States. He would probably have needed to have a piano at his disposal at some time. But then again, maybe not. Musical genius has no boilerplate that must be rigidly followed. And at a base level, every creation is created twice. First, it is born in the mind of the composer, and then it is brought to life in writing with instrumentation for others to experience. Regardless of the methodology, the need for a piano is at some point elemental in the process. It is doubtful that Hector would have had access to a piano while he was in the trenches in France. But it is plausible he could have developed the tune in his head. Songwriters often begin with notes and tunes in their head. As noted earlier, the army considered music essential and went as far as having "song leaders" to help soldiers sing in unison. In Hector's obituary, we read that he "wrote Dardanella during the war." We cannot tell when he composed the song, since he could have done so years earlier and then got around to putting it on paper later.

As for finding a piano, it is more likely that he would find access to the instrument following his return from the war. However, we do know Hector was in France and maybe Germany after the fighting ended on November 11, 1918, through April 17, 1919, for a period of five months. Then he was hospitalized. Being stationed overseas would give him plenty of opportunities to find a place where music and a piano were available. He was out of the hospital by May 7, 1919, and sailed home on July 5, 1919.

While no one knows for sure when Hector may have composed

"Dardanella," it seems logical to assume that it would have been before the November 1919 recording. As genius knows no boundaries, any timeframe prior to its release is plausible.

One could only wonder what the possibilities might have been if Hector had not been shackled by the adverse events that would overtake his life over the subsequent decade and a half. Had conditions been right to nurture his talent, who knows what he might have been capable of accomplishing? It is quite possible that "Dardanella" may have been one of Hector's minor accomplishments. It is also possible that he could have created several masterpieces if his life had offered favorable conditions and if he had not been encumbered with so many monumental challenges over such a sustained period. This is just another aspect that cannot be quantified. Hector's musical potential may have been limitless. Unfortunately, given the circumstances, not much could have been on his mind other than the challenges he continually faced. By the 1940s, we find that he was settling down, most probably due to the treatment he was receiving from weekly visits with psychiatrists. From early reports, we know that Hector wanted and sought professional help. He fought hard to get his benefits reinstated so that he could have access to critically needed psychological treatment, which was a costly endeavor back then, as it still is today.

Via Ancestry.com, we connected with a person online whose grandmother was one of Grace's sisters. She related a story about Hector's talent, of which she had first-hand knowledge. Her grandmother had married and moved from Worcester to another state. The Dale descendant we met told us how her family would make an annual trip back to Worcester. She and her grandmother took a train to Massachusetts for their visit. Although they stayed at her granduncle's house, they spent a full day with her grandaunt Grace and Alfred, as the family still called him by this name, even though they learned in 1928 that his true name was Hector. He was always referred to as Alfred by his wife's family.

As a young girl, this Dale descendant learned to play piano and had been doing so for four years before this trip to Worcester. During their visit with Grace and Alfred, at the behest of the grandmother, Alfred sat the young girl down at his piano and taught her to play a boogie-woogie song titled "Saltwater Boogie."[23] This song can be easily found on the web. It was composed in 1946 and can be used as an effective training tool when teaching piano to students. Judging from this anecdote, Hector was a knowledgeable and talented teacher. Good piano teachers understand the potential benefits of learning and playing boogie-woogie tunes. Boogie-woogie music often features a driving bass line played with the left hand while the right hand plays melodic and rhythmic patterns. This practice can enhance left-hand independence and dexterity, which is valuable for various piano styles. In addition, boogie-woogie is helpful for ear training, as it encourages students to listen carefully to the music and develop their ear for harmonies, chords, and melodic variations. These piano exercises can improve their overall musicality and ability to play by ear. From the city directories we pored over, we learned Hector also taught harmony.[24] So, by piecing the data together, we found he was a well-informed teacher and understood the muscle memory aspects of playing the piano. Had Hector not spent years struggling with amnesia and trying to cope with all the hardships he experienced because of it, his professional life would have been very different. He was continually playing "catch up" and would have been better off had he been gainfully employed and building his small business all along. Rather than closing restaurants and making the morning coffee, he could have been carving out his own place in society, fitting in, and blazing new trails.

Hector had the young student play, and she memorized the song in a matter of hours. She described Alfred as very patient and the best piano instructor she ever had. She added that it was plain to see how much her Aunt Grace and Alfred were in love. This story was so heartening to us. Grace deserved no less.

From what she remembered, this relative believes Grace lost her leg as a teenager; however, the 1930 Associated Charities letter stated that she had "worn an artificial right leg ever since she was six years old." This history in the letter came from Grace herself as an adult woman recounting her background to the Associated Charities. In either case, it makes no difference. This Dale relative recalled that Grace used crutches. This information is also verified by photographs depicting Grace using crutches, with one leg clearly missing (see figure 25). This relative further informed us that Alfred meant a lot to her grandaunt. She described Grace as the sweetest lady of all the females in her entire family. In August 1960, three years prior to Hector's passing, Grace attended her grandniece's out-of-state wedding. That would be the last time this young lady would see Grace.

Future Prospects

Consider how bleak Hector's prospects looked between 1920 and 1931. He truly had little understanding of the real world he lived in. Misfiring synapses and neurons were his soup du jour.

At times he was abandoned and neglected, abused, mistreated, punished, and victimized by his own government, which he had so nobly served. Despite the significant ways and the number of times he was subjected to unfortunate events, he managed to survive and rise above all the chaos, confusion, and mistreatment. In retrospect, for a man who at one time lost touch with reality, his mind forming a cocoon to subconsciously protect itself, his ultimate accomplishments were nothing short of remarkable.

It is still true today, as it was back then, that some veterans with mental disorders seek to end it all rather than deal with their hopeless situation. Many have had to grapple with issues like those that Hector had to contend with. In 2020, it was reported that while suicide rates were slightly lower than they had been in 2019, there were 6,146 veteran suicides, with an average of seventeen veterans committing suicide every day, according to the Veterans Health Administration.[25] That year, the suicide rate for veterans was 57.3 percent higher than for non-veteran U.S. adults, a problem that also existed during Hector's time. Little progress has been seen in terms of the raw numbers of veteran suicides over the past 20 years.[26] News of the veterans' suicide rate was part of a report that also revealed the Veterans Crisis Line had failed for ten years to save text messages for future follow-up. This was indeed a costly lesson.

Take into consideration that Hector lived during a time of great uncertainty and struggle. Times were financially tough for most Americans, including Hector and Grace. As a teenager, he went through a somber period, having lost his mother to a disease that had been around for centuries but is treatable today. Not long after losing his mother, his nuclear family split up. He voluntarily enlisted and risked his life to fight for his country. He fought in several of the most brutal battles in military history. He managed to emerge from these battles alive and physically in one piece, but the mental and emotional effects he suffered were as complex as they were grim. Many of the causes of his illness were still unknown and just being recognized by psychiatric professionals at the time, and treatments were still evolving. The science in this field was in its infancy.

Without the benefit of a roadmap or template to follow, we saw how Hector and Grace tried their best to figure out a way to eventually beat the odds. There is little doubt that Grace led the charge. Hector went from a confused, lost young man who could not hold down a menial job doing the simplest of tasks to a highly accomplished professional who taught piano, sought and earned membership to professional organizations, and influenced the lives of many people for the better. He demonstrated that his success in becoming a productive member of society by virtue of the longevity of gainful employment in his chosen field, coupled with the professional affiliations he maintained over a sustained period. He found his niche in professional settings teaching music and harmony in his community. The length of his marriage also stood the test of time. He faced arduous afflictions and oppressive obstacles. Yet he overcame these dire challenges and achieved success. His goals were few but necessary, as he longed to be a self-sustaining human being, sharing a life with someone he loved, contributing to society and improving their lot along the way. He achieved that goal with the help of Grace. Without her, things might have turned out quite differently for him.

Grace's high school education, followed by university-level business courses and work experience in a suburb of Boston, gave her knowledge of many things Hector was not aware of.[27] She was the one who knew how to get these sorts of things accomplished. Would Hector, on his own, have known how to navigate through all of this mess? Our bet is that Grace was the one who had that acumen and was aware of how to seek aid from social services and representatives of her district in Congress. Hector may not have been, due to reasons related to geography and their work history. Hector had been a cigar maker in Key West with a high school education and rigorous daily piano practice. His wife's knowledge base and circle of influence was greater than his. Chances are that Grace had the requisite knowledge and experience to identify potential resources, initiate contact with the necessary people, and do all the networking needed.

Nothing was easy for Hector, even before Grace came into his life. She was the most important person in his life and on the same level of importance that music was. Grace and music were his most valuable assets, and both helped Hector succeed over the course of his lifetime. The saying "there's someone for everyone" was proven true in this case. With no apparent special skills, Grace was Hector's greatest blessing at the time of his greatest need, which persisted for over a decade. His disease was insidious, deceptive, and not easily identifiable. She left no stone unturned to get Hector the help he needed.

Eventually, Hector received the psychological help necessary to mold him into a productive citizen, allowing him to provide for his family. The remainder of his life turned out to be one that anybody would be proud of. He had indeed reached normalcy and made inroads into a fruitful and loving existence. From the time they married, Hector maintained a close relationship with Grace's family, the only family he knew from the onset of his amnesia. There is no doubt that God put Grace in Hector's life for a reason. He and Grace were married for 42 years before he died.

The Death of Hector Francis Perez (1963)

A certified copy of Hector's death certificate revealed his true full name for the first time—Hector Francis Perez. Hector died on August 30, 1963, at 3:15 p.m. at his home, which was 4 Oakwood Place in Worcester.[28] He died of a heart attack brought on by hardening of the arteries, which had been diagnosed six years earlier. He had lived in Worcester for 42 years. He was 66 years, 8 months, and 14 days old when he passed away. His wife Grace Perez was the informant for the death certificate, a copy of which was obtained from the Registry of Vital Records and Statistics, Department of Public Health for the Commonwealth of Massachusetts. It was requested in March 2023 and is now stored in the family archives.

The death certificate noted Hector was born in East Tampa, Florida, the son of the late Charles Perez and Sarah (Velasquez) Perez. Hector's father's full name and place of birth are correct as they appear on the death certificate, as were his mother's first name and her place of birth. Her surname, however, was not "Velasquez," as recorded on the certificate; it was "Velasco." Grace may have mistakenly used Velasquez as Hector's mother's maiden name, as this was the middle name or second surname Hector used when they married in 1921 (Alfredo Velasquez Sanchez) and she was more familiar with it. She would have heard the surname Velasco very infrequently, and probably only in 1931, when Hector was reunited with his family and she learned his mother's full name.

Grace lived with Hector at the time of his death. She chose to stay for better or for worse. She was truly an exemplary woman and stood by her convictions. Grace would live another 11 years after Hector died. She passed away on July 8, 1974. Hector and Grace are both buried at St. John's Cemetery in Worcester, in a Dale family plot. When all is said and done, Grace could have easily been thought of as Hector's guardian angel. During our research, we learned that Grace wrote poetry, and we are optimistic that one day we might be able to locate and secure some of her writings and share them publicly.

On September 1, 1963, Hector's lengthy obituary appeared on page 54 of the *Worcester Telegram* complete with a photo of him. It credited the longtime piano teacher with being the composer of "Dardanella," as we previously mentioned. The obituary reported that Hector composed "Dardanella" during the war. According to his family, he soon thereafter sold the rights to the song. It was likely Grace who gave the newspaper the pertinent details about her husband's life. As we surmised earlier, this assertion about Hector writing the song probably originated with Hector himself. He had no contact with his birth family after his mother died in 1916 or at the time of his enlistment in March 1917; later, he was stricken with amnesia. If he wrote "Dardanella" during the war, it is unlikely that his birth family would have even heard the story until after he became reacquainted with them in 1931.

The subheading for the obituary referred to Hector as a piano teacher and composer. This description is interesting, as it causes one to wonder whether Hector had composed any other musical scores. The clear implication is that Hector wrote music in addition to playing the piano. Given that he was called a composer in the obituary, there must be some basis in truth for that comment, even beyond the "Dardanella" composition. It is very unlikely that Grace or anyone else just made up this story to exaggerate.

Hector taught piano lessons at his home for many years, up until two months before his death. Our Lady of Fatima hosted the funeral service at 9:00 a.m. A Solemn High Mass (which is a full ceremonial form of Mass) was offered. O'Connor Brothers Funeral Home, 592 Park Avenue in Worcester, handled the funeral arrangements. During our research, we contacted the funeral home to see whether they had any notes in Hector's file. They did not. That they even took the time to look into his file once we shared why we were looking for information was very kind. Again, kindness and goodness seem to follow Hector and Grace still.

The obituary reported that Hector was an army veteran of World War I. He left behind his widow, Grace Perez; a sister, Mrs. Dinorah Atkinson of Highlands, North Carolina; and several nieces and nephews. There was no mention of his parents, his sister Evangelina or his brother Charlie, all of whom predeceased him.

On the Find a Grave website (which is an online database of burials), a memorial was created for Hector on September 12, 2022, by a volunteer member. This memorial included all known information about him. It reported that he was born in East Tampa and not West Tampa, though both are located in Hillsborough County, Florida. Interestingly, East Tampa had a population of 800 in 1880, which expanded to 15,000 by 1900, making it one of the largest and most prosperous cities in Florida, primarily due to the founding of the cigar-centered neighborhood of Ybor City by Vicente Martinez Ybor in 1885, which brought an influx of thousands of Cubans, Spaniards, Italians, and other immigrants to the area.[29]

The online memorial has a short biography along with a hyperlink to another memorial the volunteer created for Hector's wife, Grace. There is also a link to a memorial created for his mother Sarah by another Find a Grave member with 20 years' affiliation with the group.

Hector is interred at the family gravesite located at the St. Francis Plot, Row 23, Lot 177, at St. John's Cemetery in Worcester, Worcester County, Massachusetts.

While it is true that he taught music, Hector did so much more than that. He showed others how to live and die with purpose and dignity. Family lore speaks of him being a kind and thoughtful man. He could have easily gone astray and turned to alcohol, drugs, suicide, or other harmful, destructive behavior, but he did not. He was not a lazy individual who chose not to work. He did not break things, kick the dog, beat his wife, or lash out at anyone, and he was not mean spirited. At his core, he had an affable personality, and everyone who met him liked him. Notably, Senator Walsh from Massachusetts told a reporter in 1931 after receiving Hector in his home that he was deeply moved by Hector and his situation. There was nothing in Hector's behavior that would cause one to think he felt victimized. From our research, we learned he had no chip on his shoulder. He did not present himself like that. If he was frustrated by all his troubles, he did not let it show. Instead, he would go off and play music. He conducted himself very agreeably, considering all the forces that worked against him. He was hampered by an uncommon condition, an ailment that eventually prevails over most of its victims. From all we have pieced together, he clearly knew that he could not afford to be distracted; he had to stay focused if he were going to beat this invisible ailment, amnesia.

From Grace's perspective, at first, Hector could not recall anything about his past. Then he could not hold down a job. Somewhere along the way, she saw lapses in his memory. Then the issue of his identity came into question and, while in pursuit of much-sought-after answers, he was jailed and stigmatized. The salt in the wound was that he could not access the help he needed to get back to normal because of this stigma. He then went from eight years of uncertainty to an additional three years of hell.

Through it all, Hector faced insurmountable odds and injustice. He was presented with many challenges not at all common to the average person. Then, just when it seemed as if things could not get worse, they did. Despite the unfair events that happened in their lives, Hector and Grace confronted the challenges together, with a singular focus. They stuck together through thick and thin, as the expression goes.

They faced their difficulties one step at a time, one day at a time, by putting one foot in front of the other. Like the ancient Chinese proverb says, "the journey of a thousand miles begins with a single step."[30] They were irrepressible and did not stop until they got what they were fighting for—namely, the treatment he needed. In the end, you could say they took on the system and won.

Hector was indeed the David to the government's Goliath. We are certain that Hector did not think of himself as a hero. Nevertheless, we do. The words of Joseph Campbell, famous professor on comparative mythology and "heroes," come to mind regarding Hector at this point in his life: "We're not on our journey to save the world but to save ourselves.... But in doing that, you save the world. The influence of a vital person vitalizes."[31] We are certain that Hector and Grace did not feel what they had accomplished was extraordinary or exceptional. One could argue that their pairing was divinity in action.

TEN

Understanding Wartime Trauma

History and Effects of Combat-Induced Trauma

Much of the following information is presented to offer a general overview of wartime trauma and provide a general baseline of its history, its effects, and the study and treatment of this type of trauma. Ideally, this chapter will lead you to a deeper understanding of the issue that haunted Hector and was such a prevalent part of his life for more than 15 years.

So little is understood by the public in general about wartime trauma, now known as post-traumatic stress disorder (PTSD). At best, common knowledge of this disease is fragmented and personal knowledge of its characteristics is scattered. Most people have heard of PTSD, but many cannot define it. Briefly, PTSD is the result of an individual's reaction to traumatic or shocking events, accidents, and disasters that have a lasting effect on their well-being.[1] While many of the details presented here are in depth and some of the terms used are not commonly known or understood by laypeople, it is important to understand what PTSD is holistically to grasp its true nature.

The evolution of our understanding of PTSD has been slow and painful. Wartime trauma was hard to define; therefore, it took a long time to be "officially" recognized as a psychological illness.[2] One early challenge was resistance to the idea that symptoms that were physical in nature could originate in the mind, as there was no apparent cause for the physical malady being demonstrated by the patient. It was not initially understood that psychological impacts could present as physical issues.

Symptoms of combat trauma can include flashbacks, anxiety, and frightening thoughts, all of which can be triggered by situations in everyday life, such as loud noises or a person who brings back a memory. Most people who experience a traumatic event do not develop PTSD, but for those who do, PTSD can go away on its own, or it can become chronic and last for years.

Descriptions of PTSD can be traced back to ancient Greek history and works by scholars like Hippocrates and the poet Lucretius, who wrote about people experiencing symptoms like nightmares after witnessing gruesome deaths.[3] Similar descriptions are found in *The Iliad* and *The Odyssey* as well as other classics.[4] In a 440 BC account of the battle of Marathon, Greek historian Herodotus described how an Athenian named Epizelus was suddenly stricken with blindness after seeing his comrade killed in combat. His blindness, brought on by fright and not a physical wound, persisted over many years. In the *Epic of Gilgamesh*, which dates to 2100 BC, the main character Gilgamesh witnesses the death of his closest friend, Enkidu, and is tormented by the trauma of it, experiencing recurring recollections and nightmares related to the event. Recurrent nightmares also appear in Icelandic literature, such as the *Gísli Súrsson Saga*, the events of which took place between 860 and 980 BC. In the Indian epic poem *Ramayana* (circa 5000 BC), Ravana's cousin, the demon Marrich, experiences PTSD-like symptoms (including hyperarousal, reliving trauma, and avoidance behavior) after nearly being killed by an arrow.[5] No race, nationality, religion, or culture is immune to or has a monopoly on PTSD. It is an equal opportunity offender.

In the late 1600s, Swiss physician Dr. Johannes Hofer coined the term *nostalgia* to describe Swiss soldiers who suffered from despair and homesickness, as well as classic PTSD symptoms like sleeplessness and anxiety.[6] Around the same time, German, French and Spanish doctors described similar illnesses in their military patients. Physicians wrote about nostalgia in trauma-stricken soldiers who became listless and solitary, and efforts to help them out of their lethargy did little good. Nostalgia became a common medical diagnosis that spread throughout military camps in Europe. The "disease" reached American soil during the U.S. Civil War (1861–1865).[7] Civil War soldiers exhibited the same nightmares, panic, and psychological disruptions as their predecessors, leading to research about this mysterious condition.[8]

Unfortunately, some military doctors viewed the illness as a sign of weakness and one that affected only men with a feeble will. Public ridicule was sometimes the recommended cure for nostalgia. While nostalgia described changes in veterans from a psychological perspective, other models took a physiological approach. In the United States, for example, veterans were studied, and it was found that many of them suffered from certain physical issues unrelated to wounds, such as palpitations, constricted breathing, and other cardiovascular symptoms. These symptoms were thought to arise from an overstimulation of the heart, and the condition became known as *soldier's heart*.[9] In the past several hundred years, medical doctors have described multiple PTSD-like illnesses, referred to by many terms, whose symptoms included feeling anxious and constantly on edge. Like nostalgia, soldier's heart was seen as a character defect or a personal weakness.

What made World War I different from previous wars is that improvements in weapons made combat more dangerous and frightening. Wartime technologies included tanks, flamethrowers, poison gas, much larger artillery rounds, and airplanes. During and after World War I, *shell shock*, *combat fatigue*, and *traumatic neurosis* were used to describe similar symptoms. The prevalence of what was originally referred to as shell shock meant that formal treatment for psychological trauma was needed. Soldiers who fought in World War I exhibited the classic signs of what we now recognize as PTSD, including reliving the event, avoidance, negative beliefs, and hyperarousal.[10]

British soldiers began using the term *shell shock* to describe the effects caused by exposure to military bombardments as early as 1915, when approximately 80,000 British soldiers were treated for shell shock over the course of the war.[11] The symptoms were thought to result from a kind of severe concussion to the nervous system—hence the name shell shock. Soldiers were said to have wounded minds, tremors, blurred vision, and fits, and they were unable to fight because of symptoms like fatigue, tremors, nightmares, and confusion.

Unfortunately, shell shock went from being considered a legitimate physical injury to a sign of weakness.[12] It was estimated that at least 20 percent of men developed shell shock, though the figures are murky due to physicians' reluctance to brand veterans with a psychological diagnosis that could affect disability compensation. Soldiers were typically seen as heroic and strong. Traditionalists felt a normal soldier should glory in war and betray no sign of emotion and should not succumb to terror. The soldier who developed a traumatic neurosis was thought to be constitutionally inferior, a malingerer, or a coward. When these soldiers came home unable to speak, walk or remember, with no physical reason for those shortcomings, the only possible explanation was personal weakness. Treatment methods were based on the idea that the soldier who had entered war as a hero was now behaving as a coward and needed to be snapped out of it.

But the concept of shell shock had its limitations. Cognitive and behavioral symptoms of trauma, such as nightmares, hypervigilance and avoiding triggering situations, were overlooked, as the focus was on physical symptoms. But the physical symptoms that define shell shock are often the consequences of these nonphysical symptoms. Ironically, these very same cognitive and behavioral symptoms now define PTSD.[13] The prevailing thought early in the war was that soldiers' time in the trenches with large guns caused poor nerves and physiological as well as psychological trouble. By 1916, however, medical and military authorities documented shell shock symptoms in soldiers who had been nowhere near exploding shells. These soldiers' conditions were considered *neurasthenia*—a type of nervous breakdown from war.[14] It was still encompassed by shell shock, or war neurosis. During World War I, this condition was chalked up to defective or poor moral character, just as it was during the Civil War. The sheer scale of veterans experiencing such symptoms after World War I led to the definition of *combat stress reaction*, which helped form the modern concept of PTSD.[15]

Psychological trauma experienced during the war took an unprecedented toll on veterans, many of whom suffered symptoms for the rest of their lives. These ranged from distressing memories that veterans found difficult to forget to extreme episodes of catatonia and terror when reminded of their trauma. The many principles and challenges of PTSD treatment today were first identified during World War I. Public perception of PTSD is still rooted in this past, and some of the problems discovered during World War I regarding psychological trauma still have not been resolved.

Treatment

"Treatments were harsh. Shell-shock patients could receive electroshock therapy and physical conditioning, with the aim of alleviating physical symptoms quickly. Not only were such treatments ineffective, but they were also brutal. About 80 percent of those treated were unable to serve again."[16] Treatments of the day addressed physical symptoms such as fits and tremors but were ineffective in alleviating psychological symptoms. The medical community and society at large are accustomed to looking for the simplest cause and cure for any given ailment. This approach results in a system where symptoms are discovered and cataloged and then matched with therapies that will alleviate them. Though this method works in many cases, PTSD has resisted this model.

Electroconvulsive therapies in 1918 were mostly administered without the use of anesthesia, and application in high doses for lengthy periods of up to one hour were common.[17] Treatment for traumatic neurosis also included other harsh strategies such as shaming, threats or punishment. The deepest wound was that these brutal treatments were not effective and, in some cases, caused more harm than good. As the mental health field started to expand, kinder "talking cures" were tried to rid soldiers of their symptoms.[18] Some treatments were effective, especially those talking cures that focused on the cognitive and behavioral symptoms now associated with PTSD. One army physician encouraged shell-shock patients to reconstruct their traumatic experiences, using films and simulations to help them confront their traumatic memories. These methods emphasized the cognitive and behavioral symptoms of trauma and had a much better success rate. Many modern PTSD treatments can trace their development to these talking therapies, moving away from treating only physical symptoms and placing emphasis on psychological issues, such as the distress caused by traumatic memories.

In 1941, a leading clinician, Abram Kardiner, working for the U.S. Veterans' Bureau published what would become the basis for understanding modern-day PTSD.[19] He rethought combat trauma in a much more empathetic light and speculated that these symptoms stemmed from psychological injury, rather than the soldier's flawed character. Kardiner theorized that many symptoms observed in combat veterans of World War I could be understood as resulting from chronic arousal of the autonomic nervous system—an involuntary and unconscious response. He also interpreted the irritability and explosively aggressive behavior of traumatized men as disorganized fragments of a shattered fight-or-flight response to overwhelming danger. His work in trauma-induced war neurosis helped redefine the character of those affected by these symptoms, recognizing that any man could break down under fire and that psychiatric casualties could be predicted in proportion to the severity of the individual's exposure to combat.

Work from other clinicians after World War II and the Korean War suggested that post-war symptoms could be lasting and persist anywhere from six to 20 years.[20] In some cases, these symptoms did not disappear at all. A 1951 study of 200 World War II veterans found that 10 percent still suffered from combat neurosis.[21] Evidence indicated that many of these veterans were unable to put the war behind them.

Treatment options turned toward psychoanalysis. Emotional attachments among comrades were thought to be essential to minimizing traumatic war neurosis. Those taken off the front lines for treatment often received only a week or so of care before they were placed back in the line of duty so they would not be separated from their band of brothers. When returning from war, they were asked whether they had ever talked with their families about what had happened, and the answer was invariably no. Soldiers may have tried to bury their wartime experiences and difficulties, but traumatic war neurosis did not go away.

A diagnosis called *gross stress reaction* made it into the first edition of the American Psychiatric Association's *Diagnostic and Statistical Manual of Mental Disorders* (DSM) in 1952.[22] The DSM provides the official classification of mental disorders using a common language and standard criteria. Gross stress reaction was defined as a stress disorder in response to exceptional physical or mental stress, such as a natural catastrophe or battle, occurring in people who were otherwise normal.

It was pressure from the advocacy groups that really pushed the mental health community to define PTSD. Beginning with a small march in New York in the summer of 1967, Vietnam veterans began to become activists for their own mental health care. Organizations established "rap groups" to discuss their difficulties in returning to civilian life and the terrible symptoms they experienced as a result of combat fatigue.[23] By the mid–1970s, there were hundreds of such groups around the country. Veterans had put their afflictions on the political map and redefined their symptoms as a normal response to the experience of atrocity. Society's understanding of war itself slowly began to shift as public awareness increased due to the widely televised accounts of the My Lai massacre, among other atrocities, with the horrors of war brought into American living rooms for the first time. People were gaining a better psychological understanding of the results of war.

Meanwhile, feminists participated in consciousness-raising groups, which created a forum in which to discuss their own traumas, such as rape and child abuse. As with the veterans' movement, these groups were both therapeutic and political. Out of the women's movement came crisis centers, first opened in 1971, and rape was redefined as a violent crime rather than a sex act.[24] In 1974, researchers conducted one of the first studies on rape and found that victims' symptoms matched what soldiers had experienced.[25] A pattern of symptoms (including sleeplessness, nightmares, paranoia, exaggerated startle responses, and other phobias related to the circumstances of their attack, called "rape trauma syndrome") was noted. The same symptoms observed in these studies had been noted 30 years earlier in survivors of war.

The convergence of these two political movements led to the official diagnosis of post-traumatic stress disorder, and in 1980 PTSD was added to the DSM-III.[26] Finally, trauma survivors had an official diagnosis and the validation they deserved. At first, PTSD was classified as an anxiety disorder. The latest update was in 2013, when DSM-5 was released.[27] Today PTSD is considered a trauma and a stressor-related disorder. The establishment of the PTSD diagnosis has helped in the study of the condition and in developing methods to treat it.

As the definition of PTSD has evolved, so have therapeutic techniques. Today the most popular treatments address both the physical and the mental symptoms of PTSD. Therapies range from cognitive behavioral therapy to sensorimotor processing (which involves both sensory and motor pathways and functions) to prolonged exposure therapy and other approaches.[28]

PTSD now falls into four categories: *re-experiencing* (intrusive) symptoms, which include nightmares, flashbacks and distress when reminded of the event; *avoidance* symptoms, which encompass avoiding thoughts and/or feelings about the traumatic event and avoiding things that remind one of the traumatic event, including situations, people and certain places; *hyperarousal* symptoms (physical and emotional changes), which involve being easily startled, having difficulty concentrating, experiencing anger and/or sleep issues, and engaging in reckless behavior; and *cognitive* symptoms (negative changes in thinking and mood), which entail negative thoughts about oneself or the world. Those affected by PTSD may have difficulty trusting others and find it hard to feel happy. They may also have trouble recalling important aspects of the traumatic event, and they may feel guilt or blame for or about it. Other symptoms include issues with memory loss, feelings of detachment from others, and loss of interest in previous hobbies and activities.[29]

The establishment of the PTSD diagnosis helped in the scientific study of the condition and developing evidence-based methods to treat it. A growing knowledge base from the mental health community (and increased awareness and compassion from the public) gave hope to those suffering from PTSD that true healing could now begin.

Treating PTSD can include medication, psychotherapy, or both, and the approach can vary depending on the effects of trauma on the individual and whether there were any coexisting conditions involved, such as depression or substance abuse. Psychotherapy treatment can be done in an individual setting or as part of a group.

Though the concept of shell shock shares many features with PTSD, the understanding of what constitutes trauma and the treatments for it have changed dramatically. The focus on treating underlying cognitive and behavioral symptoms has led to a great reduction in the physical consequences of trauma that were seen during World War I. The U.S. Department of Veterans Affairs estimates that nearly 14 percent of veterans returning from wars in Iraq and Afghanistan currently have PTSD.[30] A male veteran of those wars is four times more likely to develop PTSD than a man in the civilian population is. PTSD is probably at least partially responsible for the upward of sixteen veterans who commit suicide every day.[31] Service personnel are now routinely screened for symptoms of trauma before and after deployment because identifying issues early reduces the risk of developing PTSD, whereas shell-shock treatment focused on treating symptoms once they were already severe. This development represents a fundamental shift between the past and the present.

When veterans seek PTSD treatment in the VA system, policy requires that they be offered either exposure or cognitive therapy.[32] Exposure therapies are based on the idea that the fear response that gives rise to many of the traumatic symptoms can be dampened through repeated exposures to the traumatic event, whereas cognitive therapies focus on developing personal coping mechanisms, slowly changing destructive thought patterns. The most common treatment a veteran will receive includes psycho-pharmaceuticals (medications that are used to treat conditions like depression, anxiety, and psychosis). A class of drugs called SSRIs—a type of antidepressant drug that inhibits the reabsorption of serotonin by neurons, thus increasing the availability of serotonin as a neurotransmitter, which contributes to feelings of happiness—is widely used.[33]

Mental health treatment techniques include mindfulness therapies, eye movement desensitization therapy, therapies using controlled doses of MDMA (Ecstasy), virtual reality-graded exposure therapy, and hypnosis. Other creative therapies have been developed. Today the military funds research on new technologies to address PTSD, including neuro technological innovations like transcranial stimulation and neural chips, as well as novel drugs.[34] Scientific understanding has evolved a great deal since World War I.

During World War I and immediately afterward, someone other than the patient usually directed the care they received. Since then, many studies have shown that patients improve most when they have chosen their own therapy.[35] Numerous options exist now that were not available in the past. Today, even if the patient narrows their choices to those currently backed by the National Center for PTSD, they will still find themselves with five evidence-based options to consider, each of which entails a different psychomedical model of trauma and healing. These treatment options help show why people experience trauma and respond to interventions so differently. A great deal of understanding has been gained in the past one hundred years in the field, and a self-directed approach to a patient's care is at the core of these developments. This is precisely what Hector and Grace were trying to do—manage his own care. One among the two of them understood the need to take an active part in Hector's recovery from the wartime trauma he experienced. We believe that would have been Grace, with Hector included in discussions.

Other psychotherapies currently being applied for PTSD include Stress Inoculation Training, which focuses on developing skills to manage PTSD symptoms and other stressors.[36] Present-Centered Therapy is a concept of managing present-day issues affected by PTSD, and there is also Interpersonal Psychotherapy Therapy, which focuses on improving interpersonal functioning of those impacted by trauma.[37] Things have progressed a great deal in the field, but the human cost has been heartbreaking.

There is a much better understanding today of what trauma is because of the events of World War I and later wars. Many of the same challenges from a century ago are relevant today. Although modern treatments for PTSD are far more effective than those for shell shock, the stigma associated with PTSD and with the misuse of alcohol and drugs continues to be a problem. The stigma attached to mental illness still hinders people from receiving treatment, causing many to self-medicate with alcohol and or drugs instead. Self-medicating has had disastrous effects on many individuals. Such challenges are not unique to veterans. Refugees and sexual assault survivors are also deeply affected by trauma, and they often face barriers to getting proper treatment, which in turn exacerbates their PTSD.

Whereas shell shock was treated as a weakness, today PTSD is understood more compassionately. While military leaders in World War I punished soldiers for their weakness, today the ideal PTSD-afflicted veteran has taken on a role more associated with being a healthcare consumer who plays an active role in figuring out and optimizing their own therapy.

While progress has been made thanks to more than one hundred years of hindsight in studying combat-related trauma, what is still missing is an explanation as to why people have different responses to trauma and why responses vary in different historical periods. For instance, the paralysis and amnesia that typified World War I shell-shock cases are now so rare that they do not even appear as symptoms in the current DSM entry for PTSD. We still do not know enough about how soldiers' experiences and their own understandings of PTSD are being shaped by the broader social and cultural views of trauma, of war, and of gender. Although huge strides have been made in the century since World War I, PTSD remains elusive and requires continued study.

The National Institutes of Health has published detailed data regarding the prevalence of PTSD among U.S. adults aged eighteen or older.[38] It is estimated that 3.6 percent of U.S. adults had PTSD in the past year.[39] Overall, the lifetime prevalence of PTSD was 6.8 percent. Today, around 7.7 million American adults have PTSD, according to the Anxiety and Depression Association of America. The rate was higher for females (5.2 percent) than for males (1.8 percent). Some estimates say the rate of PTSD among American women is roughly 10 percent while it is around 4 percent among American males. Other studies have found that approximately 60 percent of men and 50 percent of women experience some form of trauma in their lives. In the United States, Black, Latino, and Native American populations are more likely to have PTSD than Whites.[40] PTSD can affect children as well as adults.

As laypersons, we suspect Hector's PTSD symptoms were of the cognitive type. The scant record does not show hyperarousal behaviors or avoidance symptoms. And we know for a fact he did not experience reliving the event since he had no memory of the event at all. He lost not only the memory of the traumatic event(s) but also the memory of his entire lifetime. This condition is often referred to as retrograde amnesia.[41] We know Hector's long-term memory bank was fully erased because of the severe combat trauma he experienced.

Hector's Four Known Diagnoses

Based on all the information we were able to discover throughout our research, we established that there were four professional psychological diagnoses for Hector's mental state. Three were from military doctors, while the fourth and final one was from a local Worcester psychiatrist. We do not know whether there were other diagnoses made regarding Hector's mental health; while we believe there were, we have confirmed only these four.

1. In April 1919, while still overseas, the military diagnosed Hector as having "psychoneurosis, type undetermined," which was changed from the initial misdiagnosis of alcoholism.[42] *Psychoneurosis* is no longer used in psychiatric diagnosis, while neurosis is, although the terms are interchangeable. Neurosis, as previously mentioned, is characterized as a behavioral or mental disorder of mild or moderate severity. Those afflicted with this personality disorder experience disturbing emotional symptoms such as obsessive thoughts, morbid fears, and depressive states, but without personality disorganization or loss of contact with reality. Neurosis is a term mainly used today to describe mental disorders caused by past anxiety that often has been repressed. It is distinguished from psychosis, which refers to losing touch with reality. So, it appears that after believing Hector's issues were related to alcohol abuse, the military doctors decided that he suffered from repressed anxiety. Repression occurs when one pushes thoughts and emotions out of one's mind to forget them (a survival technique). Anxiety disorders are a group of mental illnesses that cause constant and overwhelming anxiety, depression, fear, and various physical complaints without clear organic causes. However, the numerous symptoms connected with neurosis do not include memory loss. If Hector had at this time lost all memory of his life prior to military service, it should have been discovered during his interviews and the examinations conducted by military doctors over that 17-day period. They would have to have seen symptoms to warrant that diagnosis. The amnesia Hector experienced does not seem to fit in this category.

Let us not forget that almost eight months after returning to the United States, from March 6, 1920, through June 5, 1920, Hector was hospitalized for a period of ninety days for a "disease not incident to the service." That is a lengthy hospitalization. No other information was shared in the adjutant general's letters regarding that hospitalization.

2. In June and July 1928, more than nine years after the first diagnosis, Hector was again diagnosed by the military as being in a "constitutional psychopathic state, inadequate personality." As discussed earlier, the term *psychopath* was originally a general term not connected to the moral deprivation it is associated with today. Early researchers believed pervasive traits and characteristics were constitutional (that is, present at birth). In this view, personality disturbances are characterized by failure to adapt to the occupational, social, emotional, and intellectual demands of life. Most individuals diagnosed as having inadequate personalities have had average educational opportunities, and they test within normal limits on intelligence tests. Nevertheless, not only are they ineffective in all their dealings, but they also demonstrate indifference and an attitude of unconcern. They are lacking in judgment, ambition, foresight, and stamina. Although they are often good natured, their relationships are invariably shallow, and they usually are not employed, as they are too irresponsible and self-centered to work well with others. They tend to live completely in the present. Even if extra effort brings obvious results in the near future, they fail to carry through with these endeavors. According to early definitions, shiftless individuals such as vagrants, vagabonds, idlers, roamers, and the like qualify as inadequate personalities. They may become alcoholics and drug addicts, but they rarely suffer from neuroses since they are relatively insensitive to deep emotional conflict or persistent anxiety. If they are subjected to prolonged physical or social stress, they gradually deteriorate intellectually and emotionally and, in some cases, develop psychotic reactions of a schizophrenic type. In the early twentieth century, it was widely recognized that psychopaths came in many varieties, and it was important to distinguish their subtypes. The term was used as a catch-all for people acting in some psychologically puzzling manner. Overall, the diagnosis "constitutional psychopathic state, inadequate personality" indicated that the person was seen as having a long-standing, maladaptive personality style or traits that were considered problematic or incompatible with societal norms and expectations. Without knowing the exact types of behavior Hector exhibited, it is difficult to determine why the doctors assigned him this label.

Obviously, the behavior Hector demonstrated was not a serious concern at the time of his enlistment. One would think that a potential recruit might not easily hide their psychopathic tendencies during the enlistment process. An educated guess suggests Hector displayed behaviors that were not the norm soon after the war ended, as evidenced by his first hospitalization.

3. In August 1928, a month after the previous diagnosis, he was diagnosed again by the military with "psychoneurosis, hysteria acute." Hysteria has generated the most heated debates among physicians in the field. It has long been confused with neuroses and neurological pathologies such as Parkinson's disease and epilepsy. A diverse array of hysteria symptoms exists. The clinical manifestations of hysteria are numerous and multifaceted, and each main classification can be divided into several subgroups. Hysteria was among the earliest syndromes to be understood and treated by psychoanalysts. They believed that such symptoms resulted from fixations or arrested stages in an individual's early psychosexual development. As with Hector's first diagnosis in 1919, symptoms can include anxiety, depression, and various physical complaints without clear organic causes. The addition of "acute" would mean the presentation of the condition was sudden and severe. These diagnoses, made in 1928, occurred while Hector was confined to hard labor after his sentencing. One can safely surmise that Hector found himself in a hopeless situation that would drive a sane person to their furthest limits before breaking down. Once again, not enough information is known in Hector's case to determine whether this diagnosis was on point. There is nothing yet discovered to assess the validity of this theory. Again, the type of amnesia that Hector experienced does not appear to be described as a symptom of this type of mental illness. It can be understood if the harsh confinement and helplessness he was experiencing created bouts of acute hysteria. Sane people would not handle this situation well either.

4. In May and June 1930, the Associated Charities of Worcester arranged for a local psychiatrist to evaluate and diagnose Hector. He was diagnosed with "dementia praecox, remission stage," meaning premature dementia. The term *praecox* means "early" in Latin. This was used to describe mental disorders that typically manifested early in life, often in adolescence or early adulthood, and were characterized by chronic and severe psychological symptoms. *Dementia praecox* is an obsolete medical term that was used to describe what is now called schizophrenia. Also called precocious madness, it includes early advanced, mature, or sudden development of symptoms that affect intellectual and social abilities enough to interfere with daily function. Symptoms vary from patient to patient. Some of the cognitive changes observed include memory loss (usually noticed by someone else), problems communicating or finding the desired words to use, trouble with visual and spatial abilities (such as getting lost while driving), problems with reasoning or problem solving,

trouble performing complex tasks, difficulty planning and organizing, experiencing confusion and disorientation or poor coordination and control of movements. Most of these symptoms are certainly prevalent in many older adults today.

Hector and Grace initiated this final psychiatric assessment, as they were anxious for him to get help right away. He then agreed to be checked in to the local state hospital for a 30-day stay for further evaluations.

While Hector did lose his memory, the dementia praecox diagnosis may have also been another misjudgment, as his memory loss was retrograde and we do not know whether he exhibited symptoms other than amnesia, which affects one's ability to make, store, and retrieve memories. Retrograde amnesia affects memories that were formed before the onset of amnesia. The definition of retrograde amnesia fully describes what Hector suffered from.

"Remission stage" in this instance means a decrease of manifestations of the disease, so if this diagnosis was correct, there must have been some improvement seen in Hector at that point, even though he left the hospital on the thirtieth day of a 35-day stay. Hector felt his exposure to the severely mentally ill patients in the hospital was detrimental to his improvement and checked himself out. He reached this conclusion because at that point doctors had told him it would take at least one and a half years of treatment for him to see improvement. We know he was later an outpatient and went for treatment once a week. The duration of this treatment is unknown, as is the nature of and type of treatment he received.

It should come as no surprise that there was a fair amount of disagreement regarding the issues Hector experienced during the time of his care within the confines of these four known hospitalizations, which spanned a period of more than nine years. Again, without medical records to guide us, forming firmly based judgments about his condition and care is difficult, as insufficient information is available. The progression or remission of any of these diagnoses over these nine years is unknown without access to clinical notes or medical records, save the final diagnosis, which was made in 1930 and indicated that Hector was in the remission stage. It can safely be assumed he was making progress by then.

We have no further information on any outpatient treatment Hector received after these diagnoses that were reported in family correspondence and newspaper stories. Given the facts about the latter part of Hector's life, we can see a man functioning normally. He maintained a loving relationship with his wife for 42 years. In addition, he was self-employed as a music teacher for more than three decades and registered as a member of professional musicians' organizations, along with being part of a men's club at his local church. Happily, over this sustained period there were no further reported crises in his life, a miraculous ending that should inspire us all.

If you break Hector's 67-year life into thirds, you can see how dramatically things unfolded. His life was normal for roughly the first third, until his mother died when he was 19 years old. During the next third of his life, chaos ensued. The injustice that was perpetrated against him sent his life off course. If he were a planet, it would be as if there was some sort of cosmic collision that spun his rotation off its axis and Hector himself out of orbit. At this time, it was hard to tell which pole was up. It took several years for the cataclysmic rubble of his life to coalesce and for things to begin to settle down. There came to be less wobble and greater steadiness, as his rotation and orbit assumed new rhythmic resonance. Things were now humming along, and in the final third of his life, Hector found his groove. There must have been a great deal of joy and contentment experienced by Hector and Grace during their final years together. They had achieved all they set out to do. They had defeated the dark realities they were burdened with for so long, and they found their equilibrium. An influential source that helped Hector find this balance was his music, as well as Grace. As stated earlier, we feel the key to their success was their relationship.

We do not know whether anything ever "clicked" in Hector's mind and brought back his childhood memories. There was no indication from relatives interviewed that he ever regained those memories. Most likely, his amnesia lasted for the rest of his life. Yet, unquestionably, we feel he achieved self-actualization, which is the pinnacle of the five-tier "hierarchy of needs" developed by Abraham Maslow.[43] Most people do not reach this level.

There is an old axiom that seems fitting, the origin of which is debatable. The adage has been attributed to many people over the decades and is based on the melancholy notion that long after they have outlived the wars in which they fought, old soldiers are forgotten, and their passing ignored. Their sacrifices, accomplishments and lives vanish into oblivion. As the saying goes, "old soldiers never die; they just fade away." This book is our attempt to ensure that Hector does not just fade away.

Epilogue

James J. Jimenez

Evangelina "Lina" Maria Palmer was born in Cuba and is the sole reason this important family story was revived. She can be seen in figure 29 with her mother, Clara M. "Bibi" Fernandez y Perez, Hector's only niece, in 2015 (shortly before Bibi's death). Bibi's death in 2017 led Lina to discover the folder that contained the trove of letters and newspaper articles about Hector with which this story began.

Lina is the genesis behind this book and the impetus for why it is written. She has personal knowledge of her ancestral history, and over many years she has consulted and interviewed family members while taking contemporaneous notes. Of special importance were the conversations with William "Bill" Atkinson, Sr., who added much color to our known facts about our mutual relatives (figure 30).

Bill's daughter, Dinorah Anne "Dinni" Allred, Hector's grandniece, was helpful in conveying her father's stories to us (figure 31). At the time this book was being written, Dinni informed us that her father's health was deteriorating, and on December 20, 2023, Bill passed peacefully in his sleep. He was a kind and generous man, as well as a loving father. He will be missed by many. In August 2024, Dinni, too, passed peacefully surrounded by family and friends.

Lina compiled, retained, and organized many detailed handwritten notes over several decades, gathering information from multiple sources. Her meticulous recordkeeping allowed us to bring Hector's story to life so that it could be shared and live on, never to be forgotten. This was the genius of her methodology, driven by posterity and loving dedication to her family.

History has proven repeatedly that many people, places, and notable events dwindle into obscurity, and their importance becomes diminished over time until they eventually fade from consciousness, as if they never existed. This loss is due to a lack of readily available historical

Figure 29: A photograph of coauthor Lina Palmer and her mother, Clara M. "Bibi" Fernandez y Perez (1922–2017). Bibi was Hector's only niece. Coauthor Evangelina "Lina" Palmer is Hector's grandniece.

documentation. Just think about the number of family historical events you are personally aware of that remain undocumented history and will never be repeated. Those stories will vanish from memory when you pass on. Think of all the things you were told as a child and now wish you could remember. While many of us are aware of this dynamic and agree on its importance, very few take the time to make the effort, expend the energy and render the expenses needed to document our family history.

Lina understands that this knowledge and family history would surely be lost over time and become forgotten memories of events just as important to some today as they were at the time that they took place. Such stories need to be written down and made accessible so they can be passed on. She felt if this story brings hope to just one person during the challenging moments in their life, then the effort necessary to preserve it will have been worthwhile. It was her initiative, involvement, and tenacity that brought these events to life in these pages for us to read. She kept things moving forward and acted before it was too late. This is fortunate for some of us now as well as for others yet to come who will have an interest in our family history. Family stories of years gone by are intriguing to most people. The majority of this family history has been confirmed and verified through a multitude of sources.

The same is true with the various iterations of publications titled "Mis Recuerdos" (which, loosely translated, means "My Memories" or "My Recollections"), written and published by several native Cubans. Their importance lies in keeping their substance alive and sustaining the memory of these events in the present. On a personal note, I recall reading about a granduncle's involvement in Cuba's fight for self-determination in one such edition of "Mis Recuerdos." I had no prior knowledge of him or our connection and learned about him only after doing my own ancestral research. As a result, some of the struggles of the Cuban people of the late nineteenth century have crystallized for me. This information adds a new dimension not just to their lives as we get to know about them but also to our own lives.

Figure 30: William "Bill" C. Atkinson Sr., Hector's nephew and the oldest son of Dinorah and Bill Atkinson. Bill contributed insights from his recollections of our family. Bill served as a sergeant in the United States Air Force, married and had four children. Bill passed away December 20, 2023.

The recording of Hector's story has been made possible because of Lina. She embraces the concept of historical preservation and research and has been working at it for years. After reading this story, ask yourself two questions: Is the story itself important enough to keep alive, and was it worth the effort? This story is important and very much alive within Lina's immediate family. They speak about it often among themselves, reimagining the people involved and discussing key events from their lives. Ideally, this historical narrative can be found and accessed easily, available for public consumption. Who knows what the future holds in terms of how we obtain information? One day we might be able to access our family history quickly and easily, and everything will be at our fingertips, available for instant retrieval. No doubt there will be technological advances

Epilogue

Figure 31: Dinorah Anne "Dinni" Allred, granddaughter of Dinorah Perez and William Atkinson, and one of Bill Sr.'s daughters. She, too, is a grandniece of Hector's. She was instrumental in assisting her father in sharing with us treasured details and artifacts for use in this book. She passed away August 22, 2024, in Cocoa Beach, Florida.

that improve our capabilities in doing so.

Lina worked tirelessly and conducted extensive research, made numerous phone calls, sent letters, and made inquiries to bring together all the details. Her home office was bustling with activity. She verified facts and information, obtained and scanned documents, and collected photographs of people and artifacts relevant to the story. She purchased access to records, gathered evidence and arranged information in an understandable manner to present as accurate a representation as possible.

She followed up on leads and resolved potential differences in the information and reconciled conflicts. She looked for clues, developed a strategy and implemented it, making necessary adjustments along the way. Her diligence ensured that this story includes the most accurate and thorough information known, available, or discoverable. She then condensed the details for presentation in a logical and meaningful manner. Dedication to accuracy and thoroughness is paramount if you want the whole truth to be told. So are persistence and determination. Lina credits several others with providing bits of valuable information, but it was her attention to detail and proficiency at gathering data and conducting interviews that added quality to the final product and makes this story what it is—a look into the long-drawn-out, hellish battle that was Hector and Grace's lives for two decades and yet ended unbelievably well. Her systematic and logical approach to fact finding enabled Lina to produce a vivid account with wide-ranging detail.

Her ability to identify resources, persistent determination, and tirelessness resulted in a full, rich story that captures all the pertinent facts. The result is an excellent representation of people, facts, and events as they occurred. However, her journey through her own ancestral genealogy and her dedication to documenting her family's history began long before this book became a twinkle in our eyes.

Hers was a labor of love. Its importance to her cannot be understated. Her main purpose has been to share this treasured knowledge about her family in the hope that it could provide inspiration and help others in their own struggles. Mental health issues affect many people in numerous ways and can make a person feel overwhelmed by hopelessness and lead them to self-harm. Our national suicide rates show this fact, and this was an important aspect to her sharing this story. This purpose is important to her, as it is to many others as well as our huge, broad family tree. That is why getting an accurate portrayal was imperative.

Personally, I found Lina a pleasure to work with, and I owe her a debt of gratitude for allowing me to participate in this significant endeavor. Thank you, Lina, for sharing so much important family history and for introducing us to two American heroes to whom we happen to be related, both of whom encountered their share of misfortune. Despite the challenges, they managed to rise above it all. They accomplished far more together than they

Figure 32: Narrator and coauthor James J. "Jimmy" Jimenez has been researching family genealogy for over a decade, and he self-published a historical account of his immediate family and their ancestors and descendants. Born and raised in New York City, he has lived in New Jersey for more than 50 years.

could have done separately. Their greatest gift to one another was themselves. They were the key to their own survival and ultimate success.

Lina and I (your narrator) met as a DNA match on Ancestry.com (figure 32). She is my third cousin once removed. My great-grandmother Rosario Castellanos y Velasco was the younger sister of Lina's great-great-grandfather Jacinto Velasco y Valdez. Lina has an extensive family tree on Ancestry.com and has documented details and historical facts about her lineage going back two centuries. The importance of such details should not be underestimated. It is how we keep our family alive.

Appendix

We have curated a small collection, from our family archives, that includes charts, documents, letters, and newspaper articles that we feel will be helpful to readers for the purpose of tracking the chronological factual events against the evidence—to show readers the "receipts," so to speak, and share what occurred in Hector's life. We believe seeing and reading the correspondence, from close to one hundred years ago, among private and public state and national aid agencies, the U.S. Army War Department, congressional representatives, newspaper editors, the Disabled American Veterans, and family members is critical for a proper assessment of the injustice that was perpetrated against Hector by the bureaucracy of the 1920s U.S. Army. The most egregious problem came when a rogue commanding officer, apparently operating without oversight, chose not to act on the recommendation of clemency for Hector from the general court-martial members in 1928.

Timeline of Events

This timeline tracks major events that occurred in Hector's life in a chronological fashion commencing from the date of death of Hector's mother, Sarah Velasco Perez, in January 1916.

1916, January 16	Mother dies in Tampa, Florida
1917, March 27	Enlists at Fort Slocum, New York, and assigned as private to medical detachment at Fort Wadsworth, New York (see figure 21)
1917, April 3–17	Treated for German measles (see figure 39)
1917, June 11	Assigned to duty as a private with medical detachment of 15th FA (see figure 40)
1917, June 25	Transferred to medical detachment of 4th FA (see figure 39)
1917, December 12	Sailed for France with 15th FA medical detachment (see figures 33 and 34)
1918, March–November	Fought in seven campaigns—see "Battle Chart" in figure 20 (see also figure 40)
1918, July 4	Transferred to 2nd Engineers in the field of battle (see figure 40)

Appendix

1918, November 11	Armistice Day—war ends
1919, January 24–February 4	Treated for influenza overseas (see figure 39)
1919, April 17	**Hospitalized for "alcoholism, acute" (see figure 39)**
1919, April 20–May 7	**[Diagnosis 1] Psychiatric assessment/diagnosis while hospitalized: "psychoneurosis, type undetermined" (total duration: 21 days) (see figure 39)**
1919, July 5–July 14	Returned to United States via Brest, France, as "garrison prisoner" (see figure 35)
1919, August 19	Transferred to medical detachment of 36th Infantry, Hoff General Hospital #41, Fox Hills, New York (see figure 40)
1919, October 16	Under treatment in Hoff General Hospital #41, Fox Hills (see figure 40)
1919, November 20	Bandleader Ben Selvin records "Dardanella" in New York City
1919, December	"Dardanella" released
1920, March 6–June 7	Under treatment in Hoff General Hospital #41: "not incident to service" (duration: 92 days) (see figures 39 and 40)
1920, June 11–16	Under treatment in Hoff General Hospital #41: (1) not incident to service, and (2) furunculosis (duration: 6 days) (see figures 39 and 40)
1920, June 17	Furloughed (see figure 40)
1920, June 26	AWOL for 30 days; classed as "deserted" (see figure 40)
1920, July	Meets Grace, future wife
1921, July	Marriage to Grace
1928, Apr/May	Chance meeting in Worcester—recognized by a war buddy
1928, May 29	Fort Adams, Rhode Island, general court-martial, resulting in dishonorable discharge for desertion and confinement to hard labor for one year (see figure 40)
1928, June 26–July 27	**[Diagnosis 2] Psychiatric assessment/diagnosis while confined: "constitutional psychopathic state, inadequate personality" (duration: 30 days) (see figure 39)**
1928, August 3	Clemency letter written by all members of the general court-martial (see figure 36)
1928, August 9–12	**[Diagnosis 3] Psychiatric assessment/diagnoses while confined: "psychoneurosis, hysteria, acute" (constitutional psychopathic state, inadequate personality) (duration: 4 days) (see figure 39)**
1928, September 20	Court-martial orders promulgated: dishonorable discharge, forfeiture of all pay and allowance due or to become due, one-year confinement at hard labor; confinement remitted (see figure 40)
1928, September 21	Dishonorable discharge—released (see figure 40)
1930, April 16	1930 U.S. Census—Grace and Hector living apart briefly and then reunited
1930, March	Red Cross provides assistance for 30 days (see figure 37)
1930, April	Associated Charities commences giving assistance (see figure 37)

Appendix

1930, June 9	Associated Charities letter to Florida Department of Welfare (bill pending to Congress) (see figure 37)
1930, June 9	**[Diagnosis 4] Psychiatric assessment/diagnosis by local psychiatrist: "dementia praecox, remission stage"; voluntarily admits himself to state hospital (duration: 30 days) (see figure 37)**
1931, June 20	Charles Perez writes letter to Hector and Grace
1931, June 24	Grace replies to Charles' letter (see figure 38)
1931, July 3	War Department letter to Congressman Holmes (see figure 39)
1931, July 3	War Department letter to Congressman Stobbs (see figure 40)
1931, July 6	First newspaper story about Hector being found—*Key West Citizen*
1931, July 17	Chairman of DAV letter responding to the inquiry of the U.S. Marine Hospital executive officer, Captain Richard Daniel, on Hector's behalf for information on disability eligibility
1931, July 23	Senator Walsh story regarding pending bill hits newspapers
1931, July 27	W.J. Belleville letter responding to Captain Daniel of U.S. Marine Hospital Key West (see figure 41)
1931 August 2	*Worcester Telegram–USA Today* "Soldier Son—Lost Since War"
1931, September 12	Margarita Lacedonia letter, U.S. Marine Hospital, Key West, to Ruth Bryan Owen, urging support for pending congressional bill (see figure 42)
1931, December 9	Senator Walsh introduces Bill S. 851 for relief of Hector; Congressional Record (see figure 43)
1935, February 27	Newspaper story on Senate bill passing for Hector's relief
1937	WPA employment (see chapter 9)
1937	Father dies in Cuba
1942	WPA employment (see figure 24)
1940s	Employed as music teacher/has studio/listed in Worcester business directory
1950, April 30	Brother Charlie dies in Florida
1952	Sister Evangelina dies in Cuba
1954–1956	Music teacher at St. Gabriel's School of Music (see figure 44)
1955	Member, National Guild of Piano Teachers (see figures 26, 27, and 44)
1955	Member, Federation of Musicians (see figures 26 and 27)
1956–1958	Affiliation with the music department at Catholic University of America (see figure 44)
1950s–1963	Member, Men's Club, Our Lady of Fatima Church, Worcester (see figure 44)
1963, August 30	Death of Hector Francis Perez—obituary (see figure 44)
2017, May	Death of Hector's grandniece "Bibi"—author Lina Palmer discovers folder; research begins
2021	Shared story with cousin, Jimmy; joint research begins

Sheet No. 3
THIRD Class
UNITED STATES ARMY TRANSPORT SERVICE
PASSENGER LIST
OF
ORGANIZATIONS AND CASUALS
HQ. PORT OF EMBARKATION HOBOKEN, N. J.
15th F.A.
Organization (1) MEDICAL DEPARTMENT Transport Commercial Str. (2) White Star Line S.S. ADRIATIC Sailing Date DEC 12 1917 Port (3) NEW YORK CITY, N.Y.

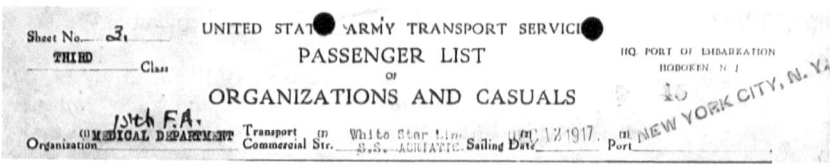

Figure 33: Army transport list (dated December 12, 1917), USA to France—Perry, Hector H.

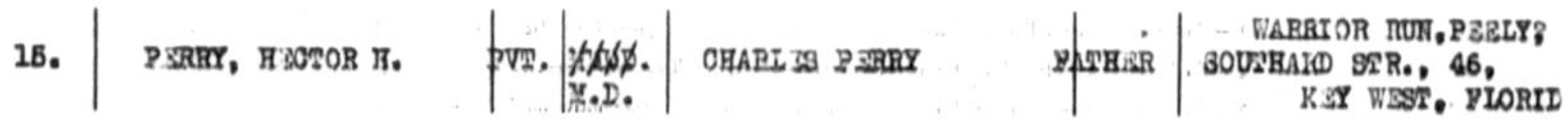

15.	PERRY, HECTOR H.	PVT.	M.D.	CHARLES PERRY	FATHER	WARRIOR RUN, PEELY? SOUTHARD STR., 46, KEY WEST, FLORID

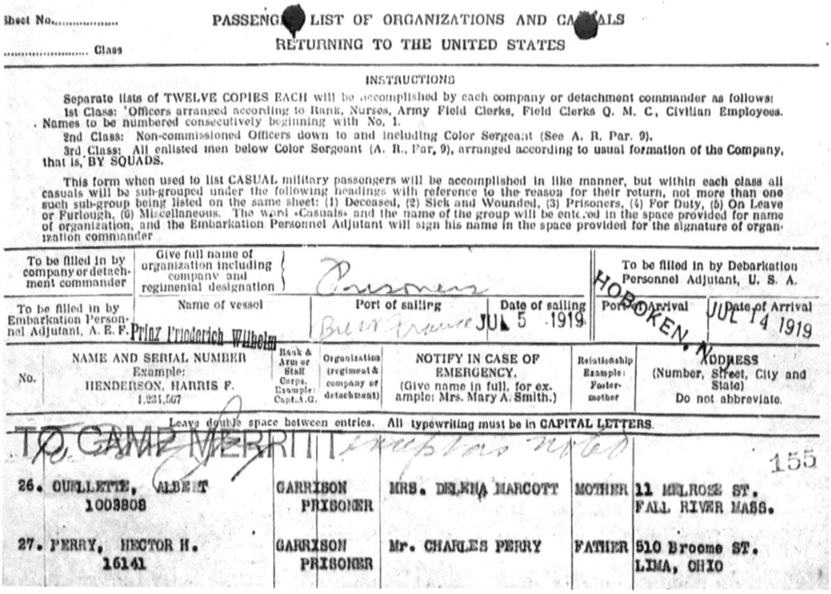

Figure 34: Army transport list (dated December 12, 1917), USA to France—Perry, Hector H.

Sheet No..................
.... Class

PASSENGER LIST OF ORGANIZATIONS AND CASUALS RETURNING TO THE UNITED STATES

INSTRUCTIONS

Separate lists of TWELVE COPIES EACH will be accomplished by each company or detachment commander as follows:
1st Class: Officers arranged according to Rank, Nurses, Army Field Clerks, Field Clerks Q. M. C., Civilian Employees. Names to be numbered consecutively beginning with No. 1.
2nd Class: Non-commissioned Officers down to and including Color Sergeant (See A. R. Par. 9).
3rd Class: All enlisted men below Color Sergeant (A. R., Par. 9), arranged according to usual formation of the Company, that is, BY SQUADS.

This form when used to list CASUAL military passengers will be accomplished in like manner, but within each class all casuals will be sub-grouped under the following headings with reference to the reason for their return, not more than one such sub-group being listed on the same sheet: (1) Deceased, (2) Sick and Wounded, (3) Prisoners, (4) For Duty, (5) On Leave or Furlough, (6) Miscellaneous. The word «Casuals» and the name of the group will be entered in the space provided for name of organization, and the Embarkation Personnel Adjutant will sign his name in the space provided for the signature of organization commander.

To be filled in by company or detachment commander — Give full name of organization including company and regimental designation: Prisoners
To be filled in by Debarkation Personnel Adjutant, U. S. A.
To be filled in by Embarkation Personnel Adjutant, A. E. F. — Name of vessel: Prinz Friederich Wilhelm — Port of sailing: Brest France — Date of sailing: JUL 5 1919 — Port of Arrival: HOBOKEN, N.J. — Date of Arrival: JUL 14 1919

No.	NAME AND SERIAL NUMBER Example: HENDERSON, HARRIS F. 1,231,567	Rank & Arm or Staff Corps. Example: Capt.A.G.	Organization (regiment & company or detachment)	NOTIFY IN CASE OF EMERGENCY. (Give name in full, for example: Mrs. Mary A. Smith.)	Relationship Example: Foster-mother	ADDRESS (Number, Street, City and State) Do not abbreviate.
	Leave double space between entries. All typewriting must be in CAPITAL LETTERS.					
	TO CAMP MERRITT except as noted					155
26.	OUELLETTE, ALBERT 1003808		GARRISON PRISONER	MRS. DELENA MARCOTT	MOTHER	11 MELROSE ST. FALL RIVER MASS.
27.	PERRY, HECTOR H. 16141		GARRISON PRISONER	Mr. CHARLES PERRY	FATHER	510 Broome ST. LIMA, OHIO

Figure 35: Army transport list (dated July 5, 1919), Brest, France, to USA—Perry, Hector H.

Appendix

NATIONAL HEADQUARTERS
2940 Melrose Ave.
Cincinnati, Ohio.
COPY

AMERICAN
DISABLED VETERNAS
OF THE WORLD WAR
NATIONAL REHABILITATION DEPARTMENT
MUNSEY BUILDING
WASHINGTON, D.C.
Ralph L. Chambers
Chairman

July 17, 1931

Mr. Richard Curd Daniel
Capt. U.S.A. & E.C.R.   Perez, Hector
U.S. Marine Hospital
Key West, Florida.

My dear Comrades

Statements contained in your letter of July 4, 1931, indicate that this veteran probably had two enlistments; the first during the period of the World War with a later re-enlistment from which he deserted.

If the veteran did have a period of honorable World War service and if he did receive disabilities during that period of service which may be held due to service, by presumption or by direct evidence, compensation may be paid to him notwithstanding the fact that he later re-enlisted and deserted.

The above statement is based upon the assumption that this veteran had an honorable period of World War service and was honorably discharged from his World War Service and upon the assumption that he deserted from an enlistment after his discharge from this period of service.

Even though there was one single period of service, if it can be shown that the veteran was of unsound mind at the time of his desertion it may be possible to secure benefits for him.

It is suggested that those interested in the claim may secure valuable assistance from Comrade T. James Gallagher, D.A.V. Rehabilitation Officer, 600 Washington Street, Boston, Mass., as it is quite probable that the case will be handled in the Boston area.

Cordially yours,

Sgd. Ralph L. Chambers

RLC:GF
Notes: Capt. Richard Curd Daniel is Dept. Executive Officer in Florida.

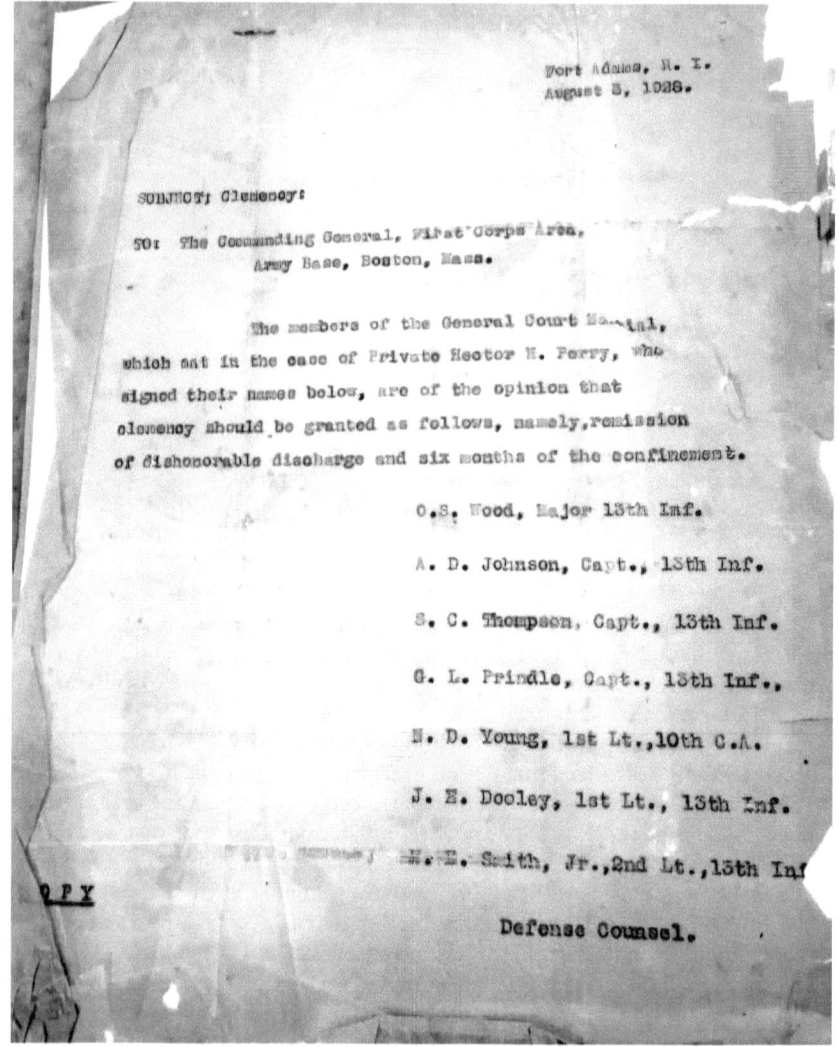

Figure 36: Letter written by the general court-martial members to their commanding officer recommending clemency for Hector. A transcription of this letter (dated August 3, 1928) is displayed in chapter 2.

THE ASSOCIATED CHARITIES
of Worcester, Massachusetts
Wetherell House, 2 State St.
Helen E. Fairbanks, General Secretary.

June 9, 1930.

RE: Hector Perry
alias
Alfredo Velasquez
Sanchez

Miss C. Adelaide Barker
Duval County Family Welfare Agency
700 West 10th Street
Jacksonville, Florida

My dear Miss Barker:

We would like to ask your assistance in locating the relatives of Hector Perry, alias Alfredo Velasquez Sanchez, now of Worcester.

Mr. Perry applied to us for aid April 14 of this year. He had been referred here by the local Red Cross who had been aiding him for a month and were unable to continue with this aid. Mr. Perry was very absent-minded and distracted at the time of his application. He did not give any information about his birthplace, relatives, and other routine questions which are asked new applicants because he said said that he was afraid that he did not know any of these facts. Upon further investigation we have found that Mr. Perry is believed to have been born in Tampa Florida, and he thinks that he was in high school at the time he left to enlist in the Army. A copy of the Army record, which is in our hands, indicates that he enlisted at Fort Slocum, New York, May 27, 1917, and left for service overseas, December 12, 1917. He participated in several battles overseas and during that time was hospitalized. He was returned to the United States July 14, 1919, and was in the United States General Hospital, Fox Hills, New York, at that time under treatment there remaining until October 16, 1919. He was also under treatment there from March 6, to June 7, 1920, and was then furloughed June 17. He deserted the service June 26, 1920, and returned to military control May 29, 1928. He was found guilty of deserting the service at the trial which took place May 29, 1928, at Fort Adams, Newport, Rhode Island, and he was dishonorably discharged from the Service September 21, of that year. Since that time Mr. Perry applied at the Boston branch of the Veteran's Bureau claiming disability and there was some contact with the Social Service Department there. Aid was not given because of his ineligibility but various attempts had been made by the Veteran's Bureau and also by the local Soldiers' Relief Department to secure an honorable discharge for Mr. Perry. At present a bill is pending to secure this and is expected to be taken up before the next session of Congress.

In July 1920, Mr. Perry met his present wife and they were married the following year in Worcester. At that time Mr. Perry was using the name of Alfredo Velasquez Sanchez and used that name in the marriage ceremony. Mrs. Sanchez, whom we shall refer to as Mrs. Perry, know practically nothing about her husband's past. She is a rather reticent lady of about thirty-four years of age. She is physically handicapped as she has worn an artificial right leg ever since she was six years old. She is rather refined and has had a high school and business school

Above and next 2 pages: Figure 37: Associated Charities letter, June 9, 1930. This was the pivotal letter that started the case of garnering support for Hector and Grace's goal of reversing the unjust sentence he had received. These three pages contain a treasure trove of facts, most of which have been corroborated by available records during our research and are included in this book.

education. She comes of average people who are now in rather poor circumstances. Mrs. Perry was apparently very much carried away by Mr. Perry who has a very agreeable and pleasing personality. She made little or inquiry into his past and married him without even knowing who his parents were or where they lived. She said that he was always popular. He is an accomplished pianist and is very fond of entertaining people with his talent. Shortly after the marriage. Very often, however, he will become very moody and go off by himself or want to play the piano by himself. Shortly after the marriage, the Perrys went to Newark, New Jersey, to live and from then on commenced a period of very irregular employment. Mr. Perry had no regular trade but was able to get jobs very easily. He never stayed at a job more than two or three months because he was extremely absent-minded and would forget to do tasks assigned to him. At the end of two years, the Newark police picked up Mr. Perry there and returned him to his home in a confused and dazed condition. The police told his wife that when he had been found he did not seem to know who he was or where he lived. Soon after this the Perrys returned to Worcester where they lived for a short time with Mrs. Perry's mother and then later in a furnished room. Mrs. Perry soon realized that she could not depend upon her husband for support and she took a job as telephone operator at Memorial Hospital in this city where she has been employed since then. Her earnings were only $12.00 and it was difficult for them to manage on this amount.

This past year, Mr. Perry was employed for a short time at a fur shop and also as a helper at the restaurant at Union Station. Both places report that he was well-liked but unreliable and undependable because of his absent-mindedness. He was dismissed at both of the places.

We found that both Mr. Perry and his wife were anxious for him to get some sort of mental treatment and they co-operated very well with us in arranging this. A local psychiatrist, Dr. Jordan, diagnosed Mr. Perry's condition as dementia praecox, remission stage, and he was committed to the Worcester State Hospital for thirty-five days observation.

This period would have ended on Thursday, June 11, but Mr. Perry left the hospital last Saturday for an indefinite visit. The doctors had thus far been unable to accomplish anything with him and when they told him that it probably would take a year or a year and a half to cure him, he became discouraged and decided to leave. He also felt that there were too many serious mental cases there and was afraid of making his condition worse. He is now extremely anxious to enter some Veterans' Hospital and we are trying to assist him in this.

In the meanwhile we had written to Washington to the Adjutant General's office to ascertain names and addresses of relatives which Mr. Perry had registered at the time of his enlistment. We just received a reply yesterday indicating that Mr. Perry's father, Charles Perry, was living at 46 Southard St., Key West, in 1918 and that his mother was listed as Clara Harrison, 510 Brown Street, Cincinnati, Ohio. There was a sister, Evangeline Perry, whose address was the same as that of the mother. As far as he remembers, his mother's name was Sarah Perry and he

3.

tried to locate her on Harrison Street in Cincinnati, Ohio. There is apparently a great deal of confusion in Mr. Perry's mind about these and we are anxious to locate these relatives if possible.

Would you kindly see if you can locate his father, Cage Perry? It is possible that the latter has moved from the address given me such a long time has elapsed, but we do hope there will be some means of tracing him or of obtaining some information. We hope to hear from you at your earliest convenience and thank you for your co-operation.

         Very truly yours,

         sgd. Helen Fairbanks,
         General Secretary.

G.R.P./MH

COPY

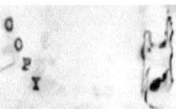

General Delivery,
June 24, 1931,
Worcester, Mass.

Dear Father:-

    I was so happy to hear from you and to know that you are also alive, for I knew he must have had a father somewhere and as you say, I'm glad it is all over with, I have found you.

    I am writing all the details about his war record to his brother in New York.

    Mrs. Fairbanks of the Associated Charities will write you the number of his bill which is going to be introduced in Congress next December.

    I was surprised to know that he had a brother and two sisters. His mind is not bad all the time, it is only at intervals and he apparently got that way in the army.

    Senator Walsh of Massachusetts thought his war record was splendid. Of course I believe Senator Walsh will try and do his best; nevertheless any other influence would help a great deal.

    I have tried to do my best taking care of him for eight years and I will always try to help him. He is a splendid fellow, his is so good. It is a shame the way he was treated after being through the thickest of fighting during the war. He was in all the big battles in France, this alone should merit an honorable discharge.

    Senator Walsh said his record was commendable. I think you have a very brave son and one to be proud of. He should be getting compensation for the service he rendered his country but he is not getting anything and it is a shame. Everybody thinks so.

    I hope your health is good. I will write you later and I want to hear real soon from you again. I thank you for your blessing for us and hope God will be good to you. We will both be glad to see you.

                                With much love,
                                Your daughter,

Figure 38: Grace's letter of June 24, 1931, written in response to her father-in-law Charles' letter. Here we see Grace, for the first time, speak with joy and relief that Hector has a family, which has been found at last.

WAR DEPARTMENT
The Adjutant General's Office
Washington

July 3, 1931.

reply refer to
AG 201- Perry, Hector H. (6-30-31)WW

Honorable Pehr G. Holmes,
    Representative in Congress,
        167 Commercial Street,
            Worcester, Mass.

My dear Mr. Holmes:

I have your letter of June 30, 1931, requesting that you be furnished with the military and medical record of Hector H. Perry, Army serial number 16,141.

The records show that Hector H. Perry, Army serial number 16,141, enlisted March 27, 1917, at Fort Slocum, New York, and was assigned to duty as a private, Medical Detachment, Fort Wadsworth, New York. He was transferred to the Medical Detachment, 4th Field Artillery June 25, 1917, sailed for foreign service December 12, 1917; returned to the United States July 14, 1919, and deserted June 26, 1920, at Hoff General Hospital, Staten Island, New York, and remained in desertion until May 29, 1928, when he surrendered to military control at Fort Adams, Rhode Island. He was tried by General Court Martial and pursuant to the sentence thereof was dishonorably discharged September 21, 1928, at Fort Adams, Rhode Island, a private, Medical Detachment.

The medical records show him treated from April 8, to 17, 1917, for German measles; January 24, to February 4, 1919, influenza, April 17, to May 7, 1919, alcoholism, acute, with change of diagnosix April 20, 1919, to psychoneurosis, type undetermined; March 6, to June 5, 1920, for a disease not incident to the service; June 11, to 16, 1920, (1) a disease not incident to the service, (2) furunculosis; June 26, to July 27, 1928, constitutional psychopathic state, inadequate personality and August 9, ot 12, 1928, psychoneurosis, hysteria, acute, (constitutional psychopathic state, inadequate personality).

Very respectfully,

C. W. Bridges (signed)
Major General,
The Adjutant General.

C O P Y

Figure 39: War Department response (dated July 3, 1931) to Congressman Holmes regarding Hector H. Perry.

War record taken from letter written by
Major General Charles W. Bridges, Adjutant
General, War Department. (published in
"The Worcester Evening Post," Monday, July 13, 1931.)

C
O
P
Y

July 3, 1931.

Hon. George R. Stobbs,
Representative in Congress,
Worcester, Mass.

My dear Mr. Stobbs:

Reference is made to your recent personal request for information regarding the military service of Hector H. Perry, Army serial number 16,141.

"The records of this office show that he enlisted May 27, 1917, at Fort Slocum, N. Y., and on June 11, 1917, was assigned to duty as a private, medical detachment of the 15th Field Artillery; left the U. S. Dec. 12, 1917, for service overseas; was transferred July 4, 1918, to the Second Engineers, served in the Toulon-Tryon defensive sector, March 24 to May 11, 1918, and in the Chateau Thierry defensive sector (Ile de France) June 6 to July 16, 1918; participated in the Aisne-Marne offensive, July 18 to July 20, 1918; served in the Marbache defensive sector, Aug. 6 to Aug. 18, 1918; in the Limey defensive sector, Sept. 9 to 11, 1918; and participated in the St. Mihiel offensive, Sept. 12 to Sept. 16, 1918, and the Meuse-Argonne offensive, Sept. 29 to Oct. 27 and Oct. 30 to Nov. 11, 1918.

"The records also show that he returned to the U. S., July 14, 1919, and was transferred to the medical detachment, 36th Infantry, Aug. 19, 1919, U.S.A. General Hospital, 41, Fox Hills, N. Y. October 16, 1919; was under treated in that hospital, March 6 to June 7, 1920, and June 12 to June 16, 1920; was furloughed June 17, 1920, and deserted the service June 26, 1920, returning to military control, May 29, 1928. He was found guilty by a general court-martial of having deserted the service of the U. S. on or about June 26, 1920, and of remaining absent in desertion until he surrendered May 29, 1928, at Fort Adams, R. I. The court sentenced him to be dishonorably discharged from the service, to forfeit all pay and allowance due or became due and to be confined at hard labor for one year. The sentence was approved by the reviewing authority, but the confinement was remitted and, as thus modified, the sentence was promulgated in general court-martial orders dated September 20, 1928.

Figure 40: War Department response (dated July 3, 1931) to Congressman Stobbs regarding Hector H. Perry.

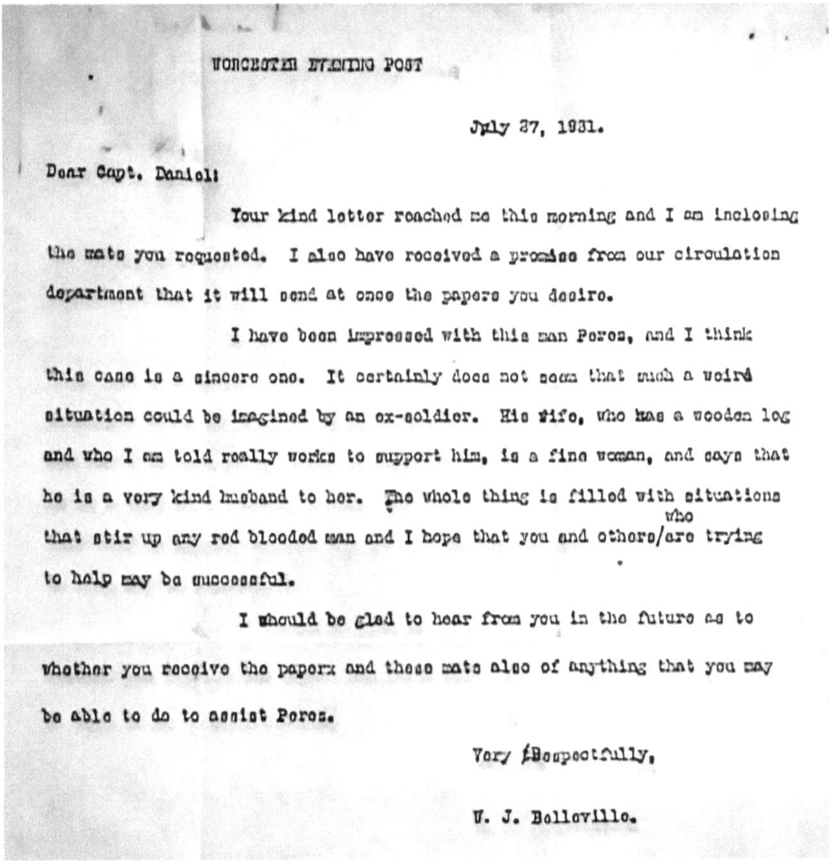

WORCESTER EVENING POST

July 27, 1931.

Dear Capt. Daniel:

    Your kind letter reached me this morning and I am inclosing the mats you requested. I also have received a promise from our circulation department that it will send at once the papers you desire.

    I have been impressed with this man Perez, and I think this case is a sincere one. It certainly does not seem that such a weird situation could be imagined by an ex-soldier. His wife, who has a wooden leg and who I am told really works to support him, is a fine woman, and says that he is a very kind husband to her. The whole thing is filled with situations that stir up any red blooded man and I hope that you and others who are trying to help may be successful.

    I should be glad to hear from you in the future as to whether you receive the papers and these mats also of anything that you may be able to do to assist Perez.

                                 Very Respectfully,

                                   W. J. Belleville.

Figure 41: Letter written by W.J. Belleville, *Worcester Evening Post* editor, on July 27, 1931, responding to an inquiry letter written by Captain Daniel of the U.S. Marine Hospital regarding Hector Perez.

Orlando, Florida.
September 12, 1931.

Honorable Ruth Bryan Owen,
C/O Chamber of Commerce,
Key West, Florida.

My dear Mrs. Owens:

    I am inclosing herewith correspondence relative to the case of Hector Perez, World War veteran, which is self-explanatory.

    Bill 3015, proposing an honorable discharge for this veteran, will be presented by Senator Walsh of Massachussetts at the next congressional session, and I am very anxious to secure your support.

    Mr. Perez was born in Tampa, Florida, and raised there and in Key West. He has a very commendable war record, a copy of which I will send you shortly. You may be interested to know that the boy's father, who is a resident of Key West, went to see him shortly after learning of this whereabouts.

    At present it appears that nothing can be done other than expediting his admission to a veterans' hospital and also having his disability service connected. From the inclosed letter, you will note that he is residing in Worcester, Mass., and therefore, will be taken care of by the Regional Office of the Veterans' Bureau in Boston.

    Assuring you that I will appreciate the interest that I know you will take in this case, I am,

Respectfully yours,

Margarita Lacedonia
(Miss) Margarita Lacedonia.

U. S. Marine Hospital,
Key West, Florida.

Figure 42 (*top and opposite*): Margarita Lacedonia's letter written on September 12, 1931, to the Honorable Ruth Bryan Owen seeking her support in favor of Hector's upcoming bill introduced by Senator David Walsh of Massachusetts.

Appendix

Orlando, Florida
September 12, 1931

Honorable Ruth Bryan Owen
C/O Chamber of Commerce,
Key West, Florida.

My dear Mrs. Owens [sic]:

I am inclosing herewith correspondence relative to the case of Hector Perez, World War veteran, which is self-explanatory.

Bill 3015, proposing an honorable discharge for this veteran, will be presented by Senator Walsh of Massachusetts at the next congressional session, and I am very anxious to secure your support.

Mr. Perez was born in Tampa, Florida, and raised there and in Key West. He has a very commendable war record, a copy of which I will send you shortly. You may be interested to know that the boy's father, who is a resident of Key West, went to see him shortly after learning of his whereabouts.

At present it appears that nothing can be done other than expediting his admission to a veterans' hospital and also having his disability service connected. From the inclosed letter, you will note that he is residing in Worcester, Mass., and therefore, will be taken care of by the Regional Office of the Veterans' Bureau in Boston.

Assuring you that I will appreciate the interest that I know you will take in this case, I am,

Respectfully yours,

(Miss) Margarita Lacedonia

U.S. Marine Hospital,
Key West, Florida.

A bill (S. 825) authorizing the enrollment of certain Indians residing in the State of Oregon;
A bill (S. 826) conferring jurisdiction upon the Court of Claims to hear and determine claims of certain bands or tribes of Indians residing in the State of Oregon; and
A bill (S. 827) authorizing the Secretary of the Interior to appraise tribal property of the Klamath and Modoc Tribes and the Yahooskin Band of Snake Indians, and for other purposes; to the Committee on Indian Affairs.
By Mr. WALSH of Massachusetts:
A bill (S. 828) granting compensation to David Samuel Goldstein; and
A bill (S. 829) granting compensation to Philip R. Roby; to the Committee on Finance.
A bill (S. 830) for the relief of Marino Ambrogi;
A bill (S. 831) for the relief of Francisco M. Belda;
A bill (S. 832) for the relief of David Wade Cameron;
A bill (S. 833) for the relief of Charles Coates;
A bill (S. 834) for the relief of Michael F. Clark;
A bill (S. 835) for the relief of William H. Connors;
A bill (S. 836) for the relief of Edward T. Costello;
A bill (S. 837) for the relief of Stephen Crotty;
A bill (S. 838) for the relief of John C. Daley;
A bill (S. 839) for the relief of Joseph Faneuf;
A bill (S. 840) for the relief of William H. Fleming;
A bill (S. 841) for the relief of Arthur B. Giroux;
A bill (S. 842) for the relief of Joseph Gorman;
A bill (S. 843) for the relief of Frank P. Hoyt;
A bill (S. 844) for the relief of John Jakmauh;
A bill (S. 845) for the relief of Gaston M. Janson;
A bill (S. 846) for the relief of Thomas F. Kenney;
A bill (S. 847) for the relief of Hector J. Langelier;
A bill (S. 848) for the relief of Albert A. Marquardt;
A bill (S. 849) for the relief of Thomas J. McDonald;
A bill (S. 850) for the relief of Michael J. Moran;
A bill (S. 851) for the relief of Hector H. Perry;
A bill (S. 852) for the relief of Henry Poole;
A bill (S. 853) for the relief of William H. Rouncevill;
A bill (S. 854) for the relief of Patrick J. Sullivan;
A bill (S. 855) for the relief of William Ray Taplin;
A bill (S. 856) for the relief of William Thibeault;
A bill (S. 857) for the relief of Robert H. Wilder;
A bill (S. 858) to provide for the retirement of August Wolters as a first sergeant in the United States Army; and
A bill (S. 859) for the advancement on the retired list of the Army of certain enlisted men; to the Committee on Military Affairs.
A bill (S. 860) for the relief of William Girard Joseph Bennett;
A bill (S. 861) for the relief of Arthur William Buckley;
A bill (S. 862) for the relief of Michael F. Calnan;
A bill (S. 863) for the relief of Edgar Joseph Casey;
A bill (S. 864) for the relief of Thomas Edward Connors;
A bill (S. 865) for the relief of Charles F. Dalton;
A bill (S. 866) for the relief of Thomas Francis Donoghue;
A bill (S. 867) for the relief of Frank D. Evans;
A bill (S. 868) for the relief of Edward A. Everett;
A bill (S. 869) for the relief of Patrick E. Farrelly;
A bill (S. 870) for the relief of William Edward Fitzgerald;
A bill (S. 871) for the relief of John Henry Fouhey;
A bill (S. 872) for the relief of Ray Funcannon;
A bill (S. 873) for the relief of Adolph Amilia Gathemann;
A bill (S. 874) for the relief of Ralph Martin George;
A bill (S. 875) for the relief of James Thomas Healy;
A bill (S. 876) for the relief of Gilbert Dennison Huntington;
A bill (S. 877) for the relief of Casimir Kaczorowski;
A bill (S. 878) for the relief of Dominick Edward Lepore;
A bill (S. 879) authorizing the Secretary of the Navy to advance on the retired list of the Navy David J. Mahoney, retired, to chief boilermaker, retired;
A bill (S. 880) for the relief of Eugene Nicolis Malgieri;
A bill (S. 881) for the relief of Thomas Joseph Malloy;
A bill (S. 882) for the relief of Edward Joseph Manning;
A bill (S. 883) for the relief of Albert Alexander Mathieson;
A bill (S. 884) for the relief of Napoleon Moran;
A bill (S. 885) for the relief of George Whittier Morse;
A bill (S. 886) for the relief of Elmer Lester Prew;
A bill (S. 887) for the relief of John W. Reardon;
A bill (S. 888) for the relief of Alvin Reaman Schmidt;
A bill (S. 889) for the relief of Samuel Stacey;
A bill (S. 890) for the relief of Francis Benedict Skiffington;
A bill (S. 891) for the relief of A. B. Thomas;
A bill (S. 892) for the relief of George William Thompson;
A bill (S. 893) for the relief of Bert Ward; and
A bill (S. 894) directing the retirement of acting assistant surgeons of the United States Navy at the age of 64 years; to the Committee on Naval Affairs.
A bill (S. 895) for the relief of William H. Ames;
A bill (S. 896) for the relief of Jessie Price Apple;
A bill (S. 897) to carry out the findings of the Court of Claims in the case of the Atlantic Works, of Boston, Mass.;
A bill (S. 898) for the relief of Capt. Asa G. Ayer;
A bill (S. 899) granting compensation to Abigail R. Bailey;
A bill (S. 900) for the relief of Anne K. Clark;
A bill (S. 901) for the relief of Warren J. Clear;
A bill (S. 902) for the relief of Willie B. Cleverly;
A bill (S. 903) for the relief of John J. Corcoran;
A bill (S. 904) for the relief of Elizabeth B. Dayton;
A bill (S. 905) for the relief of Edmund Glover Evans;
A bill (S. 906) for the relief of the International Manufacturers' Sales Co. of America (Inc.);
A bill (S. 907) for the relief of Edith N. Lindquist;
A bill (S. 908) for the relief of Edwin C. Jenney, receiver;
A bill (S. 909) for the relief of M. Grace Murphy;
A bill (S. 910) for the relief of Dean Scott;
A bill (S. 911) for the relief of Elsie M. Sears;
A bill (S. 912) for the relief of Simpson Bros. Corporation;
A bill (S. 913) for the relief of Tom Small; and
A bill (S. 914) for the relief of Katherine R. Theberge; to the Committee on Claims.
A bill (S. 915) granting a pension to Jennie B. Southwick;
A bill (S. 916) granting a pension to Emma J. Moore;
A bill (S. 917) for the relief of George E. Kenson;
A bill (S. 918) granting a pension to Henry Frank;
A bill (S. 919) granting a pension to Susie Fiedler;
A bill (S. 920) granting a pension to Mary C. Daly;
A bill (S. 921) granting an increase of pension to Mary S. Conant (with an accompanying paper);
A bill (S. 922) granting an increase of pension to Susan M. Crockett (with accompanying papers);
A bill (S. 923) granting an increase of pension to Ida May Cunningham (with accompanying papers);
A bill (S. 924) granting a pension to Beatrice E. Duke (with accompanying papers);
A bill (S. 925) granting a pension to Jennie S. Fountain (with accompanying papers);
A bill (S. 926) granting an increase of pension to Herbert W. Leach (with accompanying papers);
A bill (S. 927) granting an increase of pension to Lucy N. Teel (with accompanying papers); and
A bill (S. 928) granting a pension to Bridget A. Whittle (with accompanying papers); to the Committee on Pensions.
By Mr. NORRIS:
A bill (S. 929) relating to the taking of depositions in cases arising under section 19 of the World War veterans' act, 1924, as amended;
A bill (S. 930) to amend section 109 of the act entitled "An act to codify, revise, and amend the penal laws of the United States," approved March 4, 1909, and for other purposes;
A bill (S. 931) to amend a part of section 1 of the act of May 27, 1908, chapter 200, as amended (U. S. C., title 28, sec. 592);
A bill (S. 932) to amend an act entitled "An act to make persons charged with crimes and offenses competent witnesses in United States and Territorial courts," approved March 16, 1878, with respect to the competency of husband and wife to testify for or against each other;

Figure 43: Congressional Record S. 851 (December 9, 1931) as published by the Library of Congress.

HECTOR F. PEREZ
Composed "Dardanella"

Hector F. Perez, Piano Teacher And Composer

Hector F. Perez of 4 Oakwood Place, music teacher and composer, died Friday afternoon in his home.

He gave private piano lessons to numerous pupils at his home for many years until last June.

From 1954 to 1956, he taught music at St. Gabriel's School of Music on High Street, and from 1956 to 1958 was associated with the music department of Catholic University in Washington, D.C.

Born in East Tampa, Fla., he was a son of the late Charles and Sarah (Velasquez) Perez and lived in Worcester for 42 years.

He was an Army veteran of World War I.

During the war Mr. Perez composed "Dardanella."

According to his family, Mr. Perez soon thereafter sold the rights to it.

He was a member of the National Guild of Piano Teachers and the Men's Club of Our Lady of Fatima parish.

He leaves his widow, Grace R. (Duff) Perez; a sister, Mrs. Dinorah Atkinson of Highlands, N.C., and several nieces and nephews.

The funeral will be held Monday from O'Connor Brothers Funeral Home, 592 Park Ave., with a Solemn High Mass at 9 a.m. in Our Lady of Fatima Church. Burial will be in St. John's Cemetery.

Calling hours at the funeral home are 2 to 4 and 7 to 9 p.m. today.

Figure 44: Obituary of Hector F. Perez (August 30, 1963).

Chapter Notes

Chapter One

1. James Bovard, "Cato Institute Policy Analysis No. 47: The Last Dinosaur: The U.S. Postal Service," February 1985, https://www.cato.org/sites/cato.org/files/pubs/pdf/pa047.pdf.
2. "About Fedex: Overnight Mail," accessed December 1, 2023, https://www.fedex.com/en-us/about.html.
3. "National Records of Scotland, Statutory Births 605/00 0064," accessed January 8, 2023, https://www.ancestry.com/mediaui-viewer/collection/1030/tree/106300270/person/282443483516/media/5abdbcc7-17a7-4bb9-9472-8a1bfacb2c2c?_phsrc=aiN707&usePUBJs=true&galleryindex=5&albums=pg&showGalleryAlbums=true&tab=0&pid=282443483516&sort=-created (alternate link: https://www.ancestry.com/sharing/8095198?mark=7b22746f6b656e223a226e65334d4a62657063 4a79676f464837712f4c4958746167335831 6c79746d324b6e372b356b4d4f5461343d2 22c22746f6b656e5f76657273696f6e223a2 25632227d).
4. "1900 United States Federal Census," Ancestry.com, accessed December 3, 2023, https://www.ancestry.com/imageviewer/collections/7602/images/4114470_00555?pId=75712597.
5. "Massachusetts, U.S., Marriage Records, 1840–1915," Ancestry.com, accessed December 3, 2023, https://www.ancestry.com/imageviewer/collections/5062/images/41262_b139412-00620?pId=2512730.
6. "Memorial ID: 243466333," Find a Grave, accessed December 2, 2023, https://www.findagrave.com/memorial/243466333/edward-b-duff; "Memorial ID: 243465174," Find a Grave, accessed December 2, 2023, https://www.findagrave.com/memorial/243465174/mary-e-duff.
7. "Massachusetts, U.S., Birth Records, 1840–1915," Ancestry.com, accessed December 3, 2023, https://www.ancestry.com/imageviewer/collections/5062/images/41262_b139412-00620?pId=2512730.
8. "Certificates Issued to Many Students," *Fall River Daily Evening News*, August 31, 1921, https://www.newspapers.com/article/fall-river-daily-evening-news/136155590/.
9. Lisa Borten, "What American Education Was Like 100 Years Ago," Stacker, September 6, 2020, https://stacker.com/education/what-american-education-was-100-years-ago.
10. "City Hall Records, Marriage Intentions," *Worcester Evening Gazette*, July 7, 1921, https://www.genealogybank.com/doc/newspapers/image/v2%3A1773BDF75FF7A17E%40GB3NEWS-1793FEE2172 59C4D%402422878-179356578F8AC 747%401-179356578F8AC747?clipid=onoa cioydgxopgmhnlahbcrgzrdtimow_wmagateway016_1679002102214.
11. "1920 United States Federal Census," Ancestry.com, accessed December 3, 2023, https://www.ancestry.com/imageviewer/collections/6061/images/4311577-00311?pId=45061260.
12. "Massachusetts, U.S., Marriage Index, 1901–1955 and 1966–1970," Ancestry.com, accessed June 14, 2023, https://www.ancestry.com/imageviewer/collections/2966/images/41263_2421406273_0176-00113?pId=1229045.
13. "Massachusetts, U.S., Marriage Index, 1901–1955 and 1966–1970,"

Ancestry.com, accessed December 3, 2023, https://www.ancestry.com/imageviewer/collections/2966/images/41263_2421406273_0170-00390?pId=2153574.

14. "Last Minute Flashes," *Worcester Evening Gazette*, August 29, 1927, https://www.genealogybank.com/doc/newspapers/image/v2%3A1773BDF75FF7A17E%40GB3NEWS-17964E477307B03B%402425122-179557732ACA204E%-400-179557732ACA204E?clipid=msshwickjzfydjdeqkkuqouhzvjuzybr_wmagateway001_1679002485198.

15. "U.S., City Directories, 1822–1995," Ancestry.com, accessed December 3, 2023, https://www.ancestry.com/imageviewer/collections/2469/images/10189714?pId=512304932.

16. "1910 United States Federal Census," Ancestry.com, accessed December 3, 2023, https://www.ancestry.com/imageviewer/collections/7884/images/31111_4330112-00881?pId=11806963.

17. "Massachusetts, U.S., Town and Vital Records, 1620–1988," Ancestry.com, accessed December 2, 2023, https://www.ancestry.com/imageviewer/collections/2495/images/40143_266007__0185-00114?pId=3800284.

18. "Memorial ID: 243467883," Find a Grave, accessed December 2, 2023, https://www.findagrave.com/memorial/243467883/catherine-a-duff.

Chapter Two

1. "World War I," Wikipedia, accessed December 4, 2023, https://en.wikipedia.org/w/index.php?title=World_War_I&oldid=1188263128.

2. "American Entry into World War I, 1917," U.S. Department of State, Archive, 2001–2009, last modified January 20, 2009, accessed January 20, 2024, https://2001-2009.state.gov/r/pa/ho/time/wwi/82205.htm.

3. "Mobilizing for War: The Selective Service Act in WWI," National Archives Foundation, accessed January 21, 2024, https://www.archivesfoundation.org/documents/mobilizing-war-selective-service-act-world-war/#:~:text=On%20May%2018%2C%201917%2C%20Congress,to%20register%20for%20military%20service.

4. "New York, U.S., Abstracts of WWI Military Service, 1917–1919," Ancestry.com, accessed June 15, 2023, https://www.ancestry.com/imageviewer/collections/3030/images/40808_1120704930_0482-01124?pId=224456.

5. "Courts-martial of the United States," Wikipedia, accessed January 21, 2024, https://en.wikipedia.org/wiki/Courts-martial_of_the_United_States.

6. "Failure to Report for Duty: Desertion, AWOL, and Other Charges," FindLaw, last modified June 20, 2016, accessed January 31, 2024, https://www.findlaw.com/military/criminal-law/failure-to-report-for-duty-awol-and-other-charges.html#:~:text=Desertion%20carries%20a%20maximum%20punishment,of%20the%20court%2Dmartial.

7. "A Manual for Courts-Martial, U.S. Army, 1928 (Corrected to April 20, 1943)," Revised in the Office of the Judge Advocate General of the Army and Published by Direction of the President (Washington, DC: Government Printing Office, 1943), Appendix I, "The Articles of War," Article 58, "Desertion," https://www.ibiblio.org/hyperwar/USA/ref/MCM/index.html.

8. Dwight Sullivan, "A Matter of Life and Death: Examining the Military Death Penalty's Fairness," Death Penalty Information Center, https://deathpenaltyinfo.org/state-and-federal-info/military/the-militarys-death-penalty-system.

9. "Roll of the Dead," *Tampa Tribune*, January 22, 1916, https://www.newspapers.com/article/the-tampa-tribune-roll-of-the-dead-pere/119793016/ (alternate link: https://www.ancestry.com/mediaui-viewer/collection/1030/tree/106300270/person/282266865045/media/cd29126d-4e36-46c3-a4f4-bf23609ed797?_phsrc=aiN754&usePUBJs=true&galleryindex=1&albums=pg&showGalleryAlbums=true&tab=0&pid=282266865045&sort=-created).

10. "New York, U.S., Abstracts of WWI Military Service, 1917–1919," Ancestry.com, accessed June 15, 2023, https://www.ancestry.com/imageviewer/collections/3030/images/40808_1120704930_0482-01124?pId=224456.

11. "1880 United States Federal Census," Ancestry.com, accessed December 3, 2023, https://www.ancestry.com/imageviewer/collections/6742/images/4240

123-00097?pId=5981925; "U.S., Passport Applications, 1795–1925," Ancestry.com, accessed December 3, 2023, https://www.ancestry.com/imageviewer/collections/1174/images/USM1490_1266-0106?pId=949839.

12. "Members of the General Court-Martial" (clemency letter), First Corps Area, Boston, Massachusetts, August 3, 1928, Family Archives, Ancestry.com, accessed February 4, 2024, https://www.ancestry.com/mediaui-viewer/collection/1030/tree/106300270/person/282266865281/media/e1fa6887-1466-4e0b-bfdb-f258d795a3fb?_phsrc=aiN741&usePUBJs=true&galleryindex=1&albums=pg&showGalleryAlbums=true&tab=0&pid=282266865281&sort=-created.

13. "Death Gives Up Soldier Son," *Worcester Telegram–USA Today Network*, August 2, 1931, accessed January 20, 2024, http://imagn.com/setImages/554679/preview/22321978 (alternate link: https://www.ancestry.com/mediaui-viewer/collection/1030/tree/106300270/person/282266865281/media/921217d1-6901-46b4-a80e-af9e112a1729?_phsrc=aiN735&usePUBJs=true&galleryindex=1&albums=pg&showGalleryAlbums=true&tab=0&pid=282266865281&sort=-created).

14. "Major General C.W. Bridges to Pehr G. Holmes" (medical record letter), United States War Department, Washington, DC, July 3, 1931, Family Archives, Ancestry.com, accessed January 31, 2024, https://www.ancestry.com/mediaui-viewer/collection/1030/tree/106300270/person/282266865281/media/2131ec83-5eb6-48d6-b046-55010c65718e?_phsrc=aiN749&usePUBJs=true&galleryindex=1&albums=pg&showGalleryAlbums=true&tab=0&pid=282266865281&filter=p&sort=created.

15. "Major General Charles W. Bridges to George R. Stobbs" (war record letter), United States War Department, Washington, DC, July 3, 1931, Family Archives, Ancestry.com, accessed February 4, 2024, https://www.ancestry.com/mediaui-viewer/collection/1030/tree/106300270/person/282266865281/media/c588a91a-8ddb-4b82-826c-9a697db64a3a?_phsrc=aiN749&usePUBJs=true&galleryindex=2&albums=pg&showGalleryAlbums=true&tab=0&pid=282266865281&filter=p&sort=-created.

16. "Major General C.W. Bridges to Pehr G. Holmes" (medical record letter), United States War Department, Washington, DC, July 3, 1931, Family Archives, Ancestry.com, accessed January 31, 2024, https://www.ancestry.com/mediaui-viewer/collection/1030/tree/106300270/person/282266865281/media/2131ec83-5eb6-48d6-b046-55010c65718e?_phsrc=aiN749&usePUBJs=true&galleryindex=1&albums=pg&showGalleryAlbums=true&tab=0&pid=282266865281&filter=p&sort=-created.

Chapter Three

1. "Campaign Battles—Dates of Participation—Hector & Charles," Ancestry.com, accessed February 4, 2024, https://www.ancestry.com/mediaui-viewer/collection/1030/tree/106300270/person/282266865281/media/08882efc-8805-4ab0-8ee4-2a26dd7b3bc5?_phsrc=aiN1188&usePUBJs=true&galleryindex=1&albums=pg&showGalleryAlbums=true&tab=0&pid=282266865281&sort=-created.

2. "1900 United States Federal Census," Ancestry.com, accessed December 6, 2023, https://www.ancestry.com/imageviewer/collections/7602/images/4120049_00387?pId=34146257.

3. "1880 United States Federal Census," Ancestry.com, accessed December 5, 2023, https://www.ancestry.com/imageviewer/collections/6742/images/4240123-00139?pId=4411225.

4. "1900 United States Federal Census," Ancestry.com, accessed December 6, 2023, https://www.ancestry.com/imageviewer/collections/7602/images/4120049_00587?pId=34155417.

5. "1870 United States Federal Census," Ancestry.com, accessed January 22, 2024, https://www.ancestry.com/imageviewer/collections/7163/images/4275949_00417?pId=4101889.

6. "1880 United States Federal Census," Ancestry.com, accessed January 22, 2024, https://www.ancestry.com/imageviewer/collections/6742/images/4240123-00097?pId=5981925.

7. "1880 United Stated Federal Census," Ancestry.com, accessed December 6, 2023, https://www.ancestry.com/imageviewer/collections/6742/images/4240123-00097?pId=2702268.

8. "1880 United States Federal Census," Ancestry.com, accessed December 6, 2023, https://www.ancestry.com/imageviewer/collections/6742/images/4240123-00097?pId=2786228.

9. "1900 United Stated Federal Census," Ancestry.com, accessed December 6, 2023, https://www.ancestry.com/imageviewer/collections/7602/images/4120049_00587?pId=34155418.

10. "1910 United States Federal Census," Ancestry.com, accessed December 6, 2023, https://www.ancestry.com/imageviewer/collections/7884/images/31111_4327451-00931?pId=3055066.

11. "Florida, U.S., County Marriage Records, 1823–1982, Hillsborough County, Marriage License, February 15, 1896," Ancestry.com, accessed December 6, 2023, https://www.ancestry.com/mediaui-viewer/collection/1030/tree/106300270/person/282266865045/media/6261da5f-1ab2-4853-812e-99a23a11aca4?_phsrc=aiN819&usePUBJs=true&galleryindex=4&albums=pg&showGalleryAlbums=true&tab=0&pid=282266865045&sort=-created.

12. "1900 United Stated Federal Census," Ancestry.com, accessed December 6, 2023, https://www.ancestry.com/imageviewer/collections/7602/images/4120049_00388?pId=34146267.

13. "1900 United States Federal Census," Ancestry.com, accessed January 22, 2024, https://www.ancestry.com/imageviewer/collections/7602/images/4120049_00387?pId=34146257.

14. "United States Patent and Trademark Office, US-0687089," accessed December 6, 2023, https://image-ppubs.uspto.gov/dirsearch-public/print/downloadPdf/0687089.

15. "1910 United States Federal Census," Ancestry.com, accessed January 22, 2024, https://www.ancestry.com/imageviewer/collections/7884/images/31111_4327451-00954?pId=3055422.

16. "U.S., City Directories, 1822–1995," Ancestry.com, accessed January 22, 2024, https://www.ancestry.com/imageviewer/collections/2469/images/15247122?pId=972709640.

17. "U.S., City Directories, 1822–1995," Ancestry.com, accessed January 22, 2024, https://www.ancestry.com/imageviewer/collections/2469/images/15247122?pId=972709678.

18. "Roll of the Dead," *Tampa Tribune*, January 22, 1916, accessed January 16, 2024, https://www.newspapers.com/article/the-tampa-tribune-roll-of-the-dead-pere/119793016/.

19. "Life Expectancy in the United States," Congressional Research Service, accessed December 6, 2023, https://www.everycrsreport.com/reports/RL32792.html#_Toc194633795.

20. "Principal Causes of Death in United States Registration Area: Census Bureau Summarizes Mortality Statistics for 1917," *Public Health Reports (1896–1970)* 34, no. 27 (1919): 1474–78, accessed December 10, 2023, http://www.jstor.org/stable/4575222.

21. "Mrs. Mercedes Perez Dies Last Night," *Key West Citizen*, August 29, 1931, Ancestry.com, accessed December 7, 2023, https://www.ancestry.com/imageviewer/collections/7933/images/news-fl-ke_we_ci.1932_08_29_0004?pId=488928260.

22. "Florida Keys History Center—Monroe County's Public Library Stream," accessed January 22, 2024, https://www.flickr.com/photos/keyslibraries/9048605417/ (license link: https://creativecommons.org/licenses/by/2.0/).

23. "U.S., City Directories, 1822–1995," Ancestry.com, accessed December 7, 2023, https://www.ancestry.com/imageviewer/collections/2469/images/11968679?pId=674122081.

24. "Florida, U.S., Arriving and Departing Passenger and Crew Lists, 1898–1963," Ancestry.com, accessed December 7, 2023, https://www.ancestry.com/imageviewer/collections/8842/images/t940_45-0451?pId=2323046.

25. "U.S., City Directories, 1822–1995," Ancestry.com, accessed December 7, 2023, https://www.ancestry.com/imageviewer/collections/2469/images/11838497?pId=664099106.

26. "History of Pharmacy in the United States," Wikipedia, accessed December 7, 2023, https://en.wikipedia.org/w/index.php?title=History_of_pharmacy_in_the_United_States&oldid=1181422170; Alex Berman, "The Pharmaceutical Component of 19th-Century French Public Health and Hygiene," *Pharmacy in History* 11, no. 1 (1969), accessed December 7, 2023, http://www.jstor.org/stable/41109689.

27. "U.S., World War II Draft Registration Cards, 1942," Ancestry.com, accessed January 16, 2024, https://www.ancestry.com/imageviewer/collections/1002/images/miusa1939b_082573-01273.
28. "1920 United States Federal Census, Military and Naval Force, Germany, Coblenz," Ancestry.com, accessed January 22, 2024, https://www.ancestry.com/imageviewer/collections/6061/images/4442145_00385?pId=113162961.

Chapter Four

1. B. M. Brereton and Colin Graham Clarke, "West Indies," Encyclopedia Britannica, October 25, 2023, accessed December 7, 2023, https://www.britannica.com/place/West-Indies-island-group-Atlantic-Ocean.
2. "Hispaniola," Encyclopedia Britannica, accessed November 22, 2023, https://www.britannica.com/place/Hispaniola.
3. "Hispaniola," Wikipedia, accessed December 7, 2023, https://en.wikipedia.org/w/index.php?title=Hispaniola&oldid=1187573465.
4. "How Havana Became British for Eleven Months," *Library of Congress Blogs*, accessed December 7, 2023, https://blogs.loc.gov/law/2022/01/how-havana-became-british-for-eleven-months/.
5. "Cuba Chronology," Library of Congress Research Guides, accessed December 7, 2023, https://guides.loc.gov/world-of-1898/cuba-chronology.
6. "Republic of Cuba (1902–1959)," Wikipedia, accessed December 30, 2023, https://en.wikipedia.org/wiki/Republic_of_Cuba_(1902-1959).
7. "Ten Years' War," Wikipedia, accessed December 7, 2023, https://en.wikipedia.org/wiki/Ten_Years%27_War.
8. "The First Edition of the Modern Taino Dictionary," Taino Language Project, accessed January 22, 2024, https://www.taino-tribe.org/tedict.html.
9. "Yara, Cuba," Wikipedia, accessed December 7, 2023, https://en.wikipedia.org/w/index.php?title=Yara,_Cuba&oldid=1176606826.
10. Lars Schoultz, "A Review of the History of Havana," *Harvard Review of Latin America* (2007), accessed December 7, 2023, https://archive.revista.drclas.harvard.edu/book/book-talk-whats-most-welcoming-city-how-about-havana.
11. "1900 United States Federal Census," Ancestry.com, accessed January 22, 2024, https://www.ancestry.com/imageviewer/collections/7602/images/4120049_00387?pId=34146257.
12. "Little War," Wikipedia, accessed December 11, 2023, https://en.wikipedia.org/wiki/Little_War_(Cuba).
13. "The Pact of Zanjón," Wikipedia, accessed December 11, 2023, https://en.wikipedia.org/wiki/Pact_of_Zanjón.
14. "The Cuban War of Independence," Wikipedia, accessed December 11, 2023, https://en.wikipedia.org/wiki/Cuban_War_of_Independence.
15. "Spanish–American War," Wikipedia, accessed December 11, 2023, https://en.wikipedia.org/wiki/Spanish-American_War.
16. "The Treaty of Paris," Wikipedia, accessed December 11, 2023, https://en.wikipedia.org/wiki/Treaty_of_Paris_(1898).
17. Maryann Ward and John Devereux, "The Road Not Taken: Pre-Revolutionary Cuban Living Standards in Comparative Perspective," *Journal of Economic History* 72, issue 1 (2012), https://www.cambridge.org/core/journals/journal-of-economic-history/article/abs/road-not-taken-prerevolutionary-cuban-living-standards-in-comparative-perspective/1710F4E3173FCABE07BB7400406BF55E; "The Hemisphere: Pearl of the Antilles," *Time*, January 26, 1959, accessed December 11, 2023, https://content.time.com/time/subscriber/article/0,33009,892092-1,00.html.
18. C. Neale Ronning, *Jose Marti and the Émigré Colony in Key West: Leadership and State Formation* (New York: Praeger, 1990); "Salvador Bermúdez de Castro, Marquis de Lema," Wikipedia, accessed December 11, 2023, https://en.wikipedia.org/wiki/Salvador_Bermúdez_de_Castro,_Marquis_of_Lema.
19. Gustavo J. Godoy, "Jose Alejandro Huau: A Cuban Patriot in Jacksonville Politics," *Florida Historical Quarterly* 54, no. 2 (1975), Article 7, accessed December 11, 2023, https://stars.library.ucf.edu/cgi/viewcontent.cgi?article=3385&context=fhq.
20. C. Neale Ronning, *Jose Marti and*

the *Émigré Colony in Key West: Leadership and State Formation* (New York: Praeger, 1990).

21. Tyler J. Santana and the Tampa Historical Team, "Vicente Martinez Ybor," Tampa Historical, accessed December 11, 2023, https://tampahistorical.org/items/show/125.

22. "Upper Keys 1870 U.S. Census," Keys History, accessed December 11, 2023, http://www.keyshistory.org/census.html; "Key West," Wikipedia, accessed December 11, 2023, https://en.wikipedia.org/wiki/Key_West.

23. Dennis E. Showalter and John Graham Royde-Smith, "World War I," Encyclopedia Britannica, accessed December 9, 2023, https://www.britannica.com/event/World-War-I.

24. "The American Expeditionary Forces," Library of Congress, accessed December 12, 2023, https://www.loc.gov/collections/stars-and-stripes/articles-and-essays/a-world-at-war/american-expeditionary-forces/.

25. "American War and Military Operations Casualties: Lists and Statistics," CRS Report No. RL32492, Version 25, p. 2 (Washington, DC: Congressional Research Service, September 14, 2018), accessed December 14, 2023, https://crsreports.congress.gov/product/pdf/RL/RL32492.

26. "New York, U.S., Abstracts of WW I Military Service, 1917–1919," Ancestry.com, accessed December 14, 2023, https://www.ancestry.com/imageviewer/collections/3030/images/40808_1120704930_0482-01124?pId=224456; "World War I Enlistment Card," Ancestry.com, accessed December 14, 2023, https://www.ancestry.com/mediaui-viewer/collection/1030/tree/106300270/person/282266865282/media/aeaf0e1b-d891-4c34-b1c1-1314e0d7b004?_phsrc=aiN848&usePUBJs=true&galleryindex=4&albums=pg&showGalleryAlbums=true&tab=0&pid=282266865282&sort=-created.

27. Arlene Balkansky, "The Draft in World War I: America Volunteered Its Mass," *Library of Congress Blogs*, June 19, 2018, accessed December 14, 2023, https://blogs.loc.gov/headlinesandheroes/2018/06/wwi-draft/.

28. Eric Durr, "This World War Killer Took Almost as Many US Troops' Lives as Combat," Military.com, August 29, 2018, accessed December 14, 2023, https://www.military.com/history/this-world-war-i-killer-took-almost-as-many-us-troops-lives-as-combat.html.

29. Eric Durr, "This World War Killer Took Almost as Many US Troops' Lives as Combat," Military.com, August 29, 2018, accessed December 14, 2023, https://www.military.com/history/this-world-war-i-killer-took-almost-as-many-us-troops-lives-as-combat.html.

30. Dr. Edgar Jones, "Shell Shocked," *Monitor on Psychology* 43, no. 6 (June 2012), accessed December 14, 2023, https://www.apa.org/monitor/2012/06/shell-shocked.

31. Dr. Edgar Jones, "Shell Shocked," *Monitor on Psychology* 43, no. 6 (June 2012), accessed December 15, 2023, https://www.apa.org/monitor/2012/06/shell-shocked.

32. Pavi Sandhu, "Step Aside, Freud: Josef Breuer Is the True Father of Modern Psychotherapy," *Scientific American*, June 30, 2015, accessed December 15, 2023, https://blogs.scientificamerican.com/mind-guest-blog/step-aside-freud-josef-breuer-is-the-true-father-of-modern-psychotherapy/.

33. Daniel J. Samet, "World War I: The War That Saved Democracy," United States World War One Centennial Commission, accessed February 23, 2024, https://www.worldwar1centennial.org/index.php/communicate/press-media/wwi-centennial-news/5619-world-war-i-the-war-that-saved-democracy.html.

34. Gary Polakovic, "How Did WWI Reshape the Modern World?" *USC Today*, November 9, 2018, accessed December 15, 2023, https://today.usc.edu/impact-of-world-war-i-shaping-the-modern-world/.

35. "Military Medicine in World War I," United States World War One Centennial Commission, accessed February 23, 2024, https://www.worldwar1centennial.org/index.php/practice-of-medicine-in-ww1.html.

36. "Injuries in World War I: Psychological Injuries," United States World War One Centennial Commission, accessed February 23, 2024, https://www.worldwar1centennial.org/index.php/injuries-in-world-war-i/2592-injuries-in-world-war-i-psychological-injuries.html.

Chapter Five

1. "U.S., WWII Draft Cards Young Men, 1940–1947," Ancestry.com, accessed December 15, 2023, https://www.ancestry.com/imageviewer/collections/2238/images/44005_01_00010-01436?pId=12249158.

2. "1900 United States Federal Census," Ancestry.com, accessed December 15, 2023, https://www.ancestry.com/imageviewer/collections/7602/images/4120049_00388?pId=34146269.

3. "1910 United States Federal Census," Ancestry.com, accessed December 15, 2023, https://www.ancestry.com/imageviewer/collections/7884/images/31111_4327451-00954?pId=180178708.

4. "Memorial ID: 18264878," Find a Grave, accessed December 15, 2023, https://www.findagrave.com/memorial/18264878/francisca-velasco; "1910 United States Federal Census," Ancestry.com, accessed December 15, 2023, https://www.ancestry.com/imageviewer/collections/7884/images/31111_4327451-00803?pId=3052922.

5. "U.S., Veterans Administration Master Index, 1917–1940," Ancestry.com, accessed December 15, 2023, https://www.ancestry.com/discoveryui-content/view/5089128:61861?ssrc=pt&tid=106300270&pid=282266865282.

6. "Florida, Military Dept., Charlie E Perez," State Library and Archives of Florida, Florida Memory, accessed December 15, 2023, https://www.floridamemory.com/items/show/203671; "U.S., Headstone Applications for Military Veterans, 1861–1985," Ancestry.com, accessed December 15, 2023, https://www.ancestry.com/imageviewer/collections/2375/images/40050_2421402106_0401-01403?pId=494903.

7. "U.S., Army Transport Service Arriving and Departing Passenger Lists, 1910–1939," Ancestry.com, accessed December 15, 2023, https://www.ancestry.com/imageviewer/collections/61174/images/44509_3421606189_0303-00039?pId=3334456.

8. "U.S., Army Transport Service Arriving and Departing Passenger Lists, 1910–1939," Ancestry.com, accessed December 15, 2023, https://www.ancestry.com/imageviewer/collections/61174/images/46920_162028006074_0062-00585?pId=7161246.

9. "U.S., Army Transport Service Arriving and Departing Passenger Lists, 1910–1939," Ancestry.com, accessed December 15, 2023, https://www.ancestry.com/discoveryui-content/view/7204057:61174?ssrc=pt&tid=106300270&pid=282266865282.

10. "U.S., Veterans Administration Master Index, 1917–1940," Ancestry.com, accessed December 15, 2023, https://www.ancestry.com/discoveryui-content/view/5089128:61861?ssrc=pt&tid=106300270&pid=282266865282.

11. "1920 United States Federal Census, Military and Naval Population Abroad," Ancestry.com, accessed December 15, 2023, https://www.ancestry.com/imageviewer/collections/6061/images/4442145_00567?pId=113168857; "1920 United States Federal Census, Military and Naval Population Abroad," Ancestry.com, accessed December 15, 2023, https://www.ancestry.com/imageviewer/collections/6061/images/4442145_00385?pId=113162961.

12. "1920 United States Federal Census," Ancestry.com, accessed December 15, 2023, https://www.ancestry.com/discoveryui-content/view/7139810:6061?ssrc=pt&tid=106300270&pid=282266865279.

13. "Florida, Military Dept., Charlie E Perez," State Library and Archives of Florida, Florida Memory, accessed December 15, 2023, https://www.floridamemory.com/items/show/203671.

14. UCF Veterans Legacy Program, K-12 Instructional Packets, "Charles Ernest Perez," accessed February 5, 2024, https://vlp.cah.ucf.edu/k12.php (alternate link: https://vlp.cah.ucf.edu/instructionalmaterials/UCF-VLP-CharlesErnestPerezPacket.pdf).

15. UCF Veterans Legacy Program Institute Brochure, 2023, accessed December 15, 2023, https://online.fliphtml5.com/wqbac/jyos/#p=1.

16. "Florida, Military Dept., Charlie E Perez," State Library and Archives of Florida, Florida Memory, accessed December 15, 2023, https://www.floridamemory.com/items/show/203671?id=2.

17. "The 1973 Fire, National Personnel Records Center," National Archives,

accessed December 25, 2023, https://www.archives.gov/personnel-records-center/fire-1973.

18. "U.S., Headstone Applications for Military Veterans, 1861–1985," Ancestry.com, accessed December 15, 2023, https://www.ancestry.com/discoveryui-content/view/494903:2375?ssrc=pt&tid=106300270&pid=282266865282.

19. "Fort Hayes," Wikipedia, accessed January 7, 2024, https://en.wikipedia.org/wiki/Fort_Hayes.

20. "Florida, Military Dept., Charlie E Perez," State Library and Archives of Florida, Florida Memory, accessed December 15, 2023, https://www.floridamemory.com/items/show/203671?id=2.

21. "Silver Star," New World Encyclopedia, accessed January 7, 2024, https://www.newworldencyclopedia.org/entry/Silver_Star.

22. "How the Machine Gun Changed Combat during World War I," Norwich University, accessed December 15, 2023, https://online.norwich.edu/how-machine-gun-changed-combat-during-world-war-i.

23. "World War I Victory Medal, United States," Wikipedia, accessed December 15, 2023, https://en.wikipedia.org/wiki/World_War_I_Victory_Medal_(United_States); "World War I Victory Medal," U.S. Commission of Fine Arts, accessed December 16, 2023, https://www.cfa.gov/about-cfa/design-topics/coins-medals/world-war-i-victory-medal.

24. "Croix de Guerre 1914–1918 (France)," Wikipedia, accessed February 20, 2024, https://en.wikipedia.org/wiki/Croix_de_guerre_1914-1918_(France).

25. "1930 United States Federal Census," Ancestry.com, accessed December 15, 2023, https://www.ancestry.com/imageviewer/collections/6224/images/4639126_00422?pId=41613734; "1940 United States Federal Census," Ancestry.com, accessed December 15, 2023, https://www.ancestry.com/imageviewer/collections/2442/images/m-t0627-02668-00227?pId=5889432.

26. "Miss van Deinse Is Wed to Mr. Perez in New York," *Orlando Sentinel*, October 4, 1936, accessed December 15, 2023, https://www.newspapers.com/article/the-orlando-sentinel-marriage-of-charles/119599744/.

27. "Former Marion Girl Marries New York Man," *Marion Star* (Marion, Ohio), October 10, 1936, accessed December 15, 2023, https://www.newspapers.com/article/the-marion-star-marriage-caroline-veroni/119738536/.

28. "Personals," *Orlando Evening Star*, September 27, 1937, accessed December 15, 2023, https://www.newspapers.com/article/orlando-evening-star-charles-e-perez-m/119605067/.

29. "Personals," *St. Petersburg Times*, March 31, 1941, Ancestry.com, accessed December 15, 2023, https://www.ancestry.com/mediaui-viewer/collection/1030/tree/106300270/person/282266865282/media/c12e4a47-e337-4290-9b36-641812d7d19c?_phsrc=aiN871&usePUBJs=true&galleryindex=1&albums=pg&showGalleryAlbums=true&tab=0&pid=282266865282&sort=-created.

30. *New York National Guardsman*, September 1937, page 2, New York State Military Museum and Veterans Research Center, accessed December 15, 2023, https://museum.dmna.ny.gov/application/files/1315/7971/8920/NYNG1937_09.pdf.

31. "U.S., World War II Draft Cards Young Men, 1940–1947," Ancestry.com, accessed December 15, 2023, https://www.ancestry.com/imageviewer/collections/2238/images/44005_01_00010-01436?pId=12249158.

32. "Florida, U.S., Divorce Index, 1927–2001," Ancestry.com, accessed December 15, 2023, https://www.ancestry.com/imageviewer/collections/8837/images/FLDIV_0049-0032?pId=430198.

33. "Florida, U.S., Marriage Indexes, 1822–1875, 1927–2001," Ancestry.com, accessed December 15, 2023, https://www.ancestry.com/imageviewer/collections/8784/images/FLMAR_0326-0013?pId=1550875.

34. "U.S., Social Security Death Index," Ancestry.com, accessed December 15, 2023, https://www.ancestry.com/discoveryui-content/view/35943659:3693?ssrc=pt&tid=106300270&pid=282459275056.

35. "Bay Pines Men's Domiciliary History," U.S. Department of Veterans Affairs, accessed December 15, 2023, https://www.va.gov/bay-pines-health-care/about-us/history/.

36. "Fletcher Favors Use of $6,000,000

Funds to Aid States' Idle," Bay Pines VA Medical, accessed December 15, 2023, https://cdm15801.contentdm.oclc.org/digital/collection/p15801coll3/id/19/rec/17.

37. "U.S., City Directories, 1822–1995," Ancestry.com, accessed December 16, 2023, https://www.ancestry.com/imageviewer/collections/2469/images/11817477?pId=662586788; "Florida, U.S., State Census, 1867–1945," Ancestry.com, accessed December 16, 2023, https://www.ancestry.com/imageviewer/collections/1506/images/CSUSAFL1867_089324-00346?pId=883183.

38. "1950 United States Federal Census," Ancestry.com, accessed December 16, 2023, https://www.ancestry.com/imageviewer/collections/62308/images/43290879-Florida-059375-0007?pId=81965477.

39. "Bureau of Vital Statistics, Certificate of Death," Ancestry.com, accessed December 16, 2023, https://www.ancestry.com/mediaui-viewer/collection/1030/tree/106300270/person/282266865282/media/a275e2d0-d943-421c-974f-82eed439c014?_phsrc=aiN890&usePUBJs=true&galleryindex=8&albums=pg&showGalleryAlbums=true&tab=0&pid=282266865282&sort=-created.

40. "Other Deaths," *Miami Herald*, May 2, 1950, accessed December 16, 2023, https://www.ancestry.com/mediaui-viewer/collection/1030/tree/106300270/person/282266865282/media/5c1016bc-03a4-4b7b-9a9f-6966ada0ce74?_phsrc=aiN893&usePUBJs=true&galleryindex=7&albums=pg&showGalleryAlbums=true&tab=0&pid=282266865282&sort=-created.

41. "Memorial ID: 3974667," Find a Grave, accessed December 16, 2023, https://www.findagrave.com/memorial/3974667/charles-ernest-perez.

42. "Miami Biltmore Hotel," Wikipedia, accessed December 19, 2023, https://en.wikipedia.org/w/index.php?title=Miami_Biltmore_Hotel&oldid=1169253142.

43. "History of the Bruce W. Carter VA Medical Center," U.S. Department of Veterans Affairs, accessed December 19, 2023, https://www.va.gov/miami-health-care/about-us/history/.

44. "Memorial ID: 3974667," Find a Grave, accessed December 19, 2023, https://www.findagrave.com/memorial/3974667/charles-ernest-perez.

45. "U.S. Veterans Administration Master Index, 1917–1940," Ancestry.com, accessed December 19, 2023, https://www.ancestry.com/discoveryui-content/view/5089128:61861?ssrc=pt&tid=106300270&pid=282266865282.

46. "Memorial ID: 3974667," Find a Grave, accessed December 19, 2023, https://www.findagrave.com/memorial/3974667/charles-ernest-perez/photo.

Chapter Six

1. "Fort Slocum," Wikipedia, accessed December 19, 2023, https://en.wikipedia.org/wiki/Fort_Slocum.

2. "Roll of the Dead," *Tampa Tribune*, June 22, 1916, accessed December 19, 2023, https://www.newspapers.com/article/the-tampa-tribune-roll-of-the-dead-pere/119793016/.

3. "U.S., City Directories, 1822–1995," Ancestry.com, accessed December 19, 2023, https://www.ancestry.com/imageviewer/collections/2469/images/15247122?pId=972709640.

4. Geri Ann Galanti, "The Hispanic Family and Male-Female Relationships: An Overview," NIH National Library of Medicine, 2003, accessed December 19, 2023, https://pubmed.ncbi.nlm.nih.gov/12861920/.

5. "Seaboard Air Line Railroad," Wikipedia, accessed December 19, 2023, https://en.wikipedia.org/wiki/Seaboard_Air_Line_Railroad.

6. "New York, U.S., Abstracts of WW I Military Service, 1917–1919," Ancestry.com, accessed December 19, 2023, https://www.ancestry.com/imageviewer/collections/3030/images/40808_1120704930_0482-01124?pId=224456.

7. "New York, U.S., Abstracts of WW I Military Service, 1917–1919," Ancestry.com, accessed December 19, 2023, https://www.ancestry.com/imageviewer/collections/3030/images/40808_1120704930_0482-01124?pId=224456.

8. "Lineage and Honors, 2D Engineer Battalion," United States of America War Office, accessed December 19, 2023, updated April 18, 2024, https://history.army.mil/html/forcestruc/lineages/branches/eng/0002enbn.htm.

9. "U.S., Veterans Administration Master Index, 1917–1940," Ancestry.com,

accessed December 19, 2023, https://www.ancestry.com/discoveryui-content/view/5098786:61861?ssrc=pt&tid=106300270&pid=282266865281.

10. "Major General C.W. Bridges to Pehr G. Holmes" (medical record letter), United States War Department, Washington, DC, July 3, 1931, Family Archives, Ancestry.com, accessed January 31, 2024, https://www.ancestry.com/mediaui-viewer/collection/1030/tree/106300270/person/282266865281/media/2131ec83-5eb6-48d6-b046-55010c65718e?_phsrc=aiN749&usePUBJs=true&galleryindex=1&albums=pg&showGalleryAlbums=true&tab=0&pid=282266865281&filter=p&sort=-created.

11. "U.S., Army Transport Service Arriving and Departing Passenger Lists, 1910–1939," Ancestry.com, accessed December 19, 2023, https://www.ancestry.com/imageviewer/collections/61174/images/44509_162028006074_0179-00770?pId=937496.

12. "15th Field Artillery Regiment," Wikipedia, accessed December 19, 2023, https://en.wikipedia.org/wiki/15th_Field_Artillery_Regiment_(United_States).

13. "2nd Engineer Battalion (United States)," Wikipedia, accessed December 19, 2023, https://en.wikipedia.org/wiki/2nd_Engineer_Battalion_(United_States)#:~:text=The%202nd%20Engineer%20Regiment%20was,arrived%20in%20theater%20under%20strength (alternate link: http://www.worldwar1.com/dbc/ct_bw2eng.htm).

14. "Army and Beta Tests and Overview," Oxford Dictionary, accessed December 19, 2023, https://www.oxfordreference.com/display/10.1093/oi/authority.20110803095424949.

15. "Military Medicine in World War I," United States World War One Centennial Commission, accessed December 19, 2023, https://www.worldwar1centennial.org/index.php/practice-of-medicine-in-ww1.html.

16. "U.S., Army Transport Service Arriving and Departing Passenger Lists, 1910–1939," Ancestry.com, accessed December 19, 2023, https://www.ancestry.com/imageviewer/collections/61174/images/44509_162028006074_0179-00770?pId=937496.

17. "SS Adriatic at Southampton (1907)," Reddit, accessed December 19, 2023, https://www.reddit.com/r/Oceanlinerporn/comments/o8ebwk/ss_adriatic_at_southampton_1907/.

18. "Major General Charles W. Bridges to George R. Stobbs" (war record letter), United States War Department, Washington, DC, July 3, 1931, Family Archives, Ancestry.com, accessed December 19, 2023, https://www.ancestry.com/mediaui-viewer/collection/1030/tree/106300270/person/282266865281/media/c588a91a-8ddb-4b82-826c-9a697db64a3a?_phsrc=aiN907&usePUBJs=true&galleryindex=4&albums=pg&showGalleryAlbums=true&tab=0&pid=282266865281&sort=-created.

19. Charles Hendricks, "Combat and Construction, US Army Engineers in World War I," U.S. Army Corps of Engineers, accessed December 19, 2023, https://usace.contentdm.oclc.org/digital/api/collection/p16021coll4/id/334/download.

20. Sergeant Tatum Vayavanda, "The Battle of Belleau Wood Not Forgotten by U.S. Marines and French Soldiers," Marines: The Official Website of the United States Marine Corps, accessed December 19, 2023, https://www.marforeur.marines.mil/In-the-News/Stories/Article/Article/520993/the-battle-of-belleau-wood-not-forgotten-by-us-marines-and-french-soldiers-on-m/.

21. Colonel Bill Anderson, USMC (Ret.), "The 2D Engineers at Belleau Wood," Doughboy Center, accessed December 19, 2023, http://www.worldwar1.com/dbc/ct_bw2eng.htm.

22. "Sector Activities," Army War College, Historical Section, accessed December 19, 2023, https://history.army.mil/curriculum/wwi/docs/Additional Resources/Sector_Activities_AEF_on_Western_Front_and_Italy_1917-1918.pdf.

23. "6th Machine Gun Battalion (United States Marine Corps)," Wikipedia, accessed December 19, 2023, https://en.wikipedia.org/wiki/6th_Machine_Gun_Battalion_(United_States_Marine_Corps).

24. "2d Division Summary of Operations in the World War," American Battles Monuments Commission, accessed December 19, 2023, https://2nd-division.com/_div.misc/summary.htm.

25. "Battle of Saint-Mihiel," Wikipedia, accessed December 19, 2023,

https://en.wikipedia.org/wiki/Battle_of_Saint-Mihiel.

26. "Blood, Mud, Concrete and Barbed Wire: The Meuse-Argonne Offensive," Army Heritage Center Foundation, accessed December 19, 2023, https://www.armyheritage.org/soldier-stories-information/blood-mud-concrete-and-barbed-wire-the-meuse-argonne-offensive/.

27. "Sector Activities," Army War College, Historical Section, accessed December 19, 2023, https://history.army.mil/curriculum/wwi/docs/Additional Resources/Sector_Activities_AEF_on_Western_Front_and_Italy_1917-1918.pdf.

28. "WWI Service Cards," State Library and Archives of Florida, Florida Memory, accessed December 20, 2023, https://www.floridamemory.com/items/show/203671; "New York, U.S., Abstracts of WWI Military Service, 1917–1919," Ancestry.com, accessed December 20, 2023, https://www.ancestry.com/imageviewer/collections/3030/images/40808_1120704930_0482-01124?pId=224456.

29. "Major General Charles W. Bridges to George R. Stobbs" (war record letter), United States War Department, Washington, DC, July 3, 1931, Family Archives, Ancestry.com, accessed December 20, 2023, https://www.ancestry.com/mediauiviewer/collection/1030/tree/106300270/person/282266865281/media/c588a91a-8ddb-4b82-826c-9a697db64a3a?_phsrc=aiN909&usePUBJs=true&galleryindex=4&albums=pg&showGalleryAlbums=true&tab=0&pid=282266865281&sort=-created.

30. William T. Anderson, "Devil Dogs in Olive Drab: The 2d Engineers at Belleau Wood," Army History, updated 2022, accessed December 20, 2023, https://2nd-division.com/_div.misc/chateau.thierry/belleau.engineers.htm.

31. Ellen Terrell, "Prohibition Begins," Library of Congress Research Guides, accessed December 20, 2023, https://guides.loc.gov/this-month-in-business-history/january/prohibition.

32. Regimental Headquarters Second Engineers, "Official History of the Second Engineers in the World War, 1916–1919," Library of Congress, accessed December 20, 2023, https://tile.loc.gov/storage-services/public/gdcmassbookdig/officialhistoryo00uni/officialhistoryo00uni.pdf.

33. Hans Pohls and Stephanie Oak, "War and Military Mental Health," *American Journal of Public Health* 97, no. 12 (December 2007), accessed December 21, 2023, https://www.ncbi.nlm.nih.gov/pmc/articles/PMC2089086/.

34. "U.S., Army Transport Service Arriving and Departing Passenger Lists, 1910–1939," Ancestry.com., accessed December 20, 2023, https://www.ancestry.com/imageviewer/collections/61174/images/46920_162028006074_0145-00591?pId=7977265.

35. "Lima, Ohio," City Maps, accessed December 20, 2023, https://colgis.cityhall.lima.oh.us/zoning/.

36. "Broome Street," Wikipedia, accessed December 20, 2023, https://en.wikipedia.org/wiki/Broome_Street.

37. "U.S., Army Transport Service Arriving and Departing Passenger Lists, 1910–1939," Ancestry.com, accessed December 20, 2023, https://www.ancestry.com/imageviewer/collections/61174/images/44509_162028006074_0179-00770?pId=937496.

38. "Garrison Prisoner," Merriam Webster Dictionary, accessed December 20, 2023, https://www.merriam-webster.com/dictionary/garrison%20prisoner.

39. "General Prisoner," Merriam Webster Dictionary, accessed December 20, 2023, https://www.merriam-webster.com/dictionary/general%20prisoner.

40. "Major General Charles W. Bridges to George R. Stobbs" (war record letter), United States War Department, Washington, DC, July 3, 1931, Family Archives, Ancestry.com, accessed December 20, 2023, https://www.ancestry.com/mediauiviewer/collection/1030/tree/106300270/person/282266865281/media/c588a91a-8ddb-4b82-826c-9a697db64a3a?_phsrc=aiN911&usePUBJs=true&galleryindex=4&albums=pg&showGalleryAlbums=true&tab=0&pid=282266865281&sort=-created.

41. "Fox Hills Boasts World's Largest Army Hospital," *Staten Island Advance*, March 27, 2011, accessed December 20, 2023, https://www.silive.com/special reports/2011/03/post_1.html.

42. "List of Former United States Army Medical Units," Wikipedia, accessed December 20, 2023, https://en.wikipedia.

org/wiki/List_of_former_United_States_Army_medical_units#Debarkation_hospitals.

43. "Medical Department of the United States Army in the World War," AMEDD Center for History and Heritage, accessed December 20, 2023, https://achh.army.mil/history/book-wwi-neuropsychiatry-section1chapter3.

44. "Major General C.W. Bridges to Pehr G. Holmes" (medical record letter), United States War Department, Washington, DC, July 3, 1931, Family Archives, Ancestry.com, accessed December 20, 2023, https://www.ancestry.com/mediaui-viewer/collection/1030/tree/106300270/person/282266865281/media/2131ec83-5eb6-48d6-b046-55010c65718e?_phsrc=aiN911&usePUBJs=true&galleryindex=3&albums=pg&showGalleryAlbums=true&tab=0&pid=282266865281&sort=-created.

45. "Major General C.W. Bridges to Pehr G. Holmes" (medical record letter), United States War Department, Washington, DC, July 3, 1931, Family Archives, Ancestry.com, accessed December 20, 2023, https://www.ancestry.com/mediaui-viewer/collection/1030/tree/106300270/person/282266865281/media/2131ec83-5eb6-48d6-b046-55010c65718e?_phsrc=aiN911&usePUBJs=true&galleryindex=3&albums=pg&showGalleryAlbums=true&tab=0&pid=282266865281&sort=-created.

46. Silvano Esposito and Pasquale Pagliano, "Bacterial Skin Infections," *Reference Module in Biomedical Sciences* (2021), accessed December 29, 2023, https://www.semanticscholar.org/paper/Bacterial-Skin-Infections-Esposito-Pagliano/f99c5659a9ff9858568fc31fd8b6cb3b36ae9927.

47. "Major General Charles W. Bridges to George R. Stobbs" (war record letter), United States War Department, Washington, DC, July 3, 1931, Family Archives, Ancestry.com, accessed December 20, 2023, https://www.ancestry.com/mediaui-viewer/collection/1030/tree/106300270/person/282266865281/media/c588a91a-8ddb-4b82-826c-9a697db64a3a?_phsrc=aiN911&usePUBJs=true&galleryindex=4&albums=pg&showGalleryAlbums=true&tab=0&pid=282266865281&sort=-created.

48. "Dissociative Amnesia," *Psychology Today*, accessed December 20, 2023, https://www.psychologytoday.com/us/conditions/dissociative-amnesia; "Dissociative Fugue," *Psychology Today*, accessed December 21, 2023, https://www.psychologytoday.com/us/conditions/dissociative-fugue-psychogenic-fugue.

49. Martin Vennard, "How Can Musicians Keep Playing Despite Amnesia?" *BBC News Magazine*, November 21, 2011, accessed December 25, 2023, https://www.bbc.com/news/magazine-15791973; Gottfried Schlaug, "The Brain of Musicians: A Model for Functional and Structural Adaptation," New York Academy of Sciences, accessed December 25, 2023, https://www.musicianbrain.com/papers/Schlaug_NYAS_2001.pdf.

50. "The 1973 Fire, National Personnel Records Center," National Archives, accessed December 25, 2023, https://www.archives.gov/personnel-records-center/fire-1973.

51. Anthony D. Smith, "What Was a Constitutional Psychopath?" *Psychology Today*, February 25, 2022, accessed December 25, 2023, https://www.psychologytoday.com/us/blog/and-running/202202/what-was-constitutional-psychopath.

52. Thomas J. Orbison, MD, "Constitutional Psychopathic Inferior Personality—With or Without Psychosis," *California and Western Medicine* 30, no. 2 (February 1929), accessed December 25, 2023, https://www.psychologytoday.com/us/blog/and-running/202202/what-was-constitutional-psychopath.

53. Thomas J. Orbison, MD, "Constitutional Psychopathic Inferior Personality—With or Without Psychosis," *California and Western Medicine* 30, no. 2 (February 1929), accessed December 25, 2023, https://www.psychologytoday.com/us/blog/and-running/202202/what-was-constitutional-psychopath.

54. "Inadequate Personality," Oxford Reference, accessed December 25, 2023, https://www.oxfordreference.com/display/10.1093/oi/authority.20110810105127659.

55. Sam N., "Inadequate Personality," Psychology Dictionary, accessed December 25, 2023, https://psychologydictionary.org/inadequate-personality/.

56. "Psychoneurotic Disorders," Thomas F. Graham, American Psychological Association, accessed December 25,

2023, https://psycnet.apa.org/record/2013-44654-007.

57. "Male Hysteria," Wikipedia, accessed December 27, 2023, https://en.wikipedia.org/wiki/Male_hysteria.

58. "Conversion Disorder," Cleveland Clinic, accessed December 27, 2023, https://my.clevelandclinic.org/health/diseases/17975-conversion-disorder.

59. William B. Terhune, "Psychopathology and the Treatment of the Psychoneuroses," *New England Journal of Medicine* 198 (June 21, 1928), accessed December 27, 2023, https://www.nejm.org/doi/full/10.1056/NEJM192806211981803, DOI: 10.1056/NEJM192806211981803.

60. "Shell Shock," Wikipedia, accessed December 27, 2023, https://en.wikipedia.org/w/index.php?title=Shell_shock&oldid=1191003963.

61. "Mens Rea," Legal Information Institute, accessed December 27, 2023, https://www.law.cornell.edu/wex/mens_rea.

62. "Dissociative Amnesia," Cleveland Clinic, accessed December 2, 2023, https://my.clevelandclinic.org/health/diseases/9789-dissociative-amnesia.

63. "1930 United States Federal Census," Ancestry.com, accessed January 21, 2024, https://www.ancestry.com/imageviewer/collections/6224/images/4607707_00451?pId=768829.

64. "Massachusetts, U.S., Town and Vital Records, 1620–1988," Ancestry.com, accessed December 30, 2023, https://www.ancestry.com/imageviewer/collections/2495/images/40143_266007__0185-00114?pId=3800284.

65. "1910 United Stated Federal Census," Ancestry.com, accessed December 30, 2023, https://www.ancestry.com/imageviewer/collections/7884/images/31111_4330112-00881?pId=11806963.

66. "Massachusetts, U.S., Death Index, 1901–1980," Ancestry.com, accessed December 30, 2023, https://www.ancestry.com/imageviewer/collections/3659/images/41263_2421406273_0049-00235?pId=2808568.

67. "Massachusetts, U.S., Death Index, 1901–1980," Ancestry.com, accessed December 30, 2023, https://www.ancestry.com/imageviewer/collections/3659/images/41263_2421406273_0049-00235?pId=2804855; "Memorial ID: 190733154," Find a Grave, accessed December 30, 2023, https://www.findagrave.com/memorial/190733154/infant-conner.

68. Joe Wallace, "AWOL & Desertion, Failure to Report," Veteran.com, accessed December 29, 2023, https://veteran.com/awol/.

69. Dr. David Payne, "Trench Diseases of the First World War," Western Front Association, accessed December 29, 2023, https://www.westernfrontassociation.com/world-war-i-articles/trench-diseases-of-the-first-world-war/.

70. Frederick Holmes, "Medicine in the First World War: Venereal Disease," University of Kansas Medical Center, accessed December 29, 2023, https://www.kumc.edu/school-of-medicine/academics/departments/history-and-philosophy-of-medicine/archives/wwi/essays/medicine/venereal-disease.html.

71. Richard H. Pells and C.D. Romer, "Great Depression," Encyclopedia Britannica, accessed December 30, 2023, https://www.britannica.com/event/Great-Depression.

Chapter Seven

1. "Grace to Father-in-Law" (letter), June 24, 1931, Family Archives, Ancestry.com, accessed December 30, 2023, https://www.ancestry.com/mediauiviewer/collection/1030/tree/106300270/person/282266865281/media/6991d757-e9fa-4233-b442-70368184b6f8?_phsrc=aiN983&usePUBJs=true&galleryindex=1&albums=pg&showGalleryAlbums=true&tab=0&pid=282266865281&sort=-created.

2. "David I. Walsh," Wikipedia, accessed December 30, 2023, https://en.wikipedia.org/wiki/David_I._Walsh.

3. "George R. Stobbs," Wikipedia, accessed December 30, 2023, https://en.wikipedia.org/wiki/George_R._Stobbs.

4. "Pehr G. Holmes," Wikipedia, accessed December 30, 2023, https://en.wikipedia.org/wiki/Pehr_G._Holmes.

5. Kambiz GhaneaBassiri, "Legally White," Oregon Humanities, August 12, 2011, accessed December 30, 2023, https://www.oregonhumanities.org/rll/magazine/belong-summer-2011/legally-white/.

Notes—Chapter Seven

6. "Pehr G. Holmes," State Library of Massachusetts, accessed December 27, 2023, file:///C:/Users/owner/Downloads/ocm41543981-19411942.pdf; "Rep. George Stobbs," Government Track, accessed December 27, 2023, https://www.govtrack.us/congress/members/george_stobbs/410390.

7. "World War Adjusted Compensation Act," Wikipedia, accessed December 29, 2023, https://en.wikipedia.org/wiki/World_War_Adjusted_Compensation_Act.

8. "History Overview, Veterans Administration," U.S. Department of Veterans Affairs, accessed December 29, 2023, https://department.va.gov/history/history-overview/#:~:text=The%20second%20consolidation%20of%20federal,activities%20affecting%20war%20veterans.%E2%80%9D%20At.

9. Joni Auden Land, "The Portland Veteran Who Took on Washington, D.C., during the Great Depression," Oregon Public Broadcasting, accessed December 29, 2023, https://www.opb.org/article/2023/11/11/bonus-army-veterans-washington-dc-walter-waters/#:~:text=He%20and%20400%20other%20veterans,epicenter%20of%20a%20nationwide%20movement.

10. "House Passes Bonus Bill for WWI Veterans, June 15, 1932," *Politico* (June 2009), accessed December 29, 2023, https://www.politico.com/story/2009/06/house-passes-bonus-bill-for-wwi-veterans-june-15-1932-023722.

11. "Hooverville," Wikipedia, accessed December 29, 2023, https://en.wikipedia.org/w/index.php?title=Hooverville&oldid=1186546061.

12. Alice Kamps, "The 1932 Bonus Army: Black and White Americans Unite in March on Washington," *Pieces of History* (blog of the U.S. National Archives), July 15, 2020, accessed December 29, 2023, https://prologue.blogs.archives.gov/2020/07/15/the-1932-bonus-army-black-and-white-americans-unite-in-march-on-washington/.

13. Daniel T. Davis, "The Brave Rifles: 3d. U.S. Cavalry," American Battlefield Trust, accessed December 29, 2023, https://www.battlefields.org/learn/articles/brave-rifles-3d-us-cavalry#:~:text=Today%2C%20the%20former%20Regiment%20of,actions%20in%20the%20Mexican%20War.

14. Alice Kamps, "The 1932 Bonus Army: Black and White Americans Unite in March on Washington," *Pieces of History* (blog of the U.S. National Archives), July 15, 2020, accessed December 29, 2023, https://prologue.blogs.archives.gov/2020/07/15/the-1932-bonus-army-black-and-white-americans-unite-in-march-on-washington/.

15. "Bonus Expeditionary Forces March on Washington," National Parks Service, accessed December 29, 2023, https://www.nps.gov/articles/bonus-expeditionary-forces-march-on-washington.htm.

16. "Anacostia," National Parks Service, accessed December 29, 2023, https://www.nps.gov/anac/planyourvisit/things2do.htm.

17. Benjamin Russell Butterworth, "What World War I Taught Us about PTSD," The Conversation, accessed December 29, 2023, https://theconversation.com/what-world-war-i-taught-us-about-ptsd-105613.

18. "Father Visits Son Missing 14 Years," *Key West Citizen*, July 6, 1931, Ancestry.com, accessed December 30, 2023, https://www.ancestry.com/mediaui-viewer/collection/1030/tree/106300270/person/282266865281/media/f0f31017-87e0-4976-b47f-14eff03277fd?_phsrc=aiN994&usePUBJs=true&galleryindex=1&albums=pg&showGalleryAlbums=true&tab=0&pid=282266865281&sort=-created.

19. "World War Veteran Comes to Himself," *Worcester Telegram*, July 13, 1931, Worcester Public Library, accessed June 21, 2023, https://www.ancestry.com/mediaui-viewer/collection/1030/tree/106300270/person/282266865281/media/aaba43d5-cf6e-4959-b01e-c497a21c6c7b?_phsrc=aiN1150&usePUBJs=true&galleryindex=1&albums=pg&showGalleryAlbums=true&tab=0&pid=282266865281&sort=-created.

20. "Establish Identity of Wounded War Veteran," *Worcester Evening Gazette*, July 13, 1931, GeneologyBank.com, accessed January 25, 2024, https://www.genealogybank.com/doc/newspapers/image/v2%3A1773BDF75FF7A17E%-40GB3NEWS-1797FBDDE4C8C399%-402426536-1797A98B98B2B81E%-

402-1797A98B98B2B81E?clipid=wng pjzfzfeqxgtmalmqiwzskvwelvxjh_wma-gateway014_1679001051991.

21. "Tampan, Dazed 15 Years, Finds Out Who He Is," *Daytona Beach Journal*, July 13, 1931, GeneologyBank.com, accessed January 25, 2024, https://www.genealogybank.com/doc/newspapers/image/v2%3A14C8339FD081D3E4%-40GB3NEWS-170BF5D2F102C01E%-402426536-170BDDB133EBC1BC%400-170BDDB133EBC1BC.

22. "Relatives Find Former Tampan After 15 Years," *Tampa Tribune*, July 14, 1931, GeneologyBank.com, accessed January 25, 2024, https://www.genealogybank.com/doc/newspapers/image/v2%3A135B96627AC4A53C%-40GB3NEWS-13A4D75C5E75BF06%-402426537-139BFB1BAD189653%402-139BFB1BAD189653.

23. "Amnesia Victims Record Defended," *Boston Herald*, July 14, 1931, GeneologyBank.com, accessed January 25, 2024, https://www.genealogybank.com/doc/newspapers/image/v2%3A1386BF60B4F67060%40GB3NEWS-13E3BCB2DE5DCAB4%40242 6537-13E16EAB41F816AD%4025-13E16E AB41F816AD.

24. "Congressional Record," Congress.gov, page 21 of 47, accessed January 3, 2024, https://www.congress.gov/bound-congressional-record/1931/12/09.

25. "2nd Engineer Battalion (United States)," Wikipedia, accessed January 1, 2023, https://en.wikipedia.org/wiki/2nd_Engineer_Battalion_(United_States).

26. Frederick Holmes, "Medicine in the First World War: The Influenza Pandemic and the War," University of Kansas Medical Center, accessed December 29, 2023, https://www.kumc.edu/school-of-medicine/academics/departments/history-and-philosophy-of-medicine/archives/wwi/essays/medicine/influenza.html; George Clark, *Devil Dogs Chronicle* (Lawrence: University of Kansas Press, 2013).

27. "American War and Military Operations Casualties: Lists and Statistics," CRS Report No. RL32492, Version 25, p. 2 (Washington, DC: Congressional Research Service, September 14, 2018), accessed January 1, 2024, https://crsreports.congress.gov/product/pdf/RL/RL32492.

28. "History of the DAV," accessed January 1, 2024, https://www.dav.org/wp-content/uploads/DAVHistory_DAVWW.pdf.

29. "Cet Ex-Soldat Ent Victime D'Amnesie," *La Justice de Biddeford*, July 17, 1931, GeneologyBank.com, accessed January 25, 2024, https://www.genealogybank.com/doc/newspapers/image/v2%3A13DABF4711DD6CE5%-40GB3NEWS-13E5B08706D41BA0%-402426540-13DF17098A5F8480%401.

30. "Perez Identifies Long Lost Son," *Miami Herald*, July 19, 1931, Ancestry.com, accessed January 25, 2024, https://www.ancestry.com/mediaui-viewer/collection/1030/tree/106300270/person/282266865281/media/62a967ca-e1ff-4198-9e95-eee7cccaf7fe?_phsrc=aiN1154&useP UBJs=true&galleryindex=10&albums=pg &showGalleryAlbums=true&tab=0&pid= 282266865281&sort=-created.

31. "Amnesia Victim Returns Home," *Key West Citizen*, July 20, 1931, Ancestry.com, accessed January 25, 2024, https://www.ancestry.com/mediaui-viewer/collection/1030/tree/106300270/person/282266865281/media/b7cfe182-c2db-434e-ba12-e57b43fdf7a3?_phsrc=aiN1180 &usePUBJs=true&galleryindex=1&album s=pg&showGalleryAlbums=true&tab=0& pid=282266865281&sort=-created.

32. "Senator David I. Walsh Wants Congress to Lift Perez Discharge Stigma," *Key West Citizen*, July 23, 1931, Ancestry.com, accessed January 25, 2024, https://www.ancestry.com/mediaui-viewer/collection/1030/tree/106300270/person/282266865281/media/9db1e36c-efb9-40a9-97c7-ecd092b2d92c?_phsrc=aiN117 0&usePUBJs=true&galleryindex=1&albu ms=pg&showGalleryAlbums=true&tab= 0&pid=282266865281&sort=-created.

33. "W. J. Belleville to Captain Daniel" (letter), July 27, 1931, Family Archives, Ancestry.com, accessed January 25, 2024, https://www.ancestry.com/mediaui-viewer/collection/1030/tree/106300270/person/282266865281/media/f317ce46-85f7-4f79-979e-f8f77473cb80?_phsrc=ai N1174&usePUBJs=true&galleryindex=1& albums=pg&showGalleryAlbums=true&t ab=0&pid=282266865281&sort=-created.

34. "Death Gives Up Soldier Son," *Worcester Telegram–USA Today Network*, August 2, 1931, accessed January 20, 2024,

http://imagn.com/setImages/554679/preview/22321978.

35. "Congressional Record," Congress.gov, page 21 of 47, accessed January 3, 2024, https://www.congress.gov/bound-congressional-record/1931/12/09.

36. "Mobilizing for War: The Selective Service Act in WWI," National Archives Foundation, accessed January 4, 2024, https://www.archivesfoundation.org/documents/mobilizing-war-selective-service-act-world-war/#:~:text=On%20May%2018%2C%201917%2C%20Congress,to%20register%20for%20military%20service.

37. "Ruth Bryan Owen," Wikipedia, accessed January 4, 2024, https://en.wikipedia.org/wiki/Ruth_Bryan_Owen.

Chapter Eight

1. "Congressional Record," Congress.gov, page 21 of 47, accessed January 3, 2024, https://www.congress.gov/bound-congressional-record/1931/12/09.

2. "What Is Posttraumatic Stress Disorder (PTSD)?" American Psychiatric Association, accessed January 4, 2024, https://www.psychiatry.org/patients-families/ptsd/what-is-ptsd.

3. Benjamin Russell Butterworth, "What World War I Taught Us about PTSD," The Conversation, accessed January 4, 2024, https://theconversation.com/what-world-war-i-taught-us-about-ptsd-105613.

4. Kathy Goldschmidt and Bradley Joseph Sinkhaus, "Job Description for a Member of Congress," Congressional Management Foundation, accessed January 7, 2024, https://www.congressfoundation.org/storage/documents/CMF_Pubs/cmf-member-job-description.pdf.

5. "Gettysburg Address," Abraham Lincoln Online, accessed January 7, 2024, https://www.abrahamlincolnonline.org/lincoln/speeches/gettysburg.htm.

6. "Senate Passes Walsh's Bills," *Worcester Evening Gazette*, February 27, 1935, GeneologyBank.com, accessed January 7, 2024, https://www.genealogybank.com/doc/newspapers/image/v2%3A1773BDF75FF7A17E%-40GB3NEWS-1799C7A36B3D0F69%-402427861-1799B3D848FF51AF%401-1799B3D848FF51AF?clipid=yxbsgocktrldiqhkunjdutciwzcvjjkd_wma-gateway002_1679003306771.

7. "Depression of 1920–1921," Wikipedia, accessed January 28, 2024, https://en.wikipedia.org/wiki/Depression_of_1920-1921.

8. "Roaring Twenties," Wikipedia, accessed January 28, 2024, https://en.wikipedia.org/wiki/Roaring_Twenties.

9. Thomas Schwartz, "The Great Stock Market Crash of 1929," *Hoover Heads: The Blog of the Herbert Hoover Library and Museum*, June 15, 2022, accessed January 28, 2024, https://hoover.blogs.archives.gov/2022/06/15/the-great-stock-market-crash-of-1929-why-history-textbooks-and-the-conventional-wisdom-get-it-wrong/.

10. "Social Security Act of 1935," Social Security Administration, accessed January 28, 2024, https://www.ssa.gov/history/35act.html.

11. "New Deal Programs," Living New Deal, accessed January 28, 2024, https://livingnewdeal.org/history-of-the-new-deal/programs/.

Chapter Nine

1. "Works Progress Administration," Wikipedia, accessed January 27, 2024, https://en.wikipedia.org/wiki/Works_Progress_Administration.

2. "WPA Starts Class in Tap Dancing," *Worcester Evening Gazette*, April 24, 1937, GeneologyBank.com, accessed January 7, 2024, https://www.genealogybank.com/doc/newspapers/image/v2%3A1773BDF75FF7A17E%-40GB3NEWS-179805DEB59771D6%-402428648-1798046430CE2E9C%-406-1798046430CE2E9C?clipid=-dgbaivaqratqsiqiykpftqfmstsbkyjd_wma-gateway004_1679003077055.

3. "Federal Project Number One," Wikipedia, accessed January 7, 2024, https://en.wikipedia.org/wiki/Federal_Project_Number_One.

4. "New Deal Programs, Federal Music Project (FMP) (1935)," Living New Deal, accessed January 28, 2024, https://livingnewdeal.

org/glossary/federal-music-project-fmp-1935-1943/.

5. "Federal Music Project," Wikipedia, accessed January 7, 2024, https://en.wikipedia.org/wiki/Federal_Music_Project.

6. "Great Plains Shelterbelt," Wikipedia, accessed January 7, 2024, https://en.wikipedia.org/wiki/Great_Plains_Shelterbelt.

7. "Massachusetts Historical Records Survey Files 1936–1942," Worldcat.org, accessed January 7, 2024, https://search.worldcat.org/title/massachusetts-historical-records-survey-files-1936-1942/oclc/79840258; "Works Progress Administration (WPA) Historical Records Survey," Fort Myers–Lee County Library, accessed January 7, 2024, https://sites.rootsweb.com/~flmgs/articles/Works_Projects_AdministrationMarch2011_BM.pdf.

8. "USAT Cuba," Wikipedia, accessed January 9, 2024, https://en.wikipedia.org/wiki/USAT_Cuba; "Guests Aboard the S.S. Florida of P. & O. Line Traveling between Miami and Havana," State Library and Archives, Florida Memory, accessed January 9, 2024, http://www.floridamemory.com/items/show/251499.

9. "Florida, U.S., Arriving and Departing Passenger and Crew Lists, 1898–1963," Ancestry.com, accessed January 9, 2024, https://www.ancestry.com/imageviewer/collections/8842/images/41260_322597-00352?pId=9554330.

10. "Florida, U.S., Arriving and Departing Passenger and Crew Lists, 1898–1963," Ancestry.com, accessed January 10, 2024, https://www.ancestry.com/imageviewer/collections/8842/images/42792_DC000694-00344?pId=4929922.

11. Kristen Griffeath, "With One Voice: The American Musical Experience of World War I," National World War I Museum and Memorial, accessed January 30, 2024, https://www.theworldwar.org/sites/default/files/2022-03/with-one-voice.pdf.

12. "U.S., City Directories, 1822–1995," Ancestry.com, accessed January 7, 2024, https://www.ancestry.com/imageviewer/collections/2469/images/10637065?pId=1320449243.

13. William T. Clew, "Tracing History, Spirit of Mercy Center," Catholic Free Press, accessed January 7, 2024, https://catholicfreepress.org/news/tracing-history-spirit-of-mercy-centre.

14. "National Directory of Piano Teachers, United States of America" (1955), Ancestry.com, accessed January 7, 2024, https://www.ancestry.com/mediaui-viewer/collection/1030/tree/106300270/person/282266865281/media/9c06503e-0ce4-48ac-9228-b48a38e2b1fa?_phsrc=aiN1027&usePUBJs=true&galleryindex=2&albums=pg&showGalleryAlbums=true&tab=0&pid=282266865281&sort=-created.

15. "Clive Wearing, Amnesia Patient," Practical Psychology, accessed January 7, 2024, https://practicalpie.com/clive-wearing/.

16. "Departments of Music: History," Catholic University of America, accessed January 7, 2024, https://music.catholic.edu/about-us/history/index.html#:~:text=Music%20instruction%20has%20been%20a,was%20named%20the%20Benjamin%20T.

17. "Pianos and Their Prices," Blue Book of Pianos Online, accessed January 7, 2024, https://www.bluebookofpianos.com/spin1947.htm.

18. "Historic Buildings of Massachusetts, Our Lady of Fatima Church," Massachusetts Historic Buildings, accessed January 9, 2024, https://mass.historicbuildingsct.com/?p=6257.

19. "Victor Matrix B-23344. Dardanella / Selvin's Novelty Orchestra," Discography of American Historical Recordings, S.V., accessed January 8, 2024, https://adp.library.ucsb.edu/index.php/matrix/detail/700008515/B-23344-Dardanella.

20. YouTube Universal Music Group, "Dardanella," Bing Crosby and Louis Armstrong, Capitol Records (1960), accessed January 8, 2024, https://www.youtube.com/watch?v=MSOSxoe4XLY.

21. "Sweet Potatoes—Geoff and Maria Muldaur," Reprise Records (1972), accessed January 8, 2024, https://www.youtube.com/watch?v=0bFuHPGypIE&list=OLAK5uy_nOgAVlJnMXAcR3OsjOMdiQTzfc7L9Tpac&index=5.

22. "The Lawrence Welk Show," YouTube, accessed January 8, 2024, https://www.youtube.com/watch?v=8_Cz9qqdPwE.

23. John W. Schaum, "Saltwater Boogie, Piano Solo," Belwin, Inc., accessed January 8, 2024, https://www.youtube.com/

watch?v=qOsY1ClDak4 (alternate link: https://www.amazon.com/Saltwater-Boogie-Sheet-Music-Piano/dp/B001DXOTYG#detailBullets_feature_div).

24. "U.S., City Directories, 1822–1995," Ancestry.com, accessed January 9, 2024, https://www.ancestry.com/imageviewer/collections/2469/images/10365067?pId=520697965.

25. Matthew Miller, PhD, MPH, "VA Releases 2022 National Veteran Suicide Prevention Annual Report," accessed January 9, 2024, https://news.va.gov/108984/2022-national-veteran-suicide-prevention-annual-report/#:~:text=In%202020%2C%20there%20were%206%2C146,fell%20in%202019%20and%202020.

26. "2023 National Veteran Suicide Prevention Annual Report," U.S. Department of Veterans Affairs, accessed January 14, 2024, https://www.mentalhealth.va.gov/docs/data-sheets/2023/2023-National-Veteran-Suicide-Prevention-Annual-Report-FINAL-508.pdf.

27. "Grace R. Duff 1921 Elementary Accounting Certificate," *Fall River Daily Evening News*, August 31, 1921, accessed January 14, 2024, https://www.newspapers.com/article/fall-river-daily-evening-news-grace-r-d/123201062/.

28. "Death Certificate, Hector Francis Perez," Massachusetts Department of Public Health Registry of Vital Statistics, accessed January 14, 2024, https://www.ancestry.com/mediauiviewer/collection/1030/tree/106300270/person/282266865281/media/24f8e91e-1010-494e-aad6-1731ad49aa35?_phsrc=aiN1076&usePUBJs=true&galleryindex=1&albums=pg&showGalleryAlbums=true&tab=0&pid=282266865281&sort=-created.

29. "History of Ybor City," Wikipedia, accessed January 14, 2024, https://en.wikipedia.org/w/index.php?title=History_of_Ybor_City&oldid=1195458173.

30. "A Journey of a Thousand Miles Begins with a Single Step," Wikipedia, accessed January 13, 2024, https://en.wikipedia.org/wiki/A_journey_of_a_thousand_miles_begins_with_a_single_step.

31. John L. Brown and Ceryelle A. Moffett, *A Hero's Journey: How Educators Can Transform Schools and Improve Learning* (Alexandria, VA: Association for Supervision and Curriculum Development, 1999), 168.

Chapter Ten

1. "Post-Traumatic Stress Disorder," Substance Abuse and Mental Health Services Administration, Department of Health and Human Services, accessed January 14, 2024, https://www.samhsa.gov/mental-health/post-traumatic-stress-disorder.

2. Marc-Antoine Crocq and Louis Crocq, "From Shell Shock and War Neurosis to Posttraumatic Stress Disorder: A History of Psychotraumatology," *Dialogues in Clinical Neuroscience* 2, no. 1 (2000): 47–55, https://doi.org/10.31887/DCNS.2000.2.1/macrocq, accessed January 15, 2024, https://www.ncbi.nlm.nih.gov/pmc/articles/PMC3181586/.

3. Christos F. Kleisiaris et al., "Health Care Practices in Ancient Greece: The Hippocratic Ideal," *Journal of Medical Ethics and History of Medicine* 7, no. 6 (March 15, 2014), accessed January 14, 2024, https://www.ncbi.nlm.nih.gov/pmc/articles/PMC4263393/; Marc-Antoine Crocq and Louis Crocq, "From Shell Shock and War Neurosis to Posttraumatic Stress Disorder: A History of Psychotraumatology," *Dialogues in Clinical Neuroscience* 2, no. 1 (2000): 47–55, doi:10.31887/DCNS.2000.2.1/macrocq, accessed January 19, 2024, https://www.ncbi.nlm.nih.gov/pmc/articles/PMC3181586/.

4. Marc-Antoine Crocq and Louis Crocq, "From Shell Shock and War Neurosis to Posttraumatic Stress Disorder: A History of Psychotraumatology," *Dialogues in Clinical Neuroscience* 2, no. 1 (2000): 47–55, doi:10.31887/DCNS.2000.2.1/macrocq, accessed January 19, 2024, https://www.ncbi.nlm.nih.gov/pmc/articles/PMC3181586/.

5. Hitesh C. Sheth et al., "Anxiety Disorders in Ancient Indian Literature," *Indian Journal of Psychiatry* 52, no. 3 (2010): 289–91, doi:10.4103/0019-5545.71009, accessed January 15, 2024, https://www.ncbi.nlm.nih.gov/pmc/articles/PMC2990839/.

6. Michèle Battesti, "Nostalgia in the Army (17th–19th Centuries)," *Frontiers*

of Neurology and Neuroscience 38 (2016): 132–42, doi:10.1159/000442652, accessed January 15, 2024, https://pubmed.ncbi.nlm.nih.gov/27035922/.

7. S.C. Gwynne, "Nostalgia in the Civil War," *TimeLines*, December 5, 2019, accessed January 19, 2024, https://www.timelinesmagazine.com/publications/civil-war-courier/nostalgia-in-the-civil-war/article_7880dd3e-17a6-11ea-819c-3b6bb8b44921.html.

8. Matthew J. Friedman, MD, PhD, "History of PTSD in Veterans: Civil War to DSM-5," National Center for PTSD, U.S. Department of Veterans Affairs, accessed January 15, 2024, https://www.ptsd.va.gov/understand/what/history_ptsd.asp.

9. Dr. Matthew Friedman, "'Soldier's Heart' and 'Shell Shock': Past Names for PTSD," *Frontline*, accessed January 15, 2024, https://www.pbs.org/wgbh/pages/frontline/shows/heart/themes/shellshock.html.

10. "Voices of the First World War: Shell Shock," Imperial War Museums, accessed January 19, 2024, https://www.iwm.org.uk/history/voices-of-the-first-world-war-shell-shock.

11. Tracey Loughran, "Masculinity, Trauma and Shell Shock," *The Psychologist*, February 13, 2015, accessed January 16, 2024, https://www.bps.org.uk/psychologist/masculinity-trauma-and-shell-shock.

12. George L. Mosse, "Shell-Shock as a Social Disease," *Journal of Contemporary History* 35, no. 1 (2000): 101–8, accessed January 16, 2024, http://www.jstor.org/stable/261184.

13. Jasmeet P. Hayes et al., "Emotion and Cognition Interactions in PTSD: A Review of Neurocognitive and Neuroimaging Studies," *Frontiers in Integrative Neuroscience* 6, no. 89 (October 9, 2012), doi:10.3389/fnint.2012.00089, accessed January 19, 2024, https://www.ncbi.nlm.nih.gov/pmc/articles/PMC3466464/.

14. Caroline Alexander, "The Shock of War," *Smithsonian* magazine, accessed January 16, 2024, https://www.smithsonianmag.com/history/the-shock-of-war-55376701/.

15. Benjamin Russell Butterworth, "What World War I Taught Us about PTSD," The Conversation, accessed January 16, 2024, https://theconversation.com/what-world-war-i-taught-us-about-ptsd-105613.

16. Benjamin Russell Butterworth, "What World War I Taught Us about PTSD," The Conversation, accessed January 16, 2024, https://theconversation.com/what-world-war-i-taught-us-about-ptsd-105613.

17. "Electroconvulsive Therapy," Cleveland Clinic, accessed January 16, 2024, https://my.clevelandclinic.org/health/treatments/9302-ect-electroconvulsive-therapy.

18. Christopher Marx et al., "Talking Cure Models: A Framework of Analysis," *Frontiers in Psychology* 8 (September 2017), Article 1589, doi:10.3389/fpsyg.2017.01589, accessed January 16, 2024, https://www.ncbi.nlm.nih.gov/pmc/articles/PMC5601393/.

19. Abram Kardiner, MD, *The Traumatic Neuroses of War* (Washington, DC: National Research Council (U.S.), Committee on Problems of Neurotic Behavior, 1941), accessed January 19, 2024, https://doi.org/10.1037/10581-000; "Abram Kardiner," Wikipedia, accessed January 19, 2024, https://en.wikipedia.org/wiki/Abram_Kardiner.

20. Matthew J. Friedman, MD, PhD, Paula P. Schnurr, PhD, and Annmarie McDonagh-Coyle, MD, "Post-Traumatic Stress Disorder in the Military Veteran," National Center for PTSD, U.S. Department of Veterans Affairs, accessed January 19, 2024, https://www.ptsd.va.gov/professional/articles/article-pdf/id12012.pdf.

21. Matthew J. Friedman, MD, PhD, Paula P. Schnurr, PhD, and Annmarie McDonagh-Coyle, MD, "Post-Traumatic Stress Disorder in the Military Veteran," National Center for PTSD, U.S. Department of Veterans Affairs, accessed January 19, 2024, https://www.ptsd.va.gov/professional/articles/article-pdf/id12012.pdf.

22. Nancy C. Andreasen, "What Is Post-Traumatic Stress Disorder?" *Dialogues in Clinical Neuroscience* 13, no. 3 (2011): 240–43, doi:10.31887/DCNS.2011.13.2/, accessed January 19, 2024, https://www.ncbi.nlm.nih.gov/pmc/articles/PMC3182007/.

23. J. I. Walker, "Comparison of 'Rap'

Groups with Traditional Group Therapy in the Treatment of Vietnam Combat Veterans," *Group* 7 (1983): 48–57, https://doi.org/10.1007/BF01458250, accessed January 19, 2024, https://link.springer.com/article/10.1007/BF01458250.

24. "Rape Crisis Centers in the United States," Wikipedia, accessed January 19, 2024, https://en.wikipedia.org/wiki/Rape_crisis_centers_in_the_United_States.

25. P. Giannelli, "Rape Trauma Syndrome," *Criminal Law Bulletin* 33, no. 3 (1997): 270–79, accessed January 19, 2024, https://www.ojp.gov/ncjrs/virtual-library/abstracts/rape-trauma-syndrome-0.

26. G.J. Turnbull, "A Review of Post-Traumatic Stress Disorder. Part I: Historical Development and Classification," *Injury* 29, no. 2 (1998): 87–91, doi:10.1016/s0020-1383(97)00131-9, accessed January 19, 2024, https://pubmed.ncbi.nlm.nih.gov/10721399/.

27. "Post-Traumatic Stress Disorder," American Psychiatric Association, accessed January 19, 2024, https://www.psychiatry.org/file%20library/psychiatrists/practice/dsm/apa_dsm-5-ptsd.pdf.

28. "Clinical Practice Guideline for the Treatment of Post-Traumatic Stress Disorder," American Psychiatric Association, accessed January 19, 2024, https://www.apa.org/ptsd-guideline/treatments (alternate link: https://www.apa.org/ptsd-guideline/treatments/recommendations-summary-table.pdf).

29. "Post-Traumatic Stress Disorder," Mayo Clinic, accessed January 19, 2024, https://www.mayoclinic.org/diseases-conditions/post-traumatic-stress-disorder/symptoms-causes/syc-20355967.

30. "PTSD in Iraq and Afghanistan Veterans," U.S. Department of Veterans Affairs, accessed January 19, 2024, https://www.publichealth.va.gov/epidemiology/studies/new-generation/ptsd.asp.

31. Charles R. Hooper, "Suicide Among Veterans," American Addiction Centers, accessed January 19, 2024, https://americanaddictioncenters.org/veterans/suicide-among-veterans.

32. Mike Richman, "Prolonged Exposure or Cognitive Processing Therapy?" VA Research Communications, accessed January 19, 2024, https://www.research.va.gov/currents/0122-Prolonged-exposure-or-cognitive-processing-therapy.cfm.

33. "Medications for PTSD," National Center for PTSD, U.S. Department of Veterans Affairs, accessed January 19, 2024, https://www.ptsd.va.gov/understand_tx/meds_for_ptsd.asp.

34. "Darpa and the Brain Initiative," Defense Advanced Research Projects Agency, accessed January 19, 2024, https://www.darpa.mil/program/our-research/darpa-and-the-brain-initiative; J. Difede, J. Cukor, K. Wyka, et al., "D-Cycloserine Augmentation of Exposure Therapy for Post-Traumatic Stress Disorder: A Pilot Randomized Clinical Trial," *Neuropsychopharmacology* 39 (2014): 1052–58, https://doi.org/10.1038/npp.2013.317, accessed January 19, 2024, https://pubmed.ncbi.nlm.nih.gov/24217129/.

35. Kim Eckart, "PTSD Symptoms Improve When Patient Chooses Form of Treatment, Study Shows," University of Washington News, October 19, 2018, accessed January 19, 2024, https://www.washington.edu/news/2018/10/19/ptsd-symptoms-improve-when-patient-chooses-form-of-treatment-study-shows/.

36. "Stress Inoculation Training for Post-Traumatic Stress Disorder," Society for Clinical Psychology, accessed January 19, 2024, https://div12.org/treatment/stress-inoculation-training-for-post-traumatic-stress-disorder/.

37. M. Tracie Shea, "Present-Centered Therapy for PTSD," National Center for PTSD, U.S. Department of Veterans Affairs, accessed January 19, 2024, https://www.ptsd.va.gov/professional/treat/txessentials/present_centered_therapy.asp; Kathryn L. Bleiberg and John C. Markowitz, "Interpersonal Psychotherapy for PTSD: Treating Trauma without Exposure," *Journal of Psychotherapy Integration* 29, no. 1 (2019): 15–22, doi:10.1037/int0000113, accessed January 19, 2024, https://www.ncbi.nlm.nih.gov/pmc/articles/PMC6750225/.

38. "Past Year Prevalence of Post-Traumatic Stress Disorder Among Adults," National Comorbidity Survey Replication (NCS-R), accessed January 19, 2024, https://www.nimh.nih.gov/health/statistics/post-traumatic-stress-disorder-ptsd.

39. "Anxiety Disorders: Facts and Statistics," Anxiety and Depression Association of America, accessed January 19, 2024, https://adaa.org/understanding-anxiety/facts-statistics.

40. "Addressing Diversity in PTSD Treatment: Disparities in Treatment Engagement and Outcome Among Patients of Color," National Center for PTSD, U.S. Department of Veterans Affairs, accessed January 19, 2024, https://www.ptsd.va.gov/professional/articles/article-pdf/id1554318.pdf.

41. "Retrograde Amnesia," Wikipedia, accessed January 20, 2024, https://en.wikipedia.org/wiki/Retrograde_amnesia.

42. Thomas F. Graham, "Psychoneurotic Disorders," American Psychological Association, accessed December 25, 2023, https://psycnet.apa.org/record/2013-44654-007.

43. "Maslow's Hierarchy of Needs," Wikipedia, accessed January 20, 2024, https://en.wikipedia.org/wiki/Maslow%27s_hierarchy_of_needs.

Bibliography

"2d Division Summary of Operations in the World War." American Battles Monuments Commission. Accessed December 19, 2023. https://2nd-division.com/_div.misc/summary.htm.

"2nd Engineer Battalion (United States)." Wikipedia. Accessed December 19, 2023. https://en.wikipedia.org/wiki/2nd_Engineer_Battalion_(United_States).

"6th Machine Gun Battalion (United States Marine Corps)." Wikipedia. Accessed December 19, 2023. https://en.wikipedia.org/wiki/6th_Machine_Gun_Battalion_(United_States_Marine_Corps).

"15th Field Artillery Regiment." Wikipedia. Accessed December 19, 2023. https://en.wikipedia.org/wiki/15th_Field_Artillery_Regiment_(United_States).

"1870 United States Federal Census." Ancestry.com. Accessed January 22, 2024. https://www.ancestry.com/imageviewer/collections/7163/images/4275949_00417?pId=4101889.

"1880 United States Federal Census." Ancestry.com. Accessed December 3, 2023. https://www.ancestry.com/imageviewer/collections/6742/images/4240123-00097?pId=5981925.

"1900 United States Federal Census." Ancestry.com. Accessed December 3, 2023. https://www.ancestry.com/imageviewer/collections/7602/images/4114470_00555?pId=75712597.

"1910 United States Federal Census." Ancestry.com. Accessed December 3, 2023. https://www.ancestry.com/imageviewer/collections/7884/images/31111_4330112-00881?pId=11806963.

"1920 United States Federal Census." Ancestry.com. Accessed December 3, 2023. https://www.ancestry.com/imageviewer/collections/6061/images/4311577-00311?pId=45061260.

"1920 United States Federal Census, Military and Naval Force, Germany, Coblenz." Ancestry.com. Accessed January 22, 2024. https://www.ancestry.com/imageviewer/collections/6061/images/4442145_00385?pId=113162961.

"1920 United States Federal Census, Military and Naval Population Abroad." Ancestry.com. Accessed December 15, 2023. https://www.ancestry.com/imageviewer/collections/6061/images/4442145_00567?pId=113168857.

"1930 United States Federal Census." Ancestry.com. Accessed December 15, 2023. https://www.ancestry.com/imageviewer/collections/6224/images/4639126_00422?pId=41613734.

"1940 United States Federal Census." Ancestry.com. Accessed December 15, 2023. https://www.ancestry.com/imageviewer/collections/2442/images/m-t0627-02668-00227?pId=5889432.

"1950 United States Federal Census." Ancestry.com. Accessed December 16, 2023. https://www.ancestry.com/imageviewer/collections/62308/images/43290879-Florida-059375-0007?pId=81965477.

"The 1973 Fire, National Personnel Records Center." National Archives. Accessed

December 25, 2023. https://www.archives.gov/personnel-records-center/fire-1973.

"2023 National Veteran Suicide Prevention Annual Report." U.S. Department of Veterans Affairs. Accessed January 14, 2024. https://www.mentalhealth.va.gov/docs/data-sheets/2023/2023-National-Veteran-Suicide-Prevention-Annual-Report-FINAL-508.pdf.

"About Fedex: Overnight Mail." Accessed December 1, 2023. https://www.fedex.com/en-us/about.html.

"Abram Kardiner." Wikipedia. Accessed January 19, 2024. https://en.wikipedia.org/wiki/Abram_Kardiner.

"Addressing Diversity in PTSD Treatment: Disparities in Treatment Engagement and Outcome Among Patients of Color." National Center for PTSD, U.S. Department of Veterans Affairs. Accessed January 19, 2024. https://www.ptsd.va.gov/professional/articles/article-pdf/id1554318.pdf.

Alexander, Caroline. "The Shock of War." *Smithsonian* magazine, September 2010. Accessed January 16, 2024. https://www.smithsonianmag.com/history/the-shock-of-war-55376701/.

"American Entry into World War I, 1917." U.S. Department of State, Archive, 2001–2009. Last modified January 20, 2009. Accessed January 20, 2024. https://2001-2009.state.gov/r/pa/ho/time/wwi/82205.htm.

"The American Expeditionary Forces." Library of Congress. Accessed December 12, 2023. https://www.loc.gov/collections/stars-and-stripes/articles-and-essays/a-world-at-war/american-expeditionary-forces/.

"American War and Military Operations Casualties: Lists and Statistics." CRS Report No. RL32492, Version 25, p. 2 (Washington, DC: Congressional Research Service, September 14, 2018). Accessed December 14, 2023. https://crsreports.congress.gov/product/pdf/RL/RL32492.

"Amnesia Victim Returns Home." *Key West Citizen*, July 20, 1931. Ancestry.com. Accessed January 25, 2024. https://www.ancestry.com/mediaui-viewer/collection/1030/tree/106300270/person/282266865281/media/b7cfe182-c2db-434e-ba12-e57b43fdf7a3?_phsrc=aiN1180&usePUBJs=true&galleryindex=1&albums=pg&showGalleryAlbums=true&tab=0&pid=282266865281&sort=-created.

"Amnesia Victims Record Defended." *Boston Herald*, July 14, 1931. GenealogyBank.com. Accessed January 25, 2024. https://www.genealogybank.com/doc/newspapers/image/v2%3A1386BF60B4F67060%40GB3NEWS-13E3BCB2DE5DCAB4%402426537-13E16EAB41F816AD%4025-13E16EAB41F816AD.

"Anacostia." National Parks Service. Accessed December 29, 2023. https://www.nps.gov/anac/planyourvisit/things2do.htm.

Anderson, Colonel Bill, USMC (Ret.). "The 2D Engineers at Belleau Wood." Doughboy Center. Accessed December 19, 2023. http://www.worldwar1.com/dbc/ct_bw2eng.htm.

Anderson, William T. "Devil Dogs in Olive Drab: The 2d Engineers at Belleau Wood." Army History, updated 2022. Accessed December 20, 2023. https://2nd-division.com/_div.misc/chateau.thierry/belleau.engineers.htm.

Andreasen, Nancy C. "What Is Post-Traumatic Stress Disorder?" *Dialogues in Clinical Neuroscience* 13, no. 3 (2011): 240–43. doi:10.31887/DCNS.2011.13.2/. Accessed January 19, 2024. https://www.ncbi.nlm.nih.gov/pmc/articles/PMC3182007/.

"Anxiety Disorders: Facts and Statistics." Anxiety and Depression Assn of America. Accessed January 19, 2024. https://adaa.org/understanding-anxiety/facts-statistics.

"Army and Beta Tests and Overview." Oxford Dictionary. Accessed December 19, 2023. https://www.oxfordreference.com/display/10.1093/oi/authority.20110803095424949.

Balkansky, Arlene. "The Draft in World War I: America 'Volunteered its Mass.'" *Library of Congress Blogs*, June 19, 2018. Accessed December 14, 2023. https://blogs.loc.gov/headlinesandheroes/2018/06/wwi-draft/.

Battesti, Michèle. "Nostalgia in the Army (17th–19th Centuries)." *Frontiers of Neurology and Neuroscience* 38 (2016): 132–42. doi:10.1159/000442652. Accessed January 15, 2024. https://pubmed.ncbi.nlm.nih.gov/27035922/.

Bibliography

"Battle of Saint-Mihiel." Wikipedia. Accessed December 19, 2023. https://en.wikipedia.org/wiki/Battle_of_Saint-Mihiel.

"Bay Pines Men's Domiciliary History." U.S. Department of Veterans Affairs. Accessed December 15, 2023. https://www.va.gov/bay-pines-health-care/about-us/history/.

Berman, Alex. "The Pharmaceutical Component of 19th-Century French Public Health and Hygiene." *Pharmacy in History* 11, no. 1 (1969). Accessed December 7, 2023. http://www.jstor.org/stable/41109689.

Bleiberg, Kathryn L., and John C. Markowitz. "Interpersonal Psychotherapy for PTSD: Treating Trauma without Exposure." *Journal of Psychotherapy Integration* 29, no. 1 (2019): 15–22. doi:10.1037/int0000113. Accessed January 19, 2024. https://www.ncbi.nlm.nih.gov/pmc/articles/PMC6750225/.

"Blood, Mud, Concrete and Barbed Wire: The Meuse-Argonne Offensive." Army Heritage Center Foundation. Accessed December 19, 2023. https://www.armyheritage.org/soldier-stories-information/blood-mud-concrete-and-barbed-wire-the-meuse-argonne-offensive/.

"Bonus Expeditionary Forces March on Washington." National Parks Service. Accessed December 29, 2023. https://www.nps.gov/articles/bonus-expeditionary-forces-march-on-washington.htm.

Borten, Lisa. "What American Education Was Like 100 Years Ago." Stacker, September 6, 2020. Accessed December 2, 2023. https://stacker.com/education/what-american-education-was-100-years-ago.

Bovard, James. "Cato Institute Policy Analysis No. 47: The Last Dinosaur: The U.S. Postal Service." February 1985. https://www.cato.org/sites/cato.org/files/pubs/pdf/pa047.pdf.

Brereton, B.M., and Colin Graham Clarke. "West Indies." Encyclopedia Britannica, October 25, 2023. Accessed December 7, 2023. https://www.britannica.com/place/West-Indies-island-group-Atlantic-Ocean.

"Broome Street." Wikipedia. Accessed December 20, 2023. https://en.wikipedia.org/wiki/Broome_Street.

Brown, John L., and Ceryelle A. Moffett. *A Hero's Journey: How Educators Can Transform Schools and Improve Learning*. Alexandria, VA: Association for Supervision and Curriculum Development, 1999.

"Bureau of Vital Statistics, Certificate of Death." Ancestry.com. Accessed December 16, 2023. https://www.ancestry.com/mediaui-viewer/collection/1030/tree/106300270/person/282266865282/media/a275e2d0-d943-421c-974f-82eed439c014?_phsrc=aiN890&usePUBJs=true&galleryindex=8&albums=pg&showGalleryAlbums=true&tab=0&pid=282266865282&sort=-created.

Butterworth, Benjamin Russell. "What World War I Taught Us about PTSD." The Conversation. Accessed December 29, 2023. https://theconversation.com/what-world-war-i-taught-us-about-ptsd-105613.

"Campaign Battles—Dates of Participation—Hector & Charles." Ancestry.com. Accessed February 4, 2024. https://www.ancestry.com/mediaui-viewer/collection/1030/tree/106300270/person/282266865281/media/08882efc-8805-4ab0-8ee4-2a26dd7b3bc5?_phsrc=aiN1188&usePUBJs=true&galleryindex=1&albums=pg&showGalleryAlbums=true&tab=0&pid=282266865281&sort=-created.

"Certificates Issued to Many Students." *Fall River Daily Evening News*, August 31, 1921. https://www.newspapers.com/article/fall-river-daily-evening-news/136155590/.

"Cet Ex-Soldat Est Victime D'Amnesie." *La Justice de Biddeford*, July 17, 1931. GenealogyBank.com Accessed January 25, 2024. https://www.genealogybank.com/doc/newspapers/image/v2%3A13DABF4711DD6CE5%40GB3NEWS-13E5B08706D41BA0%402426540-13DF17098A5F8480%401.

"City Hall Records, Marriage Intentions." *Worcester Evening Gazette*, July 7, 1921. https://www.genealogybank.com/doc/newspapers/image/v2%3A1773BDF75FF7A17E%-40GB3NEWS-1793FEE217259C4D%402422878-179356578F8AC747%401-179356578F8AC747?clipid=onoacioydgxopgmhnlahbcrgzrdtimow_wma-gateway016_1679002102214.

Clark, George. *Devil Dogs Chronicle*. Lawrence: University of Kansas Press, 2013.

Bibliography

Clew, William T. "Tracing History, Spirit of Mercy Center." Catholic Free Press. Accessed January 7, 2024. https://catholicfreepress.org/news/tracing-history-spirit-of-mercy-centre.

"Clinical Practice Guideline for the Treatment of Post-Traumatic Stress Disorder." American Psychiatric Association. Accessed January 19, 2024. https://www.apa.org/ptsd-guideline/treatments. Alternate link: https://www.apa.org/ptsd-guideline/treatments/recommendations-summary-table.pdf.

"Clive Wearing, Amnesia Patient." Practical Psychology. Accessed January 7, 2024. https://practicalpie.com/clive-wearing/.

"Congressional Record." Congress.gov, page 21 of 47. Accessed January 3, 2024. https://www.congress.gov/bound-congressional-record/1931/12/09.

"Conversion Disorder." Cleveland Clinic. Accessed December 27, 2023. https://my.clevelandclinic.org/health/diseases/17975-conversion-disorder.

"Courts-martial of the United States." Wikipedia. Accessed January 21, 2024. https://en.wikipedia.org/wiki/Courts-martial_of_the_United_States.

Crocq, Marc-Antoine, and Louis Crocq. "From Shell Shock and War Neurosis to Posttraumatic Stress Disorder: A History of Psychotraumatology." *Dialogues in Clinical Neuroscience* 2, no. 1 (2000): 47–55. doi:10.31887/DCNS.2000.2.1/macrocq. Accessed January 19, 2024. https://www.ncbi.nlm.nih.gov/pmc/articles/PMC3181586/.

"Croix de Guerre 1914–1918 (France)." Wikipedia. Accessed February 20, 2024. https://en.wikipedia.org/wiki/Croix_de_guerre_1914-1918_(France).

"Cuba Chronology." Library of Congress Research Guides. Accessed December 7, 2023. https://guides.loc.gov/world-of-1898/cuba-chronology.

"The Cuban War of Independence." Wikipedia. Accessed December 11, 2023. https://en.wikipedia.org/wiki/Cuban_War_of_Independence.

"Dardanella." YouTube. Accessed January 8, 2024. https://www.youtube.com/watch?v=cgLeNIfgFuY.

"Darpa and the Brain Initiative." Defense Advanced Research Projects Agency. Accessed January 19, 2024. https://www.darpa.mil/program/our-research/darpa-and-the-brain-initiative.

"David I. Walsh." Wikipedia. Accessed December 30, 2023. https://en.wikipedia.org/wiki/David_I._Walsh.

Davis, Daniel T. "The Brave Rifles: 3d. U.S. Cavalry." American Battlefield Trust. Accessed December 29, 2023. https://www.battlefields.org/learn/articles/brave-rifles-3d-us-cavalry#:~:text=Today%2C%20the%20former%20Regiment%20of,actions%20in%20the%20Mexican%20War.

"Death Certificate, Hector Francis Perez." Massachusetts Department of Public Health Registry of Vital Statistics. Accessed January 14, 2024. https://www.ancestry.com/mediaui-viewer/collection/1030/tree/106300270/person/282266865281/media/24f8e91e-1010-494e-aad6-1731ad49aa35?_phsrc=aiN1076&usePUBJs=true&galleryindex=1&albums=pg&showGalleryAlbums=true&tab=0&pid=282266865281&sort=-created.

"Death Gives Up Soldier Son." *Worcester Telegram–USA Today Network*, August 2, 1931. Accessed January 20, 2024. http://imagn.com/setImages/554679/preview/22321978. Alternate link: https://www.ancestry.com/mediaui-viewer/collection/1030/tree/106300270/person/282266865281/media/921217d1-6901-46b4-a80e-af9e112a1729?_phsrc=aiN735&usePUBJs=true&galleryindex=1&albums=pg&showGalleryAlbums=true&tab=0&pid=282266865281&sort=-created.

"Departments of Music: History." Catholic University of America. Accessed January 7, 2024. https://music.catholic.edu/about-us/history/index.html#:~:text=Music%20instruction%20has%20been%20a,was%20named%20the%20Benjamin%20T.

"Depression of 1920–1921." Wikipedia. Accessed January 28, 2024. https://en.wikipedia.org/wiki/Depression_of_1920-1921.

Difede, J., J. Cukor, K. Wyka, et al. "D-Cycloserine Augmentation of Exposure Therapy for Post-Traumatic Stress Disorder: A Pilot Randomized Clinical Trial." *Neuropsychopharmacology* 39 (2014): 1052–58. https://doi.org/10.1038/npp.2013.317. Accessed January 19, 2024. https://pubmed.ncbi.nlm.nih.gov/24217129/.

Bibliography

"Dissociative Amnesia." Cleveland Clinic. Accessed December 2, 2023. https://my.clevelandclinic.org/health/diseases/9789-dissociative-amnesia.

"Dissociative Amnesia." *Psychology Today*. Accessed December 20, 2023. https://www.psychologytoday.com/us/conditions/dissociative-amnesia.

"Dissociative Fugue." *Psychology Today*. Accessed December 21, 2023. https://www.psychologytoday.com/us/conditions/dissociative-fugue-psychogenic-fugue.

Durr, Eric. "This World War Killer Took Almost as Many US Troops' Lives as Combat." Military.com, August 29, 2018. Accessed December 14, 2023. https://www.military.com/history/this-world-war-i-killer-took-almost-as-many-us-troops-lives-as-combat.html.

Eckart, Kim. "PTSD Symptoms Improve When Patient Chooses Form of Treatment, Study Shows." University of Washington News, October 19, 2018. Accessed January 19, 2024. https://www.washington.edu/news/2018/10/19/ptsd-symptoms-improve-when-patient-chooses-form-of-treatment-study-shows/.

"Electroconvulsive Therapy." Cleveland Clinic. Accessed January 16, 2024. https://my.clevelandclinic.org/health/treatments/9302-ect-electroconvulsive-therapy.

Esposito, Silvano, and Pasquale Pagliano. "Bacterial Skin Infections." *Reference Module in Biomedical Sciences* (2021). Accessed December 29, 2023. https://www.semanticscholar.org/paper/Bacterial-Skin-Infections-Esposito-Pagliano/f99c5659a9ff9858568fc31fd8b6cb3b36ae9927.

"Establish Identity of Wounded War Veteran." *Worcester Evening Gazette*, July 13, 1931. GeneologyBank.com. Accessed January 25, 2024. https://www.genealogybank.com/doc/newspapers/image/v2%3A1773BDF75FF7A17E%40GB3NEWS-1797FBDDE4C8C399%402426536-1797A98B98B2B81E%402-1797A98B98B2B81E?clipid=wngpjzfzfeqxgtmalmqiwzskvwelvxjh_wma-gateway014_1679001051991.

"Failure to Report for Duty: Desertion, AWOL, and Other Charges." FindLaw. Last modified June 20, 2016. Accessed January 31, 2024. https://www.findlaw.com/military/criminal-law/failure-to-report-for-duty-awol-and-other-charges.html#:~:text=Desertion%20carries%20a%20maximum%20punishment,of%20the%20court%2Dmartial.

"Father Visits Son Missing 14 Years." *Key West Citizen*, July 6, 1931. Ancestry.com. Accessed December 30, 2023. https://www.ancestry.com/mediaui-viewer/collection/1030/tree/106300270/person/282266865281/media/f0f31017-87e0-4976-b47f-14eff03277fd?_phsrc=aiN994&usePUBJs=true&galleryindex=1&albums=pg&showGalleryAlbums=true&tab=0&pid=282266865281&sort=-created.

"Federal Music Project." Wikipedia. Accessed January 7, 2024. https://en.wikipedia.org/wiki/Federal_Music_Project.

"Federal Project Number One." Wikipedia. Accessed January 7, 2024. https://en.wikipedia.org/wiki/Federal_Project_Number_One.

"The First Edition of the Modern Taino Dictionary." Taino Language Project. Accessed January 22, 2024. https://www.taino-tribe.org/tedict.html.

"Fletcher Favors Use of $6,000,000 Funds to Aid States' Idle." Bay Pines VA Medical. Accessed December 15, 2023. https://cdm15801.contentdm.oclc.org/digital/collection/p15801coll3/id/19/rec/17.

"Florida, Military Dept., Charlie E Perez." State Library and Archives of Florida, Florida Memory. Accessed December 15, 2023. https://www.floridamemory.com/items/show/203671.

"Florida, U.S., Arriving and Departing Passenger and Crew Lists, 1898–1963." Ancestry.com. Accessed January 9, 2024. https://www.ancestry.com/imageviewer/collections/8842/images/41260_322597-00352?pId=9554330.

"Florida, U.S., Arriving and Departing Passenger and Crew Lists, 1898–1963." Ancestry.com. Accessed December 7, 2023. https://www.ancestry.com/imageviewer/collections/8842/images/t940_45-0451?pId=2323046.

"Florida, U.S., Arriving and Departing Passenger and Crew Lists, 1898–1963." Ancestry.com. Accessed January 10, 2024. https://www.ancestry.com/imageviewer/collections/8842/images/42792_DC000694-00344?pId=4929922.

"Florida, U.S., County Marriage Records, 1823–1982, Hillsborough County, Marriage

License, February 15, 1896." Ancestry.com. Accessed December 6, 2023. https://www.ancestry.com/mediaui-viewer/collection/1030/tree/106300270/person/282266865045/media/6261da5f-1ab2-4853-812e-99a23a11aca4?_phsrc=aiN819&usePUBJs=true&galleryindex=4&albums=pg&showGalleryAlbums=true&tab=0&pid=282266865045&sort=-created.

"Florida, U.S., Divorce Index, 1927–2001." Ancestry.com. Accessed December 15, 2023. https://www.ancestry.com/imageviewer/collections/8837/images/FLDIV_0049-0032?pId=430198.

"Florida, U.S., Marriage Indexes, 1822–1875, 1927–2001." Ancestry.com. Accessed December 15, 2023. https://www.ancestry.com/imageviewer/collections/8784/images/FLMAR_0326-0013?pId=1550875.

"Florida, U.S., State Census, 1867–1945." Ancestry.com. Accessed December 16, 2023. https://www.ancestry.com/imageviewer/collections/1506/images/CSUSAFL1867_089324-00346?pId=883183.

"Florida Keys History Center—Monroe County's Public Library Stream." Accessed January 22, 2024. https://www.flickr.com/photos/keyslibraries/9048605417/. License link: https://creativecommons.org/licenses/by/2.0/.

"Former Marion Girl Marries New York Man." *Marion Star* (Marion, Ohio), October 10, 1936. Accessed December 15, 2023. https://www.newspapers.com/article/the-marion-star-marriage-caroline-veroni/119738536/.

"Fort Hayes." Wikipedia. Accessed January 7, 2024. https://en.wikipedia.org/wiki/Fort_Hayes.

"Fort Slocum." Wikipedia. Accessed December 19, 2023. https://en.wikipedia.org/wiki/Fort_Slocum.

"Fox Hills Boasts World's Largest Army Hospital." *Staten Island Advance*, March 27, 2011. Accessed December 20, 2023. https://www.silive.com/specialreports/2011/03/post_1.html.

Friedman, Matthew J. "'Soldier's Heart' and 'Shell Shock': Past Names for PTSD." *Frontline*, Accessed January 15, 2024. https://www.pbs.org/wgbh/pages/frontline/shows/heart/themes/shellshock.html.

Friedman, Matthew J., MD, PhD. "History of PTSD in Veterans: Civil War to DSM-5." National Center for PTSD, U.S. Department of Veterans Affairs. Accessed January 15, 2024. https://www.ptsd.va.gov/understand/what/history_ptsd.asp.

Friedman, Matthew J., MD, PhD, Paula P. Schnurr, PhD, and Annmarie McDonagh-Coyle, MD. "Post-Traumatic Stress Disorder in the Military Veteran." National Center for PTSD, U.S. Department of Veterans Affairs. Accessed January 19, 2024. https://www.ptsd.va.gov/professional/articles/article-pdf/id12012.pdf.

Galanti, Geri Ann. "The Hispanic Family and Male-Female Relationships: An Overview." NIH National Library of Medicine, 2003. Accessed December 19, 2023. https://pubmed.ncbi.nlm.nih.gov/12861920/.

"Garrison Prisoner." Merriam Webster Dictionary. Accessed December 20, 2023. https://www.merriam-webster.com/dictionary/garrison%20prisoner.

"General Prisoner." Merriam Webster Dictionary. Accessed December 20, 2023. https://www.merriam-webster.com/dictionary/general%20prisoner.

"George R. Stobbs." Wikipedia. Accessed December 30, 2023. https://en.wikipedia.org/wiki/George_R._Stobbs.

"Gettysburg Address." Abraham Lincoln Online. Accessed January 7, 2024. https://www.abrahamlincolnonline.org/lincoln/speeches/gettysburg.htm.

GhaneaBassiri, Kambiz. "Legally White." Oregon Humanities, August 12, 2011. Accessed December 30, 2023. https://www.oregonhumanities.org/rll/magazine/belong-summer-2011/legally-white/.

Gianelli, P. "Rape Trauma Syndrome." *Criminal Law Bulletin* 33, no. 3 (1997): 270–79. Accessed January 19, 2024. https://www.ojp.gov/ncjrs/virtual-library/abstracts/rape-trauma-syndrome-0.

Godoy, Gustavo G. "Jose Alejandro Huau: A Cuban Patriot in Jacksonville Politics." *Florida Historical Quarterly* 54, no. 2 (1975), Article 7. Accessed December 11, 2023. https://stars.library.ucf.edu/cgi/viewcontent.cgi?article=3385&context=fhq.

Goldschmidt, Kathy, and Bradley Joseph Sinkhaus. "Job Description for a Member of Congress." Congressional Management Foundation. Accessed January 7, 2024. https://www.congressfoundation.org/storage/documents/CMF_Pubs/cmf-member-job-description.pdf.
"Grace R. Duff 1921 Elementary Accounting Certificate." *Fall River Daily Evening News*, August 31, 1921. Accessed January 14, 2024. https://www.newspapers.com/article/fall-river-daily-evening-news-grace-r-d/123201062/.
"Grace to Father-in-Law" (letter). June 24, 1931. Family Archives. Ancestry.com. Accessed December 30, 2023. https://www.ancestry.com/mediaui-viewer/collection/1030/tree/106300270/person/282266865281/media/6991d757-e9fa-4233-b442-70368184b6f8?_phsrc=aiN983&usePUBJs=true&galleryindex=1&albums=pg&showGalleryAlbums=true&tab=0&pid=282266865281&sort=-created.
Graham, Thomas F. "Psychoneurotic Disorders." American Psychological Association. Accessed December 25, 2023. https://psycnet.apa.org/record/2013-44654-007.
"Great Plains Shelterbelt." Wikipedia. Accessed January 7, 2024. https://en.wikipedia.org/wiki/Great_Plains_Shelterbelt.
Griffeath, Kristen. "With One Voice: The American Musical Experience of World War I." National World War I Museum and Memorial. Accessed January 30, 2024. https://www.theworldwar.org/sites/default/files/2022-03/with-one-voice.pdf.
"Guests Aboard the S.S. Florida of P. & O. Line Traveling between Miami and Havana." State Library and Archives, Florida Memory. Accessed January 9, 2024. http://www.floridamemory.com/items/show/251499.
Gwynne, S.C. "Nostalgia in the Civil War." *TimeLines*, December 5, 2019. Accessed January 19, 2024. https://www.timelinesmagazine.com/publications/civil-war-courier/nostalgia-in-the-civil-war/article_7880dd3e-17a6-11ea-819c-3b6bb8b44921.html.
Hayes, Jasmeet P., et al. "Emotion and Cognition Interactions in PTSD: A Review of Neurocognitive and Neuroimaging Studies." *Frontiers in Integrative Neuroscience* 6, no. 89 (October 9, 2012). doi:10.3389/fnint.2012.00089. Accessed January 19, 2024. https://www.ncbi.nlm.nih.gov/pmc/articles/PMC3466464/.
"The Hemisphere: Pearl of the Antilles." *Time*, January 26, 1959. Accessed December 11, 2023. https://content.time.com/time/subscriber/article/0,33009,892092-1,00.html.
Hendricks, Charles. "Combat and Construction, US Army Engineers in World War I." U.S. Army Corps of Engineers. Accessed December 19, 2023. https://usace.contentdm.oclc.org/digital/api/collection/p16021coll4/id/334/download.
"Hispaniola." Encyclopedia Britannica. Accessed November 22, 2023. https://www.britannica.com/place/Hispaniola.
"Hispaniola." Wikipedia. Accessed December 7, 2023. https://en.wikipedia.org/w/index.php?title=Hispaniola&oldid=1187573465.
"Historic Buildings of Massachusetts, Our Lady of Fatima Church." Massachusetts Historic Buildings. Accessed January 9, 2024. https://mass.historicbuildingsct.com/?p=6257.
"History of Pharmacy in the United States." Wikipedia. Accessed December 7, 2023. https://en.wikipedia.org/w/index.php?title=History_of_pharmacy_in_the_United_States&oldid=1181422170.
"History of the Bruce W. Carter VA Medical Center." U.S. Department of Veterans Affairs. Accessed December 19, 2023. https://www.va.gov/miami-health-care/about-us/history/.
"History of the DAV." Accessed January 1, 2024. https://www.dav.org/wp-content/uploads/DAVHistory_DAVWW.pdf.
"History of Ybor City." Wikipedia. Accessed January 14, 2024. https://en.wikipedia.org/w/index.php?title=History_of_Ybor_City&oldid=1195458173.
"History Overview, Veterans Administration." U.S. Department of Veterans Affairs. Accessed December 29, 2023. https://department.va.gov/history/history-overview/#:~:text=The%20second%20consolidation%20of%20federal,activities%20affecting%20war%20veterans.%E2%80%9D%20At.
Holmes, Frederick. "Medicine in the First World War: The Influenza Pandemic and the War." University of Kansas Medical Center. Accessed December 29, 2023. https://www.

kumc.edu/school-of-medicine/academics/departments/history-and-philosophy-of-medicine/archives/wwi/essays/medicine/influenza.html.

Holmes, Frederick. "Medicine in the First World War: Venereal Disease." University of Kansas Medical Center. Accessed December 29, 2023. https://www.kumc.edu/school-of-medicine/academics/departments/history-and-philosophy-of-medicine/archives/wwi/essays/medicine/venereal-disease.html.

Hooper, Charles R. "Suicide Among Veterans." American Addiction Centers. Accessed January 19, 2024. https://americanaddictioncenters.org/veterans/suicide-among-veterans.

"Hooverville." Wikipedia. Accessed December 29, 2023. https://en.wikipedia.org/w/index.php?title=Hooverville&oldid=1186546061.

"House Passes Bonus Bill for WWI Veterans, June 15, 1932." *Politico* (June 2009). Accessed December 29, 2023. https://www.politico.com/story/2009/06/house-passes-bonus-bill-for-wwi-veterans-june-15-1932-023722.

"How Havana Became British for Eleven Months." *Library of Congress Blogs*. Accessed December 7, 2023. https://blogs.loc.gov/law/2022/01/how-havana-became-british-for-eleven-months/.

"How the Machine Gun Changed Combat during World War I." Norwich University. Accessed December 15, 2023. https://online.norwich.edu/how-machine-gun-changed-combat-during-world-war-i.

"Inadequate Personality." Oxford Reference. Accessed December 25, 2023. https://www.oxfordreference.com/display/10.1093/oi/authority.20110810105127659.

"Injuries in World War I: Psychological Injuries." United States World War One Centennial Commission. Accessed February 23, 2024. https://www.worldwar1centennial.org/index.php/injuries-in-world-war-i/2592-injuries-in-world-war-i-psychological-injuries.html.

Jones, Dr. Edgar. "Shell Shocked." *Monitor on Psychology* 43, no. 6 (June 2012). Accessed December 14, 2023. https://www.apa.org/monitor/2012/06/shell-shocked.

"A Journey of a Thousand Miles Begins with a Single Step." Wikipedia. Accessed January 13, 2024. https://en.wikipedia.org/wiki/A_journey_of_a_thousand_miles_begins_with_a_single_step.

Kamps, Alice. "The 1932 Bonus Army: Black and White Americans Unite in March on Washington." *Pieces of History* (blog of the U.S. National Archives), July 15, 2020. Accessed December 29, 2023. https://prologue.blogs.archives.gov/2020/07/15/the-1932-bonus-army-black-and-white-americans-unite-in-march-on-washington/.

Kardiner, Abram, MD. *The Traumatic Neuroses of War*. Washington, DC: National Research Council (U.S.), Committee on Problems of Neurotic Behavior, 1941. Accessed January 19, 2024. https://doi.org/10.1037/10581-000.

"Key West." Wikipedia. Accessed December 11, 2023. https://en.wikipedia.org/wiki/Key_West.

Kleisiaris, Christos F., et al. "Health Care Practices in Ancient Greece: The Hippocratic Ideal." *Journal of Medical Ethics and History of Medicine* 7, no. 6 (March 15, 2014). Accessed January 19, 2024. https://www.ncbi.nlm.nih.gov/pmc/articles/PMC4263393/.

Land, Joni Auden. "The Portland Veteran Who Took on Washington, D.C., during the Great Depression." Oregon Public Broadcasting. Accessed December 29, 2023. https://www.opb.org/article/2023/11/11/bonus-army-veterans-washington-dc-walter-waters/#:~:text=He%20and%20400%20other%20veterans,epicenter%20of%20a%20nationwide%20movement.

"Last Minute Flashes." *Worcester Evening Gazette*, August 29, 1927. https://www.genealogybank.com/doc/newspapers/image/v2%3A1773BDF75FF7A17E%40GB3NEWS-17964E477307B03B%402425122-179557732ACA204E%400-179557732ACA204E?clipid=msshwickjzfydjdeqkkuqouhzvjuzybr_wma-gateway001_1679002485198.

"The Lawrence Welk Show." YouTube. Accessed January 8, 2024. https://www.youtube.com/watch?v=8_Cz9qqdPwE.

"Life Expectancy in the United States." Congressional Research Service. Accessed December 6, 2023. https://www.everycrsreport.com/reports/RL32792.html#_Toc194633795.

Bibliography

"Lima, Ohio." City Maps. Accessed December 20, 2023. https://colgis.cityhall.lima.oh.us/zoning/.

"Lineage and Honors, 2D Engineer Battalion." United States of America War Office. Accessed December 19, 2023. https://history.army.mil/html/forcestruc/lineages/branches/eng/0002enbn.htm.

"List of Former United States Army Medical Units." Wikipedia. Accessed December 20, 2023. https://en.wikipedia.org/wiki/List_of_former_United_States_Army_medical_units#Debarkation_hospitals.

"Little War." Wikipedia. Accessed December 11, 2023. https://en.wikipedia.org/wiki/Little_War_(Cuba).

Loughran, Tracey. "Masculinity, Trauma and Shell Shock." *The Psychologist*, February 13, 2015. Accessed January 16, 2024. https://www.bps.org.uk/psychologist/masculinity-trauma-and-shell-shock.

"Major General Charles W. Bridges to George R. Stobbs" (war record letter). United States War Department, Washington, DC, July 3, 1931. Family Archives. Ancestry.com. Accessed February 4, 2024. https://www.ancestry.com/mediaui-viewer/collection/1030/tree/106300270/person/282266865281/media/c588a91a-8ddb-4b82-826c-9a697db64a3a?_phsrc=aiN749&usePUBJs=true&galleryindex=2&albums=pg&showGalleryAlbums=true&tab=0&pid=282266865281&filter=p&sort=-created.

"Major General C.W. Bridges to Pehr G. Holmes" (medical record letter). United States War Department, Washington, DC, July 3, 1931. Family Archives. Ancestry.com. Accessed January 31, 2024. https://www.ancestry.com/mediaui-viewer/collection/1030/tree/106300270/person/282266865281/media/2131ec83-5eb6-48d6-b046-55010c65718e?_phsrc=aiN749&usePUBJs=true&galleryindex=1&albums=pg&showGalleryAlbums=true&tab=0&pid=282266865281&filter=p&sort=-created.

"Male Hysteria." Wikipedia. Accessed December 27, 2023. https://en.wikipedia.org/wiki/Male_hysteria.

"A Manual for Courts-Martial, U.S. Army, 1928 (Corrected to April 20, 1943)." Revised in the Office of the Judge Advocate General of the Army and Published by Direction of the President. Washington, DC: Government Printing Office, 1943. Appendix I, "The Articles of War," Article 58, "Desertion." https://www.ibiblio.org/hyperwar/USA/ref/MCM/index.html.

Marx, Christopher, et al. "Talking Cure Models: A Framework of Analysis." *Frontiers in Psychology* 8 (September 2017), Article 1589. doi:10.3389/fpsyg.2017.01589. Accessed January 16, 2024. https://www.ncbi.nlm.nih.gov/pmc/articles/PMC5601393/.

"Maslow's Hierarchy of Needs." Wikipedia. Accessed January 20, 2024. https://en.wikipedia.org/wiki/Maslow%27s_hierarchy_of_needs.

"Massachusetts, U.S., Birth Records, 1840–1915." Ancestry.com. Accessed December 3, 2023. https://www.ancestry.com/imageviewer/collections/5062/images/41262_b139412-00620?pId=2512730.

"Massachusetts, U.S., Death Index, 1901–1980." Ancestry.com. Accessed December 30, 2023. https://www.ancestry.com/imageviewer/collections/3659/images/41263_2421406273_0049-00235?pId=2808568.

"Massachusetts, U.S., Marriage Index, 1901–1955 and 1966–1970." Ancestry.com. Accessed December 3, 2023. https://www.ancestry.com/imageviewer/collections/2966/images/41263_2421406273_0170-00390?pId=2153574.

"Massachusetts, U.S., Marriage Index, 1901–1955 and 1966–1970." Ancestry.com. Accessed June 14, 2023. https://www.ancestry.com/imageviewer/collections/2966/images/41263_2421406273_0176-00113?pId=1229045.

"Massachusetts, U.S., Marriage Records, 1840–1915." Ancestry.com. Accessed December 3, 2023. https://www.ancestry.com/imageviewer/collections/2511/images/41262_b139334-00417?pId=12561222.

"Massachusetts, U.S., Town and Vital Records, 1620–1988." Ancestry.com. Accessed December 2, 2023. https://www.ancestry.com/imageviewer/collections/2495/images/40143_266007__0185-00114?pId=3800284.

"Massachusetts Historical Records Survey Files 1936–1942." Worldcat.org. Accessed

January 7, 2024. https://search.worldcat.org/title/massachusetts-historical-records-survey-files-1936-1942/oclc/79840258.

"Medical Department of the United States Army in the World War." AMEDD Center for History and Heritage. Accessed December 20, 2023. https://achh.army.mil/history/book-wwi-neuropsychiatry-section1chapter3.

"Medications for PTSD." National Center for PTSD, U.S. Department of Veterans Affairs. Accessed January 19, 2024. https://www.ptsd.va.gov/understand_tx/meds_for_ptsd.asp.

"Members of the General Court-Martial" (clemency letter). First Corps Area. Boston, Massachusetts, August 3, 1928. Family Archives. Ancestry.com. Accessed February 4, 2024. https://www.ancestry.com/mediauiviewer/collection/1030/tree/106300270/person/282266865281/media/e1fa6887-1466-4e0b-bfdb-f258d795a3fb?_phsrc=aiN741&usePUBJs=true&galleryindex=1&albums=pg&showGalleryAlbums=true&tab=0&pid=282266865281&sort=-created.

"Memorial ID: 18264878." Find a Grave. Accessed December 15, 2023. https://www.findagrave.com/memorial/18264878/francisca-velasco.

"Memorial ID: 190733154." Find a Grave. Accessed December 30, 2023. https://www.findagrave.com/memorial/190733154/infant-conner.

"Memorial ID: 243465174." Find a Grave. Accessed December 2, 2023. https://www.findagrave.com/memorial/243465174/mary-e-duff.

"Memorial ID: 243466333." Find a Grave. Accessed December 2, 2023. https://www.findagrave.com/memorial/243466333/edward-b-duff.

"Memorial ID: 243467883." Find a Grave. Accessed December 2, 2023. https://www.findagrave.com/memorial/243467883/catherine-a-duff.

"Memorial ID: 3974667." Find a Grave. Accessed December 16, 2023. https://www.findagrave.com/memorial/3974667/charles-ernest-perez.

"Mens Rea." Legal Information Institute. Accessed December 27, 2023. https://www.law.cornell.edu/wex/mens_rea.

"Miami Biltmore Hotel." Wikipedia. Accessed December 19, 2023. https://en.wikipedia.org/w/index.php?title=Miami_Biltmore_Hotel&oldid=1169253142.

"Military Medicine in World War I." United States World War One Centennial Commission. Accessed December 19, 2023. https://www.worldwar1centennial.org/index.php/practice-of-medicine-in-ww1.html.

Miller, Matthew, PhD, MPH. "VA Releases 2022 National Veteran Suicide Prevention Annual Report." Accessed January 9, 2024. https://news.va.gov/108984/2022-national-veteran-suicide-prevention-annual-report/#:~:text=In%202020%2C%20there%20were%206%2C146,fell%20in%202019%20and%202020.

"Miss van Deinse Is Wed to Mr. Perez in New York." *Orlando Sentinel*, October 4, 1936. Accessed December 15, 2023. https://www.newspapers.com/article/the-orlando-sentinel-marriage-of-charles/119599744/.

"Mobilizing for War: The Selective Service Act in WWI." National Archives Foundation. Accessed January 21, 2024. https://www.archivesfoundation.org/documents/mobilizing-war-selective-service-act-world-war/#:~:text=On%20May%2018%2C%201917%2C%20Congress,to%20register%20for%20military%20service.

Mosse, George L. "Shell-Shock as a Social Disease." *Journal of Contemporary History* 35, no. 1 (2000): 101–8. Accessed January 16, 2024. http://www.jstor.org/stable/261184.

"Mrs. Mercedes Perez Dies Last Night." *Key West Citizen*, August 29, 1931. Ancestry.com. Accessed December 7, 2023. https://www.ancestry.com/imageviewer/collections/7933/images/news-fl-ke_we_ci.1932_08_29_0004?pId=488928260.

N., Sam. "Inadequate Personality." Psychology Dictionary. Accessed December 25, 2023. https://psychologydictionary.org/inadequate-personality/.

"National Directory of Piano Teachers, United States of America." 1955. Ancestry.com. Accessed January 7, 2024. https://www.ancestry.com/mediaui-viewer/collection/1030/tree/106300270/person/282266865281/media/9c06503e-0ce4-48ac-9228-b48a38e2b1fa?_phsrc=aiN1027&usePUBJs=true&galleryindex=2&albums=pg&showGalleryAlbums=true&tab=0&pid=282266865281&sort=-created.

"National Records of Scotland, Statutory Births 605/00 0064." Accessed January 8,

2023. https://www.ancestry.com/mediaui-viewer/collection/1030/tree/106300270/person/282443483516/media/5abdbcc7-17a7-4bb9-9472-8a1bfacb2c2c?_phsrc=aiN707&usePUBJs=true&galleryindex=5&albums=pg&showGalleryAlbums=true&tab=0&pid=282443483516&sort=-created. Alternate link: https://www.ancestry.com/sharing/8095198?mark=7b22746f6b656e223a226e65334d4a626570634a79676f464837712f4c49587461673358316c79746d324b6e372b356b4d4f5461343d222c22746f6b656e5f76657273696f6e223a225632227d.
"New Deal Programs." Living New Deal. Accessed January 28, 2024. https://livingnewdeal.org/history-of-the-new-deal/programs/.
"New Deal Programs, Federal Music Project (FMP) (1935)." Living New Deal. Accessed January 28, 2024. https://livingnewdeal.org/glossary/federal-music-project-fmp-1935-1943/.
"New York, U.S., Abstracts of WW I Military Service, 1917–1919." Ancestry.com. Accessed June 15, 2023. https://www.ancestry.com/imageviewer/collections/3030/images/40808_1120704930_0482-01124?pId=224456.
New York National Guardsman, 1924–1940. New York State Military Museum and Veterans Research Center. Accessed December 15, 2023. https://museum.dmna.ny.gov/application/files/1315/7971/8920/NYNG1937_09.pdf.
Orbison, Thomas J., MD. "Constitutional Psychopathic Inferior Personality—With or Without Psychosis." *California and Western Medicine* 30, no. 2 (February 1929). Accessed December 25, 2023. https://www.psychologytoday.com/us/blog/and-running/202202/what-was-constitutional-psychopath.
"Other Deaths." *Miami Herald*, May 2, 1950. Accessed December 16, 2023. https://www.ancestry.com/mediaui-viewer/collection/1030/tree/106300270/person/282266865282/media/5c1016bc-03a4-4b7b-9a9f-6966ada0ce74?_phsrc=aiN893&usePUBJs=true&galleryindex=7&albums=pg&showGalleryAlbums=true&tab=0&pid=282266865282&sort=-created.
"The Pact of Zanjón." Wikipedia. Accessed December 11, 2023. https://en.wikipedia.org/wiki/Pact_of_Zanjón.
"Past Year Prevalence of Post-Traumatic Stress Disorder Among Adults." National Comorbidity Survey Replication (NCS-R). Accessed January 19, 2024. https://www.nimh.nih.gov/health/statistics/post-traumatic-stress-disorder-ptsd.
Payne, Dr. David. "Trench Diseases of the First World War." Western Front Association. Accessed December 29, 2023. https://www.westernfrontassociation.com/world-war-i-articles/trench-diseases-of-the-first-world-war/.
"Pehr G. Holmes." State Library of Massachusetts. Accessed December 27, 2023. file:///C:/Users/owner/Downloads/ocm41543981-19411942.pdf.
"Pehr G. Holmes." Wikipedia. Accessed December 30, 2023. https://en.wikipedia.org/wiki/Pehr_G._Holmes.
Pells, Richard H., and C.D. Romer. "Great Depression." Encyclopedia Britannica. Accessed December 30, 2023. https://www.britannica.com/event/Great-Depression.
"Perez Identifies Long Lost Son." *Miami Herald*, July 19, 1931. Ancestry.com. Accessed January 25, 2024. https://www.ancestry.com/mediaui-viewer/collection/1030/tree/106300270/person/282266865281/media/62a967ca-e1ff-4198-9e95-eee7cccaf7fe?_phsrc=aiN1154&usePUBJs=true&galleryindex=10&albums=pg&showGalleryAlbums=true&tab=0&pid=282266865281&sort=-created.
"Personals." *Orlando Evening Star*, September 27, 1937. Accessed December 15, 2023. https://www.newspapers.com/article/orlando-evening-star-charles-e-perez-m/119605067/.
"Personals." *St. Petersburg Times*, March 31, 1941. Accessed December 15, 2023. https://www.ancestry.com/mediauiviewer/collection/1030/tree/106300270/person/282266865282/media/c12e4a47-e337-4290-9b36-641812d7d19c?_phsrc=aiN871&usePUBJs=true&galleryindex=1&albums=pg&showGalleryAlbums=true&tab=0&pid=282266865282&sort=-created.
"Pianos and Their Prices." Blue Book of Pianos Online. Accessed January 7, 2024. https://www.bluebookofpianos.com/spin1947.htm.
Pohls, Hans, and Stephanie Oak. "War and Military Mental Health." *American Journal of*

Public Health 97, no. 12 (December 2007). Accessed December 21, 2023. https://www.ncbi.nlm.nih.gov/pmc/articles/PMC2089086/.

Polakovic, Gary. "How Did WWI Reshape the Modern World?" *USC Today*, November 9, 2018. Accessed December 15, 2023. https://today.usc.edu/impact-of-world-war-i-shaping-the-modern-world/.

"Post-Traumatic Stress Disorder." American Psychiatric Association. Accessed January 19, 2024. https://www.psychiatry.org/file%20library/psychiatrists/practice/dsm/apa_dsm-5-ptsd.pdf.

"Post-Traumatic Stress Disorder." Mayo Clinic. Accessed January 19, 2024. https://www.mayoclinic.org/diseases-conditions/post-traumatic-stress-disorder/symptoms-causes/syc-20355967.

"Post-Traumatic Stress Disorder." Substance Abuse and Mental Health Services Administration, Department of Health and Human Services. Accessed January 14, 2024. https://www.samhsa.gov/mental-health/post-traumatic-stress-disorder.

"Principal Causes of Death in United States Registration Area: Census Bureau Summarizes Mortality Statistics for 1917." *Public Health Reports (1896–1970)* 34, no. 27 (1919): 1474–78. Accessed December 10, 2023. http://www.jstor.org/stable/4575322.

"PTSD in Iraq and Afghanistan Veterans." U.S. Department of Veterans Affairs. Accessed January 19, 2024. https://www.publichealth.va.gov/epidemiology/studies/new-generation/ptsd.asp.

"Rape Crisis Centers in the United States." Wikipedia. Accessed January 19, 2024. https://en.wikipedia.org/wiki/Rape_crisis_centers_in_the_United_States.

Regimental Headquarters Second Engineers. "Official History of the Second Engineers in the World War, 1916–1919." Library of Congress. Accessed December 20, 2023. https://tile.loc.gov/storageservices/public/gdcmassbookdig/officialhistoryo00uni/officialhistoryo00uni.pdf.

"Relatives Find Former Tampan After 15 Years." *Tampa Tribune*, July 14, 1931. GeneologyBank.com. Accessed January 25, 2024. https://www.genealogybank.com/doc/newspapers/image/v2%3A135B96627AC4A53C%40GB3NEWS-13A4D75C5E75BF06%-402426537-139BFB1BAD189653%402-139BFB1BAD189653.

"Rep. George Stobbs." Government Track. Accessed December 27, 2023. https://www.govtrack.us/congress/members/george_stobbs/410390.

"Republic of Cuba (1902–1959)." Wikipedia. Accessed December 30, 2023. https://en.wikipedia.org/wiki/Republic_of_Cuba_(1902-1959).

"Retrograde Amnesia." Wikipedia. Accessed January 20, 2024. https://en.wikipedia.org/wiki/Retrograde_amnesia.

Richman, Mike. "Prolonged Exposure or Cognitive Processing Therapy?" VA Research Communications. Accessed January 19, 2024. https://www.research.va.gov/currents/0122-Prolonged-exposure-or-cognitive-processing-therapy.cfm.

"Roaring Twenties." Wikipedia. Accessed January 28, 2024. https://en.wikipedia.org/wiki/Roaring_Twenties.

"Roll of the Dead." *Tampa Tribune*, January 22, 1916. https://www.newspapers.com/article/the-tampa-tribune-roll-of-the-dead-pere/119793016/. Alternate link: https://www.ancestry.com/mediaui-viewer/collection/1030/tree/106300270/person/282266865045/media/cd29126d-4e36-46c3-a4f4-bf23609ed797?_phsrc=aiN754&usePUBJs=true&galleryindex=1&albums=pg&showGalleryAlbums=true&tab=0&pid=282266865045&sort=-created.

Ronning, C. Neale. *Jose Marti and the Émigré Colony in Key West: Leadership and State Formation*. New York: Praeger, 1990.

"Ruth Bryan Owen." Wikipedia. Accessed January 4, 2024. https://en.wikipedia.org/w/index.php?title=Ruth_Bryan_Owen.

"Salvador Bermudez de Castro, Marquis de Lema." Wikipedia. Accessed December 11, 2023. https://en.wikipedia.org/wiki/SalvadorBermúdez_de_Castro,_Marquis_of_Lema.

Samet, Daniel J. "World War I: The War That Saved Democracy." United States World War One Centennial Commission. Accessed February 23, 2024. https://www.

worldwar1centennial.org/index.php/communicate/press-media/wwi-centennial-news/5619-world-war-i-the-war-that-saved-democracy.html.

Sandhu, Pavi. "Step Aside, Freud: Josef Breuer Is the True Father of Modern Psychotherapy." *Scientific American*, June 30, 2015. Accessed December 15, 2023. https://blogs.scientificamerican.com/mind-guest-blog/step-aside-freud-josef-breuer-is-the-true-father-of-modern-psychotherapy/.

Santana, Tyler J., and the Tampa Historical Team. "Vicente Martinez Ybor." Tampa Historical. Accessed December 11, 2023. https://tampahistorical.org/items/show/125.

Schaum, John W. "Saltwater Boogie, Piano Solo." Belwin, Inc. Accessed January 8, 2024. https://www.youtube.com/watch?v=qOsY1ClDak4.

Schlaug, Gottfried. "The Brain of Musicians: A Model for Functional and Structural Adaptation." New York Academy of Sciences. Accessed December 25, 2023. https://www.musicianbrain.com/papers/Schlaug_NYAS_2001.pdf.

Schoultz, Lars. "A Review of the History of Havana." *Harvard Review of Latin America* (2007). Accessed December 7, 2023. https://archive.revista.drclas.harvard.edu/book/book-talk-whats-most-welcoming-city-how-about-havana.

Schwartz, Thomas. "The Great Stock Market Crash of 1929." *Hoover Heads: The Blog of the Herbert Hoover Library and Museum*, June 15, 2022. Accessed January 28, 2024. https://hoover.blogs.archives.gov/2022/06/15/the-great-stock-market-crash-of-1929-why-history-textbooks-and-the-conventional-wisdom-get-it-wrong/.

"Seaboard Air Line Railroad." Wikipedia. Accessed December 19, 2023. https://en.wikipedia.org/wiki/Seaboard_Air_Line_Railroad.

"Sector Activities." Army War College, Historical Section. Accessed December 19, 2023. https://history.army.mil/curriculum/wwi/docs/AdditionalResources/Sector_Activities_AEF_on_Western_Front_and_Italy_1917-1918.pdf.

"Senate Passes Walsh's Bills." *Worcester Evening Gazette*, February 27, 1935. GeneologyBank.com. Accessed January 7, 2024. https://www.genealogybank.com/doc/newspapers/image/v2%3A1773BDF75FF7A17E%40GB3NEWS-1799C7A36B3D0F69%402427861-1799B3D848FF51AF%401-1799B3D848FF51AF?clipid=yxbsgocktrldiqhkunjdutciwzcvjjkd_wma-gateway002_1679003306771.

"Senator David I. Walsh Wants Congress to Lift Perez Stigma." *Key West Citizen*, July 23, 1931. Ancestry.com. Accessed January 25, 2024. https://www.ancestry.com/mediaui-viewer/collection/1030/tree/106300270/person/282266865281/media/9db1e36c-efb9-40a9-97c7-ecd092b2d92c?_phsrc=aiN1170&usePUBJs=true&galleryindex=1&albums=pg&showGalleryAlbums=true&tab=0&pid=282266865281&sort=-created.

Shea, M. Tracie. "Present-Centered Therapy for PTSD." National Center for PTSD, U.S. Department of Veterans Affairs. Accessed January 19, 2024. https://www.ptsd.va.gov/professional/treat/txessentials/present_centered_therapy.asp.

"Shell Shock." Wikipedia. Accessed December 27, 2023. https://en.wikipedia.org/w/index.php?title=Shell_shock&oldid=1191003963.

Sheth, Hitesh C., et al. "Anxiety Disorders in Ancient Indian Literature." *Indian Journal of Psychiatry* 52, no. 3 (2010): 289–91. doi:10.4103/0019-5545.71009. Accessed January 15, 2024. https://www.ncbi.nlm.nih.gov/pmc/articles/PMC2990839/.

Showalter, Dennis E., and John Graham Royde-Smith. "World War I." Encyclopedia Britannica. Accessed December 9, 2023. https://www.britannica.com/event/World-War-I.

"Silver Star." New World Encyclopedia. Accessed January 7, 2024. https://www.newworldencyclopedia.org/entry/Silver_Star.

Smith, Anthony D. "What Was a Constitutional Psychopath?" *Psychology Today*, February 25, 2022. Accessed December 25, 2023. https://www.psychologytoday.com/us/blog/and-running/202202/what-was-constitutional-psychopath.

"Social Security Act of 1935." Social Security Administration. Accessed January 28, 2024. https://www.ssa.gov/history/35act.html.

"Spanish–American War." Wikipedia. Accessed December 11, 2023. https://en.wikipedia.org/wiki/Spanish-American_War.

"SS Adriatic at Southampton (1907)." Reddit. Accessed December 19, 2023. https://www.reddit.com/r/Oceanlinerporn/comments/o8ebwk/ss_adriatic_at_southampton_1907/.

"Stress Inoculation Training for Post-Traumatic Stress Disorder." Society for Clinical Psychology. Accessed January 19, 2024. https://div12.org/treatment/stress-inoculation-training-for-post-traumatic-stress-disorder/.

Sullivan, Dwight. "A Matter of Life and Death: Examining the Military Death Penalty's Fairness." Death Penalty Information Center. https://deathpenaltyinfo.org/state-and-federal-info/military/the-militarys-death-penalty-system.

"Sweet Potatoes—Geoff and Maria Muldaur." Reprise Records (1972). Accessed January 8, 2024. https://www.youtube.com/watch?v=0bFuHPGyplE&list=OLAK5uy_nOgAVlJnMXAcR3OsjOMdiQTzfc7L9Tpac&index=5.

"Tampan, Dazed 15 Years, Finds Out Who He Was." *Daytona Beach Journal*, July 13, 1931. GeneologyBank.com. Accessed January 25, 2024. https://www.genealogybank.com/doc/newspapers/image/v2%3A14C8339FD081D3E4%40GB3NEWS-170BF5D2F102C01E%-402426536-170BDDB133EBC1BC%400-170BDDB133EBC1BC.

"Ten Years' War." Wikipedia. Accessed December 7, 2023. https://en.wikipedia.org/wiki/Ten_Years%27_War.

Terhune, William B. "Psychopathology and the Treatment of the Psychoneuroses." *New England Journal of Medicine* 198 (June 21, 1928). Accessed December 27, 2023. https://www.nejm.org/doi/full/10.1056/NEJM192806211981803.

Terrell, Ellen. "Prohibition Begins." Library of Congress Research Guides. Accessed December 20, 2023. https://guides.loc.gov/this-month-in-business-history/january/prohibition.

"The Treaty of Paris." Wikipedia. Accessed December 11, 2023. https://en.wikipedia.org/wiki/Treaty_of_Paris_(1898).

Turnbull, G.J. "A Review of Post-Traumatic Stress Disorder. Part I: Historical Development and Classification." *Injury* 29, no. 2 (1998): 87–91. doi:10.1016/s0020-1383(97)00131-9. Accessed January 19, 2024. https://pubmed.ncbi.nlm.nih.gov/10721399/.

UCF Veterans Legacy Program, K–12 Instructional Packets. "Charles Ernest Perez." Accessed February 5, 2024. https://vlp.cah.ucf.edu/k12.php. Alternate link: https://vlp.cah.ucf.edu/instructionalmaterials/UCF-VLP-CharlesErnestPerezPacket.pdf.

UCF Veterans Legacy Program Institute Brochure, 2023. Accessed December 15, 2023. https://online.fliphtml5.com/wqbac/jyos/#p=1.

"United States Patent and Trademark Office, US-0687089." Accessed December 6, 2023. https://image-ppubs.uspto.gov/dirsearch-public/print/downloadPdf/0687089.

"Upper Keys 1870 U.S. Census." Keys History. Accessed December 11, 2023. http://www.keyshistory.org/census.html.

"U.S., Army Transport Service Arriving and Departing Passenger Lists, 1910–1939." Ancestry.com. Accessed December 15, 2023. https://www.ancestry.com/discoveryui-content/view/7204057:61174?ssrc=pt&tid=106300270&pid=282266865282.

"U.S., Army Transport Service Arriving and Departing Passenger Lists, 1910–1939." Ancestry.com. Accessed December 15, 2023. https://www.ancestry.com/imageviewer/collections/61174/images/44509_3421606189_0303-00039?pId=3334456.

"U.S., Army Transport Service Arriving and Departing Passenger Lists, 1910–1939." Ancestry.com. Accessed December 15, 2023. https://www.ancestry.com/imageviewer/collections/61174/images/46920_162028006074_0062-00585?pId=7161246.

"U.S., City Directories, 1822–1995." Ancestry.com. Accessed December 3, 2023. https://www.ancestry.com/imageviewer/collections/2469/images/10189714?pId=512304932.

"U.S., Headstone Applications for Military Veterans, 1861–1985." Ancestry.com. Accessed December 15, 2023. https://www.ancestry.com/imageviewer/collections/2375/images/40050_2421402106_0401-01403?pId=494903.

"U.S., Passport Applications, 1795–1925." Ancestry.com. Accessed December 3, 2023. https://www.ancestry.com/imageviewer/collections/1174/images/USM1490_1266-0106?pId=949539.

"U.S., Social Security Death Index." Ancestry.com. Accessed December 15, 2023. https://www.ancestry.com/discoveryui-content/view/35943659:3693?ssrc=pt&tid=106300270&pid=282459275056.

"U.S., Veterans Administration Master Index, 1917–1940." Ancestry.com. Accessed

December 15, 2023. https://www.ancestry.com/discoveryui-content/view/5089128:61861?ssrc=pt&tid=106300270&pid=282266865282.
"U.S., Veterans Administration Master Index, 1917–1940." Ancestry.com. Accessed December 19, 2023. https://www.ancestry.com/discoveryui-content/view/5098786:61861?ssrc=pt&tid=106300270&pid=282266865281.
"U.S., World War II Draft Cards Young Men, 1940–1947." Ancestry.com. Accessed December 15, 2023. https://www.ancestry.com/imageviewer/collections/2238/images/44005_01_00010-01436?pId=12249158.
"U.S., World War II Draft Registration Cards, 1942." Ancestry.com. Accessed January 16, 2024. https://www.ancestry.com/imageviewer/collections/1002/images/miusa1939b_082573-01273.
"USAT Cuba." Wikipedia. Accessed January 9, 2024. https://en.wikipedia.org/wiki/USAT_Cuba.
Vayavanda, Sergeant Tatum. "The Battle of Belleau Wood Not Forgotten by U.S. Marines and French Soldiers." Marines: The Official Website of the United States Marine Corps. Accessed December 19, 2023. https://www.marforeur.marines.mil/In-the-News/Stories/Article/Article/520993/the-battle-of-belleau-wood-not-forgotten-by-us-marines-and-french-soldiers-on-m/.
Vennard, Martin. "How Can Musicians Keep Playing Despite Amnesia?" *BBC News Magazine*, November 21, 2011. Accessed December 25, 2023. https://www.bbc.com/news/magazine-15791973.
"Victor Matrix B-23344. Dardanella / Selvin's Novelty Orchestra." Discography of American Historical Recordings, S.V. Accessed January 8, 2024. https://adp.library.ucsb.edu/index.php/matrix/detail/700008515/B-23344-Dardanella.
"Voices of the First World War: Shell Shock." Imperial War Museums. Accessed January 19, 2024. https://www.iwm.org.uk/history/voices-of-the-first-world-war-shell-shock.
Walker, J.I. "Comparison of 'Rap' Groups with Traditional Group Therapy in the Treatment of Vietnam Combat Veterans." *Group* 7 (1983): 48–57. https://doi.org/10.1007/BF01458250. Accessed January 19, 2024. https://link.springer.com/article/10.1007/BF01458250.
Wallace, Joe. "AWOL & Desertion, Failure to Report." Veteran.com. Accessed December 29, 2023. https://veteran.com/awol/.
Ward, Maryann, and John Devereaux. "The Road Not Taken: Pre-Revolutionary Cuban Living Standards in Comparative Perspective." *Journal of Economic History* 72, issue 1 (2012). Accessed December 11, 2023. https://www.cambridge.org/core/journals/journal-of-economic-history/article/abs/road-not-taken-prerevolutionary-cuban-living-standards-in-comparative-perspective/1710F4E3173FCABE07BB7400406BF55E.
"What Is Posttraumatic Stress Disorder (PTSD)?" American Psychiatric Association. Accessed January 4, 2024. https://www.psychiatry.org/patients-families/ptsd/what-is-ptsd.
"W. J. Belleville to Captain Daniel" (letter). July 27, 1931. Family Archives. Ancestry.com. Accessed January 25, 2024. https://www.ancestry.com/mediaui-viewer/collection/1030/tree/106300270/person/282266865281/media/f317ce46-85f7-4f79-979e-f8f77473cb80?_phsrc=aiN1174&usePUBJs=true&galleryindex=1&albums=pg&showGalleryAlbums=true&tab=0&pid=282266865281&sort=-created.
"Works Progress Administration." Wikipedia. Accessed January 27, 2024. https://en.wikipedia.org/wiki/Works_Progress_Administration.
"Works Progress Administration (WPA) Historical Records Survey." Fort Myers–Lee County Library. Accessed January 7, 2024. https://sites.rootsweb.com/~flmgs/articles/Works_Projects_AdministrationMarch2011_BM.pdf.
"World War Adjusted Compensation Act." Wikipedia. Accessed December 29, 2023. https://en.wikipedia.org/wiki/World_War_Adjusted_Compensation_Act.
"World War I." Wikipedia. Accessed December 4, 2023. https://en.wikipedia.org/w/index.php?title=World_War_I&oldid=1188263128.
"World War I Enlistment Card." Ancestry.com. Accessed December 14, 2023. https://www.

ancestry.com/mediaui-viewer/collection/1030/tree/106300270/person/282266865282/media/aeaf0e1b-d891-4c34-b1c1-1314e0d7b004?_phsrc=aiN848&usePUBJs=true&galleryindex=4&albums=pg&showGalleryAlbums=true&tab=0&pid=282266865282&sort=-created.

"World War I Victory Medal." U.S. Commission of Fine Arts. Accessed December 16, 2023. https://www.cfa.gov/about-cfa/design-topics/coins-medals/world-war-i-victory-medal.

"World War I Victory Medal, United States." Wikipedia. Accessed December 15, 2023. https://en.wikipedia.org/wiki/World_War_I_Victory_Medal_(United_States).

"World War Veteran Comes to Himself." *Worcester Telegram*, July 13, 1931. Worcester Public Library. Accessed June 21, 2023. https://www.ancestry.com/mediaui-viewer/collection/1030/tree/106300270/person/282266865281/media/aaba43d5-cf6e-4959-b01e-c497a21c6c7b?_phsrc=aiN1150&usePUBJs=true&galleryindex=1&albums=pg&showGalleryAlbums=true&tab=0&pid=282266865281&sort=-created.

"WPA Starts Class in Tap Dancing." *Worcester Evening Gazette*, April 24, 1937. GeneologyBank.com. Accessed January 7, 2024. https://www.genealogybank.com/doc/newspapers/image/v2%3A1773BDF75FF7A17E%40GB3NEWS-179805DEB59771D6%402428648-1798046430CE2E9C%406-1798046430CE2E9C?clipid=dgbaivaqratqsiqiykpftqfmstsbkyjd_wma-gateway004_1679003077055.

"WWI Service Cards." State Library and Archives of Florida, Florida Memory. Accessed December 20, 2023. https://www.floridamemory.com/items/show/203671.

"Yara, Cuba." Wikipedia. Accessed December 7, 2023. https://en.wikipedia.org/w/index.php?title=Yara,_Cuba&oldid=1176606826.

YouTube Universal Music Group. "Dardanella." Bing Crosby and Louis Armstrong. Capitol Records (1960). Accessed January 8, 2024. https://www.youtube.com/watch?v=MSOSxoe4XLY.

Index

abscess 79, 95
absent minded 14, 27, 90-91, 94, 141
adjudication 20, 106
Adjutant General of the War Department 68, 71-72, 74, 92-93, 103-105, 110, 124, 136, 138, 174
SS *Adriatic* 67-68
Aisne-Marne American Cemetery 45
Aisne-Marne offensive sector 45, 48, 51, 59, 68-69, 72, 74, 107, 118
alcoholism 76-77, 104-106, 137, 173-174, 186
Allies 4, 18, 40, 69, 102
Allred, Dinorah Anne "Dinni" Atkinson 178, 181
American Disabled Veterans 7, 117-120, 129, 185, 189
American Expeditionary Forces 38, 40, 43, 51, 67-68, 70, 75, 109, 118
American Legion 54-57
American Red Cross 7, 89-90, 95, 99, 112, 117, 123, 143
American Psychiatric Association 168
Amerindian 35
amnesia 25, 41, 61, 67, 80, 85, 87, 113-114, 116, 121-123, 126-127, 129, 133, 135, 138, 151, 158, 160-161, 163, 172-173, 175-177
Ancestry.com 3, 46, 157, 183
Armistice Day 20, 70, 76, 186
Armstrong, Louis 155
army psychiatrists 22, 79, 138
Associated Charities of Worcester 7, 64, 89-90, 92-93, 95, 98-102, 114, 117, 123, 125, 158, 175, 186, 191
Atkinson, William "Bill," Sr. 5, 45, 50, 57, 71, 178, 180

Barker, Miss C. Adelaide 90
Bay Pines National Cemetery 44-45, 56-58
Bayamo, Cuba 36
Belgium, Antwerp 44, 49
Belleville, William J. 123, 125, 187, 197
Belmont Street 146, 151
Benjamin T. Rome School of Music 152
Bermudez de Castro y O'Lawler, Salvador 38
Biltmore Hotel 58

Black, Johnny S.
Bloomingdale Asylum 143
Bonus Expeditionary Forces 109-110, 139
The Boston Herald 112-113, 116
Bowen, William C. 19
Brest, France 44, 78, 94, 186, 188
Breuer, Josef 41
Bridges, Maj. Gen. Charles W. 93, 103, 105-107, 124
Britain 35, 42
British Expeditionary Forces 41, 70, 166
Broward, Napoleon Bonaparte 37
Brown, Gen. Preston 23, 127
Bruce W. Carter VA Medical Center 58

Camp Bois-l'Évêque 69
Caribbean Sea 3, 35-36
Carrefour de la Croix 69
Castellanos y Velasco, Rosario 3, 26, 183
Castro, Fidel 3, 7
Catholic Church 2, 149, 153, 187
Catholic University of America 152, 187
Central Powers 4, 18, 42
Cespedes, Carlos Manuel de 36
Chambers, Ralph L. 118, 120, 121, 189
Château-Thierry: *defensive sector (Ile de France)* 68, 107; *spring offensive* 68; S.S. 49
clemency: 22-23, 75, 85, 88, 126, 138, 185; letter 22-23, 84, 124, 186, 190
Cluster, Dick 36
Columbus, Christopher 35-36
Columbus Barracks, Ohio 46, 52, 60
combat trauma 83, 164, 168, 173
Congress: 12, 18-19, 40, 51, 90-91, 93, 98, 100-101, 104, 106-109, 112, 116-117, 119, 121, 123, 128-129, 131-133, 140, 160, 187, 200; bill 90, 101, 113, 116, 129, 140, 143, 187; inquiry 23, 71, 74, 93, 102, 104, 127, 140; records 7, 187, 200; 72nd 106, 117, 131
constitutional psychopathic state 22-23, 75, 82-83, 104-105, 174, 186
Coolidge, Pres. Calvin 108, 109
Coral Gables, Florida 57, 58
Croix de Guerre 50, 51, 69, 72, 118

241

Index

Cuba 2, 3, 7, 9, 26–27, 29–30, 32–33, 35–39, 53, 67, 99, 146–148, 178, 187
Cull, Nicholas J. 42

Dale, Grace Marie 12
Dale, William B. 12
Daniel, Capt. Richard Curd 118–121, 125, 129, 187, 189, 197
Dardanella 153–157, 161–162, 186
David and Goliath 76, 141, 163
Daytona Beach, Florida 112–114
Daytona Beach Journal 113–114
death penalty 20
dementia praecox, remission stage 92–93, 175–176, 187
desertion 20, 23, 63, 71, 73–75, 87, 89, 91, 103–104, 107, 111, 114–115, 119–120, 134, 186, 189
Devil Dogs (teufel hunden) 69, 72, 118
diagnoses 5, 15, 22–24, 31, 75–80, 82–84, 88, 92–94, 104–106, 108, 136–138, 161, 165–166, 168–170, 173–176, 186–187
Diagnostic and Statistical Manual of Mental Disorders (DSM) 168
Diaz, Charles 37, 39
dishonorable discharge 20, 22–23, 63, 71, 75, 78, 84, 86, 88–90, 95–96, 98, 100, 108, 110–111, 113, 116–119, 121, 123, 126–127, 131–134, 140, 143, 186
Dolan, Elizabeth A. 13
Dominican Republic 35
Dooley, 1st Lt. J.E. 22
Duval County Family Welfare Agency 89–90, 101, 117, 125
Duval Street 31, 33, 45, 122

ecstasy 171
Eisenhower, Dwight D. 110
"El Grito de Yara" ("The Cry of Yara") 36
Elizabeth Street 27, 43
Emergency Officers' Retirement Act 134
Epic of Gilgamesh 165
Estellencs 2
Europe 4, 18, 40, 42, 49, 68, 74, 135, 142, 165
eye movement desensitization and reprocessing (EMDR) therapy 171

Fairbanks, Helen E. 89–90, 92, 98
Federal Project Number One 144
Federation of Musicians 151–152, 187
Fernandez, Honorable Judge Carlos B. 3
Fernandez, Clara Maria "Bibi" 2
Fernandez, Esteban Silvestre Quintanal Barroso 32, 146
Field Artillery: 4th 63, 66, 104, 185; 15th 63, 66–67, 79, 107, 185
Find a Grave 15, 59, 162
SS *Finland* 44
First Army Corps 23, 127
First Division 56
Fletcher, Sen. Duncan U. 56

Florida 3, 4, 5, 16, 21, 26–27, 29–38, 40, 43–46, 53–54, 56–62, 89–90, 101, 111–112, 117–118, 120–125, 128–129, 148, 161–162, 181, 185, 187, 189, 199
SS *Florida* 146
Florida Keys Public Library Archives 32
Florida National Cemetery Administration's Veterans Legacy Program 45
Foch, Supreme Allied Commander Ferdinand 70
Fort Adams, Rhode Island 19–20, 22–23, 60, 75, 83, 91, 95, 103–104, 107, 115, 121, 124, 138, 186
Fort Slocum, New York 60, 62, 66, 90, 104, 107, 185
Fort Wadsworth, New York 66–67, 104, 185
Fourragere 50–51
Fox Hills Hospital, New York 79, 91, 94–95, 103, 107, 113, 115, 122, 126, 138, 186
France 18, 38, 40, 42, 43, 44, 45, 50, 64, 66, 67, 68, 71, 75, 78, 93, 94, 100, 101, 107, 117, 121, 134, 155, 156, 185, 186, 188
Franklin Street 14
furlough 20, 84, 87, 89, 94, 111, 113, 115, 126, 137, 139–140
furunculosis 79, 94, 104, 186

Gallagher, T. James, 119–120, 189
garrison prisoner 78, 105–106, 186
General Bailey Post 54, 56
general court-martial 20, 22–24, 62–64, 71, 75–76, 82, 84, 87, 98, 104, 106–107, 111, 113–115, 124, 131, 138, 140–141, 149, 185–186, 190, 205
general prisoner 78
general secretary 64, 89, 90, 92, 98, 12
German submarine 18
Germany 18, 19, 45, 69, 77, 78, 93, 156
Gómez, Gen. Máximo 35
Granma Province 36
Great Depression 95, 108–109, 142, 144
Greater Antilles 35–36
La Grippe 94
La Guerra Chiquita (The Little War) 36
La Guerra de Independencia Cubana (The Cuban War of Independence) 37, 39
La Guerra de los Diez Años (The Ten Years War) 26, 36
Gulf of Guacanayabo 36

Haiti, Republic of 35
Hamilton Heights, NY 53
hard labor 20, 76, 85–86, 107–108, 112, 115–116, 126, 137, 175, 186
Harding, Pres. Warren G. 109
Harrison, Clara 64, 92
Harrison Street 64, 92
Hatuey, Taíno (Cacique chief) 36
Havana 3, 29, 32–33, 35–36, 38, 61, 99, 146–149
Hernandez, Rafael 36

Index

Herodotus 165
Hillsborough County 38, 162
Hispanic 49, 61
Historical Records Survey Projects 146
The History of Havana 36
Hoboken, New Jersey 43, 44, 78, 94
Hofer, Dr. Johannes 165
Hoff General Hospital 63, 79, 83, 94, 104, 186
Holmes, Pehr G. 102–104, 106–107, 116–117, 187, 195
honorable discharge 90–91, 96, 100, 113, 116–117, 127–129, 132–133, 135, 143, 199
Hoover, Pres. Herbert 109
House of Representatives 101–102, 128, 132
Hundred Days Offensive 70
hysteria 23, 75, 83, 105, 175, 186

The Iliad 165
inadequate personality disorder 22–23, 75, 82–83, 104–105, 141, 174, 186
Indigenous people 36
infantry 22, 59, 68, 79, 94, 107, 110, 186; Infantry Division 51–52, 66, 186; Infantry Regiment 43, 45, 56
influenza 70, 76, 93–94, 104–105, 128, 137, 186
Interpersonal Psychotherapy Therapy (IPT) 171
Ireland 13, 150
La Isla Española 35
Italy 2, 18, 70

Jacksonville, FL 37–38, 62, 89–90, 101
Japan 18
Jimenez, James J. 3, 7–9, 178, 182
Johnson, Capt. A.D. 22
La Justice de Biddeford 121

Kardiner, Abram 168
Key West, Florida 1, 26–27, 29–34, 36–38, 40, 43–46, 53, 56, 63–64, 92, 98–99, 112, 117–120, 122–126, 128–129, 146–147, 160, 187, 189, 199
The Key West Citizen 31, 112, 122–124, 187
Koblenz, Germany 77, 93
Korean War 168

Lacedonia, Margarita 1, 120, 128–129, 187, 198–199
Lancaster County, South Carolina 26
Latin American Pharmacy 33
letters 1, 5, 7, 13, 17, 61, 66, 71, 89, 93, 99, 106–107, 110–111, 117, 120, 124, 126, 135, 138, 149, 151, 174, 178, 181, 185
Limey defensive sector 69, 107
Lincoln, Pres. Abraham 133
Lucy-le-Bocage Aisne Marne American Cemetery 45
Lusitania 18

MacArthur, Gen. Douglas 109–110
machine guns 45, 49, 69

Macon, Georgia 33
Main Street, Worcester 12, 18–19, 113, 123
USS *Maine* 37
malaria 94
Manhattan 53, 78
Manzanillo, Cuba 36
Marbache defensive sector 69, 107
Marine Brigade (4th Marine Brigade) 69, 72, 74, 118
Marine Corps 68
Marion, Ohio 53
Marrich 165
Marx, Judge Robert 119
Maslow, Abraham 177
McAuley, Catherine 150
McCarthy and Fisher, Inc. 154
MDMA 171
Medical Detachment 63, 66–67, 79, 80, 94, 104, 107, 133, 185–186
medical record 24, 56, 79, 82, 88, 93, 102, 104–105, 137, 176
Memorial (Find-a-a-Grave) 15, 59, 162
Memorial Hospital 16, 91
mens rea 86–87, 114
mental issues 21, 24, 60, 65, 77, 93, 106, 110, 135, 137–139, 155, 172–173, 175
Metz 70
Meuse-Argonne American Cemetery 45
Meuse-Argonne offensive 45, 51, 69–70, 107, 119
Mexican American War 19
Mexico 19, 35
The Miami Herald 57, 122
Middle East 18
Midnight at the Oasis 155
military control 23, 63–64, 82, 91, 104, 107–108
military enlistment card 45–46, 48, 99
Mis Recuerdos 38, 179–180
Monroe County, Florida 38, 40
Mora, Claudia R. 26, 62
mulatto 34, 45
Muldaur, Geoff 155
Muldaur, Maria 155
music teacher 27, 150, 176, 187

National Archives 39, 46, 78, 95, 136
National Cemetery Administration's Veterans Legacy Program 45
National Center for PTSD 171
National Directory of Piano Teachers, United States of America 151
National Institute of Health 172
National Personnel Records Administration (Center) 65, 80–81
Nazareth Home for Boys 150
neurasthenia 167
neurosis 77, 105, 166–168, 173
New Chalmers Street 62
New Deal 142, 144
New England Journal of Medicine 83

Index

New York 4–5, 21, 26, 30, 34, 37, 39–40, 43–44, 48–49, 52–54, 56–57, 60–63, 66, 79, 81, 90–91, 94, 99–100, 113, 116–117, 121–122, 124, 149, 154–155, 169, 182, 185–186
Newark, New Jersey 16, 87, 91
Newport, RI 91
North Shore Hotel 57
nostalgia 165–166

Oakwood Place 160
O'Brien, "Dynamite" Johnny 37
O'Connor Brothers Funeral Home 162
The Odyssey 165
official military personnel files 74, 80
Orange Court Hotel 57
Orbison, Dr. Thomas J. 82
Orlando, Florida 34, 53–54, 57, 99, 124, 199
Orlando Sentinel 53
Our Lady of Fatima Church 153, 162, 187
Owen, Rep. Ruth Bryan 128–129, 187, 198–199

Pact of Zanjón 36–37
Palmer, Evangelina M. 1, 7–8, 81, 178–179, 187
Palmer Bestard, Gabriel 2
Parkinson's disease 175
Patton, Gen. George S. 110
Paul, John 152
Pearl of the Antilles 37
Peninsular and Occidental (P & O) Steamship Company 146
Perez, Agusto 26, 61
Perez, Charles 26–27, 30–31, 53, 64, 67, 78, 92, 98–99, 112, 115, 122–124, 126, 129, 161, 187
Perez, Charles E. "Charlie" 27, 29, 34, 40, 43–50, 52–62, 65, 71–72, 74, 99–100, 122, 124, 162, 187
Perez, Dinorah (Mrs. William P. Atkinson) 27, 29, 33–34, 44, 52–53, 57, 61, 65, 99, 112, 124, 149, 162, 180
Perez, Dolores "Lola" 26, 45, 61, 129
Perez, Evangelina 27, 29–30, 32–34, 52, 60–61, 64–65, 92, 146–149, 153, 162, 187
Perez, Jose I. 26, 30, 40, 62
Perez, Ramon 26, 61
Perez (née Velasco), Sarah 26–27, 29–32, 53, 61, 64–65, 92, 99, 149, 153, 161–162, 185
Perry, Hector H. 20–21, 25, 40, 60, 62, 67, 73, 78, 96, 104, 106–107, 112, 117, 131–133, 135, 145–146, 195–196
Pershing, Gen. John J. 69–70, 72, 118, 149
Philippines 36–37
Phillips Exeter Academy 102
Portland, Oregon 109
post office 53, 99, 124
post traumatic stress disorder (PTSD) 41, 110, 131–133, 141, 164–172
present-centered therapy (PCT) 171
Prindle, Capt. G.L. 22

SS *Prinz Friedrich Wilhelm* 78, 94
prison 23, 96, 108, 114–115, 126, 137; prisoner 78, 105, 186
private 22, 45, 47, 63, 66–67, 104, 107, 185; First Class 47
prohibition 77
psychiatry 22–23, 75–77, 79, 83, 138, 143, 159, 168, 173, 176, 186–187
psychoneurosis 22, 75, 77, 79, 83–84, 94, 104–106, 137, 173, 175, 186
psychosis 105, 137, 171, 173
psychopath 22–23, 75, 82–83, 104–105, 174, 186
psychotherapy 77, 170–171

Racehorse Division 118
Ramayana 165
RCA (Radio Corporation of America) 154
Record of Service Form 62–63, 71
Red Star Line 44
Regular Army 46, 62
relief bills 109, 116, 131–132, 134, 140
remission sentence 22, 75, 126; stage 92–93, 175–176, 187
repression 173
Richmond Avenue 54
Riverside Drive 53
Rolo, Juan Perez 38
Romagne-sous-Montfaucon, France 45
Roosevelt, Pres. Franklin Delano 144
Russell's Cornet Band of Key West 32
Russia 18, 51

safety appliance 27–29
St. Augustine National Cemetery 45
St. Gabriel's School of Music 150, 187
St. John's Cemetery 161–162
St. Louis, Missouri 80–81
Saint Mihiel 51, 69–70, 72
St. Petersburg, Florida 45, 54
Sanchez, Alfred (Alfredo) Velasquez 13–20, 25, 88, 90–91, 113–114, 115, 121, 157–157, 161
SARS-CoV-2 (COVID-19) 41
schizophrenia 175
Scotland 12
Second Battle of the Marne 69
Second Engineers 66, 68–69, 72, 74, 77, 107, 118, 133, 185
Sector Activities of the American Expeditionary Forces 70
Seidenberg Avenue 27, 29
Selective Service Act 19, 40
Selvin, Ben 154, 186
Senate 109, 127, 131–132, 134, 187; Bill S.851 131, 134, 187
shell shock 41–42, 77, 85, 94, 137, 166–168, 170, 172
Silver Star 48–50, 52
Sisters of Mercy Order 150
Smith, 2nd Lt. N.E., Jr. 22
Social Security Act 142

Index

Social Services 95, 117, 160
Soissons, France 48, 59, 71
soldier's heart 165–166
Southampton 67
Southard Steet
Spain 2, 3, 35–37
Spaniards 36, 162
Spanish American War 35, 37–38, 42
Spanish flu 4, 18, 40, 41, 70, 93, 105
Spanish oppression 26, 29
State Library and Archives of Florida 45
Staten Island. New York 63, 66, 80, 94–95, 103–104, 126
Stobbs, George R. 71–72, 102–103, 106–107, 112, 115–117, 124, 187, 196
stress inoculation training (SIT) 171
stress reaction 167–168
Survey of Federal Archives 146
Syrians 102

Taíno 36
Tampa, Florida 16, 21, 27, 29–30, 32–34, 37–38, 49, 52, 60–62, 90, 99, 112–115, 129, 146, 161–162
The Tampa Tribune 29, 113, 115
telephone operator 14, 91
Texas 19, 53, 57
Thompson, Capt. S.C. 22
Toulon-Troyon defensive sector 68, 93, 107
transcranial stimulation 171
traumatic neurosis 41, 85, 166–169
Treaty of Paris 37
trench disease 94; fever 94; foot 94; mouth 94
tribunal 20, 22, 75, 85, 88, 124
tuberculosis (TB) 29, 31, 94
typhoid 94

Uniform Code of Military Justice 20
Union Canadian Center in Worcester, MA 144
United Kingdom 18
U.S. Army 7, 9, 18
U.S. Army Air Service 69
United States Army Medical Corps 82
United States Department of State List of Cuba Prohibited Accommodations 3
U.S. General Hospital 63, 79, 83, 91, 94, 104, 107, 186
U.S. Marine Hospital 117–120, 125, 128–129, 187, 189, 197, 199
U.S. Patent 27–29
U.S. Veterans Association Center for Soldiers 56

Velasco, Antonio 32
Velasco, Evaristo 26
Velasco, Francisca de Leon y Silvera 27, 43
Velasco, Margarita 26
Velasco, Sarah 26–27, 29–32, 53, 61, 64–65, 92, 99, 149, 153, 161–162, 185
Velasco y Valdez, Jacinto 3, 29, 36, 183
Victory Medal 50–52
virtual reality-graded exposure therapy 171

Walsh, Sen. David I. 100–101, 116–117, 123–124, 127, 129, 131–132, 134, 163, 187, 198–199
War Department 19–20, 37, 58, 71, 93, 102–103, 106–108, 110, 115–116, 123–124, 136, 138, 185, 195–196
wartime trauma 83, 164, 171
Washington, D.C. 5, 62, 66, 92, 103–104, 109, 118, 120, 131, 152, 189
Washington Daily News 110
Welk, Lawrence 155
West Indies 3, 35
Western Front 4, 19, 52, 67, 69, 70, 139
White Star Line 67
Winden Lane 27, 43
Worcester, Massachusetts 12, 13, 16, 18, 19, 64, 75, 80, 89–93, 95, 98, 99, 100, 101, 102, 104, 106, 107, 110, 112–114, 117, 121–126, 128–129, 134, 143–144, 146, 147–151, 154, 157, 160–162, 173, 175, 186–187, 197, 199
Worcester District Medical Society 93
The Worcester Evening Gazette 13, 14, 113–114, 134, 144
The Worcester Evening Post 106–107, 123, 125, 197
Worcester State Asylum 15
The Worcester Telegram 113, 125, 161, 187
Works Progress Administration (WPA) 144, 187; music program 144, 150; survey project 144, 146
World War Adjusted Compensation Act 108
World War I 2, 4, 7, 9, 18, 20, 38, 40–44, 49–52, 56–57, 59, 66, 68–70, 82, 108–110, 113, 115, 118–119, 128, 141, 149, 162, 166–168, 170–172
World War II draft card 34, 54, 144–145, 150–151

Ybor, Vicente Martinez 38, 162
Ybor City, Florida 162
Young, 1st Lt. N.D. 22

Zimmerman telegram 18